ISBN 0-916054-64-0
$10.95

THE POLITICS OF PROSECUTION:

Jim Thompson, Richard Nixon, Marje Everett & the Trial of Otto Kerner

by Hank Messick
Author of LANSKY

GANGSTERS, crooked politicians, amoral businessmen aren't new to Chicago or the rest of the country, and so long as the citizen can maintain a faith in the machinery of justice he's inclined to accept the theory that the fleas come with the dog.

The importance of this book lies in the detailed, intriguing study of how our federal judicial system was prostituted for political gain and personal profit . . .

Otto Kerner, Jr., son-in-law of Anton "Boss" Cermak—the man who built the unique political organization known as the Chicago Machine—inadverently made himself a tempting target when he won the image of "Mr. Clean". As Governor of Illinois and as a sitting federal appellate court judge, he appeared untarnished and untarnishable. Abruptly, thanks to the allegations of one person, Marje Lindheimer Everett, he is made to appear vulnerable. The Nixon White House moved quickly. Ironically, Mrs. Everett is motivated by hatred of another naive.

in trouble it is
he seemed will-

ting, fact-filled
in Illinois, es-
ory of Kerner
:h of this ma-
lf, but the *real*
:cision to get
to ultimately

f a number of
lom of Infor-
: to document
rocess. Grand
; was turned
ights of indi-
vithout apol-
demand that
done. If har-
witness was
:. If, on the
:nt to prose-
certain well
ls of justice

again and
documents,
1 the court-
itted in the
: politics of

ppened and
righteningly
and again.
1 be ruined
stice, but a

er again be

Books by Hank Messick

The Silent Syndicate

Syndicate in the Sun

Syndicate Wife

Syndicate Abroad

Secret File

LANSKY

John Edgar Hoover

The Mobs and the Mafia

Private Lives of Public Enemies

Beauties and the Beasts

Gangs and Gangsters

Kidnapping

BARBOZA

King's Mountain

The Only Game in Town

The Politics of Prosecution

Jim Thompson, Marje Everett,
Richard Nixon
& The Trial of Otto Kerner

Hank Messick

CAROLINE HOUSE BOOKS • OTTAWA, ILLINOIS

ISBN: 0-916054-64-0
Library of Congress Catalogue Card Number 77-15915

Manufactured in the United States of America

Caroline House Books/Green Hill Publishers, Inc., Ottawa, Illinois 61350

In memory of my father,
G. F. Messick,
a good man.

He was no politician
for he was tender with the tenderness of a man,
and politicians are jackals preying on a people,
scavengers of the public treasuries,
wreckers of the faith of the citizenry,
holding honor more lightly than gain.

— ABE LINCOLN, SCHAEFER O'NEILL

*My name is Truth and I am the most
elusive captive in the universe.*

CARL SANDBURG

Contents

Abbreviations

AP — Arlington Park
BJC — Balmoral Jockey Club
CHR — Chicago Harness Racing, Inc.
CTE — Chicago Thoroughbred Enterprises, Inc.
IRB — Illinois Racing Board
IRE — Illinois Racing Enterprises, Inc.
LF — Lincoln Fields
O.K. — Otto Kerner, Jr.
SP — Sportsman's Park
T.I. — Ted Isaacs
WP — Washington Park
WPTA — Washington Park Trotting Association
W.S.M. — William S. Miller

*Speak the truth and shame
the Devil.*

Foreword

The manner in which the lives of an assortment of individuals were altered when the business of horse racing got mixed up with machine politics and Nixon-era justice is the concern of this book.

Best known of these individuals was the late Otto Kerner, former governor of Illinois and at the time of his indictment a federal appellate court judge. A man still revered in certain circles, was he guilty as charged or was he prosecuted for political reasons? Could the answer to both questions be "Yes"?

There is Theodore "Ted" Isaacs, Kerner's friend and business consultant. Was he also Kerner's bagman? Did he sacrifice himself at the trial in a vain effort to save Kerner?

A key figure is Mrs. Marje Lindheimer Everett, formerly known as the Queen of Illinois Racing. It was Mrs. Everett who set in motion the events that exposed the great scandal, yet she managed to testify for both sides during the trial and moved to California a wealthy woman. How did she obtain her power? Why did she blow the whistle? Why did the United States Attorney call her a "public servant" before the trial and a "briber" after it was over?

The U.S. Attorney was James "Big Jim" Thompson, an admittedly ambitious man. His successful prosecution of Kerner led ultimately to his election as governor and made him a potential Republican candidate for the presidency. Was his goal justice or political advancement? Were his methods proper? Is he a dedicated public servant or a ruthless man on the make, another Nixon?

Kerner's attorney was Paul Connolly, the handsome law partner of Edward Bennett Williams. Was his professional reputation justified? Did he make a deal with Mrs. Everett or was his kindness to her the mark of a gentleman? Were his courtroom tactics proper? Why did he repeatedly enrage the presiding judge?

What of the role of the late Mayor Daley in the events that caused the scandal? Two of his former law partners, William J. Lynch and George Schaller, represented Mrs. Everett in confidential matters. Were they unaware of backdated documents and offers of racetrack stock to a gaggle of politicians? How important was *clout*? Kerner was known as "Mr. Clean," but his father-in-law was the legendary Boss Cermak, the man who created the political machine Daley ruled. Had corruption become a way of life in the racing industry?

In the background were shadowy figures such as John Mitchell, the only former attorney general of the United States to go to prison; a mysterious private eye who worked for both Daley and Mrs. Everett; and Internal Revenue Service officials who organized the highly secret Project CRIMP. Did these IRS men make the business of "getting Otto's ass," as Thompson so inelegantly put it, a sport, a big-game hunt at a time when the law of the jungle was in vogue in Washington? How far were they willing to go to bag their prize?

Finally, there is William S. Miller, appointed to the Illinois Racing Board by Adlai Stevenson, Sr., and named chairman by Otto Kerner. Why did Marje Everett hate him? Why did the government indict him and then drop the charges? Was Miller a good man trying to keep the racing industry afloat on a sea of corruption?

It was Miller who made it possible for me to write this book. Early in 1976, former IRS Special Agent Peter Stufflebeam brought Miller to my Florida home. I was in very poor health at the time, facing a fast of one hundred days. We talked. As part of the pressure to make him "flip" — turn government witness — he had been hit with a multimillion dollar civil tax suit. The criminal trial was long over, but the tax suit was alive and growing as interest and penalty charges piled up. Miller, who had reached the age when he needed to put his affairs in order, retained me to study the record and give him an expert opinion as to whether he should continue to fight or seek a compromise. In other words, did the IRS have a case?

Accepting the job, I was soon buried in a paper blizzard: thousands upon thousands of pages of trial transcripts, Grand Jury transcripts, court rulings, investigative reports, and confidential documents obtained under the Freedom of Information Act. To these I added some records of my own.

The white-haired Miller — self-made businessman and millionaire, former horse breeder, horse racer, and racetrack owner — asked only that I put the picture together and give him an honest opinion. And then, his voice shaking just a bit, he added:

"If you find I'm a crook I'll give you my home on the ocean at Golden Beach."

I am, frankly, something of a cynic when it comes to self-made millionaires who dabble in politics and racing. In fact a reviewer once complained that "Messick thinks everyone is crooked." Not so, of course; in a long career as investigative reporter–author, I've retained the ability to recognize an honest man and to distinguish certain shades of difference in the less-than-honest. In any case, I approached Miller's files with a certain skepticism, and I asked some very personal questions.

The results of my study become apparent in the pages that follow. Suffice it to say that the story, together with my returning strength, awakened my ambitions as a writer. The facts as I collected them simply demanded to be written in book form. Stufflebeam and others had toyed with the idea and had abandoned it as too complex, so the field was clear. Miller had no objections, but he made it clear he would have no part of the project. It would be my responsibility. The facts cited would be selected by me, the opinions voiced would be mine alone, and the profits, if any, from publication would also be entirely mine.

Additional research was necessary. In Chicago I discovered new information which shocked Miller, who, somehow, had managed to retain illusions. As always there were those who would not talk, content, apparently, to let the record speak for them. The record was massive enough, and sometimes its contradictions were more revealing than a consistent narrative. The adage that liars need good memories was proven true once more.

Eventually satisfied that as much of the truth was in my hands as possible, I began writing. Condensing a million or more words, much of the language highly technical and complex, into a readable book is no easy task. I attempted to present the facts in more or less chronological order, after giving sufficient background, in the belief the reader is entitled — if he or she desires — to make an independent evaluation as the complicated story unfolds. In Chapter Twelve I give MY verdict.

Did justice triumph or was it prostituted? Did the ends justify the means? Read and decide. The answer could be important for your future and mine. And if in the reading you find yourself more than slightly fascinated by this unique look at things as they really were, so much the better. It might even make you angry.

HANK MESSICK
Treetops
Peace River, Arcadia

*My fellow Americans, the long dark
night for America is about to end.*

RICHARD M. NIXON, 1969

1
The Opportunity

It began in 1969. For some it was a time to visit the sick and bury the
dead for the shadow of President Nixon was long on the land. For
millions it was a time of waiting, of transition. After eight years, the
Republicans had returned to power. And for those who had helped win
the narrow victory, it was time to prepare for the next battle by using
the agencies of government to cripple the opposition.

Among those who recognized the mood of the victors was Mrs.
Marjorie Lindheimer Everett. She began cultivating George E. Mahin, "director of transition" for Richard B. Ogilvie, the new Republican
governor of Illinois. Mahin was cool to her social invitations, but quick
to respond when she asked for help at the Chicago-area racetracks she
once controlled and still operated for an outside conglomerate. Mahin
introduced her to John Walsh, a special agent of the Intelligence
Division of the Internal Revenue Service. Aware that Marje, as she was
known to the press and the racing industry, had been close to powerful
Democrats including Mayor Daley, Walsh was happy to give advice
and accept information.

It was late October before Marje made her move. On a Friday
afternoon she called Mahin and urgently requested that he and Walsh
meet with her the next morning. Mahin suggested Monday would be
more convenient, but the lady would brook no delay. Mahin agreed,
called Walsh just as he was quitting his office, and obtained his reluc-
tant consent.

The session began at ten o'clock Saturday morning at Mahin's
Michigan Avenue apartment. Unprepared, Mrs. Mahin managed a
lunch of pea soup and sandwiches. It quickly became apparent that
Mrs. Everett's ire was directed at William S. Miller, former chairman
of the Illinois Racing Board and now chief stockholder of Chicago

1

Harness Racing, Inc. The urgency stemmed from the fact that the IRB, now Republican dominated, was about to award racing dates for 1970. Miller had received dates in the past and expected as a matter of routine to obtain them again. Marje was attempting to harm two birds with one stone. If Chicago Harness could be denied dates, it would hurt not only Miller whom she had come to hate but it would damage another new enemy, Philip Levin of Gulf & Western, the conglomerate which purchased her racing empire earlier in the year and retained her to manage it. If Chicago Harness, a tenant at one of Gulf & Western's tracks, was denied racing dates, it would cost G & W more than a million dollars in rents and concession income. A poor way to manage a business, perhaps, but Mrs. Everett had her reasons.

Mahin was more interested in Miller than was Walsh for racing was state business. The special agent drew the witness on, exploiting her anger at Miller to get information on others. The technique was successful. Marje disclosed that she gave $45,000 in 1960 for Otto Kerner's gubernatorial campaign. Miller was supposed to deliver the money, but she was certain he had not done so. She was equally sure he had not paid taxes on the windfall. All they needed to do was check his tax returns.

As the sympathetic questions continued, Mrs. Everett opened up more and still more. "Racing," she declared, "is a dirty business, and to survive you have to play dirty too." For example, she had been forced to sell racing stock to a number of politicians at prices that amounted to extortion. Miller had forced her to do it, she said, during his tenure as racing board chairman.

Who were the politicians? She listed a dozen names, Republicans as well as Democrats. Walsh was impressed but hid his feelings. Marje impatiently played her trump card and named former Governor Otto Kerner, Jr. The payoff, she added, was all part of Miller's master plan. After all, while Miller had been appointed to the board by Adlai Stevenson, it had been Kerner who made him chairman and who combined the harness racing board with the flat racing commission to give him even greater authority.

The state official looked at the federal agent. If true, this was dynamite, a gift from heaven. In that 1960 election Kerner led the Democrats to victory by a majority of 482,000 votes and thus made it possible for John F. Kennedy to squeak by with less than 9,000. Moreover, Illinois had been a decisive state in that election. With a few more votes there and in Texas, Nixon would have become president in 1961.

After winning another decisive victory in 1964, the Mr. Clean of Illinois politics quit politics early in 1968 to become, as his father before him, a federal appellate court judge. Ogilvie, a former Cook County sheriff, had little trouble that fall in beating the Democrat substitute and Nixon, of course, had won the state easily.

A scandal tarnishing the still popular Kerner? It sounded too wonderful to be true. How reliable was the witness? In some circles she had the reputation of being ruthless, a worthy successor to her father, Benjamin Franklin Lindheimer. Ben had built the racing empire consisting of Arlington, Washington, and Balmoral tracks. Upon his death in 1960 it had been left to Mrs. Everett to operate. With help from Miller, her father's friend, she had greatly enlarged it by introducing harness racing at Washington Park, and had reportedly sold out to Gulf & Western for more than twenty million. Was she capable of smearing Kerner just to revenge herself on Miller? Perhaps, but considering the state of political morality in Illinois, her tale might very well be true. Kerner was the magic word. No one in Washington would give a damn about Miller or a bunch of state legislators, but Kerner was known nationally. He had headed a Presidential Commission on Civil Disorders, and its report bore his name. Somehow he had risen through the ranks of the Chicago Machine without being tainted. If Mrs. Everett's story could make indictments possible, the prosecution would be of vast importance to Republican politicians in Illinois and perhaps the nation.

When the meeting broke up late in the afternoon, Walsh borrowed the telephone. He called his wife to say he wouldn't be home for dinner and he called his immediate supervisor, John Foy, and told him he was coming over with something very interesting indeed.

Marje left the apartment well satisfied that the wheels were turning. By Monday, she believed, top officials in Springfield and Washington would be informed and the word would go out to deny racing dates to Miller's corporation. There had been no need to spell out a formal agreement — Mahin understood the terms and future cooperation would depend on how well her desires were met.

The Internal Revenue Service considered the report of great importance, and its top officials had no desire to share it with the Justice Department. Indeed, the IRS distrusted its own people in the district office in Chicago. Some of them were too close to Mayor Daley. Walsh was quietly transferred to the regional office and the preliminary investigation was "bootlegged" — as a top official put it — out of there until the district office could be completely reorganized and a new team of investigators brought in from other cities.

The probe began under the assumption that if nothing else, it would put a crimp into the political machine currently bossed by Daley but assembled in 1932 by Kerner's father-in-law, Anton "Boss" Cermak. Soon the investigative activity was being referred to as Project Crimp, since the men involved needed to call it something. Deciding, as the work continued, that a more formal designation was desirable, Special Agent Walsh found words to fit the nickname and so created the acronym meaning *Corruption (Racing) Influence Money Politicians*. Project CRIMP became official. In time some investigators joked that the letters really meant "Corrupt Republicans Investigating Marje's Pals." When top officials heard the joke they were not amused and word went out from the national office forbidding the use of acronyms as code words for official probes. Thus an investigation of tax havens in the Bahamas became "Project Haven." Operation Leprechaun got its name because the agent in charge of a probe of political corruption in Miami was inspired by the green ink in his pen.

Great secrecy was maintained about Project CRIMP. Nixon's first commissioner of internal revenue, Randolph Thrower, was asked to come to Chicago for a briefing in order to reduce the chance of a leak. Interestingly enough, however, very little was said in those first months about the role of Marje Everett. Instead, the impression was given that Walsh had somehow developed a whole host of informants with inside information, each supporting the other independently.

Late in 1970, the IRS decided the case was far enough along to be entrusted to the Justice Department. Details were given to a group of high officials headed by Henry Peterson, and a federal strike force was assigned. Nevertheless, the Intelligence Division of IRS continued to provide most of the manpower. Walsh, however, was promoted and transferred to Cincinnati as other men hunted for evidence to substantiate Marje's allegations. The need to build a solid case was stressed — an unsuccessful prosecution of such a man as Otto Kerner would hurt as much as his conviction would help the Republican cause. Yet confidence was high. Former White House aide Charles Colson has since

Photo by Minerva Wagner

HANK MESSICK is the author of sixteen books. A prize-winning investigative journalist, he is a leading expert on organized crime and corruption in America. Born in Happy Valley, North Carolina, he received degrees in journalism from the University of North Carolina and an MA in English from Iowa State University. He became nationally-known during his years as a reporter for the *Louisville Courier-Journal* (1956-63), and has since devoted his time to writing books, serving as a consultant to newspapers, governors and state investigating committees. He has written for *The Nation*, *Rolling Stone* and other magazines. His books have been widely-published abroad, with his *Lanksy* being responsible for Israel deporting crime syndicate boss Meyer Lansky after it was published there.

Mr. Messick resides in Fort Lauderdale, Florida with his wife. He has three children.

related a conversation late in 1970 at the Nixon compound on Key Biscayne. Attorney General John Mitchell was there and happily assured everyone that thanks to the current investigation Mayor Daley wouldn't be so powerful the next time around.

The politics of prosecution would pay off in Illinois, Mitchell predicted, and for once he was right. Ironically, however, the principal beneficiary would be a political unknown, James "Big Jim" Thompson, whose goal in the years following Project CRIMP became the presidency which Nixon had so thoroughly disgraced.

To understand how this incredible chapter in the history of justice developed, it is perhaps necessary first to go back in time and tell how the Chicago Machine came into being.

A hundred years ago if men were knaves,
Why, people called them so.

Chicago, 1896

2
The Machine

In 1903, Lincoln Steffens visited Chicago to write another article in his "Shame of Our Cities" series. He anticipated no problems for "the evil of Chicago was obvious, general, bold." Yet he didn't write as planned. More intriguing than the political bosses, he decided, were the unique methods of the reformers.

Walter L. Fisher, head of the Municipal Voters League, explained the situation. The reformers weren't seeking "good government" because they realized that, given the ethnic subdivisions of the city's population and the ignorance of many of its citizens, it would be impossible to achieve sufficient strength. The goal, then, was "representative government," and that meant, Steffens decided, the reformers played politics like the grafters but did so to obtain a fair share of the spoils for the public interest: a school here, a paved street there, a park over here. As Steffens wrote:

> The methods of these League reformers were the methods of politics: they dealt with each ward according to the actual situation there. They got the facts, knew the candidates, politicians, parties, grafts, and the people in a ward, and then, with this information, by publicity and by *trading* they swung the anonymous minority that followed the League all together *to one side and one ultimate purpose.* [Emphasis added]

This use of practical politics was not wisdom, Steffens decided. Rather was it "a sort of instinct, the Chicago instinct."

Instead of another muckraking article citing the city's acceptance of an alliance between gangsters, crooked businessmen, and corrupt politicians, Steffens wrote about reformers attempting to justify the

6

means by the limited goals they set for themselves; he wrote about the "Chicago instinct" to wheel and deal in the interest of "realism." And because Steffens by now had become influential, his article caused reformers in other cities to follow Chicago's example. Some of them, Steffens noted, got results of a sort: "not good government, not normal representative government, but — a temporary betterment."

In the decades that followed, no reformer attempted to give Chicago — or Cook County — good government. That simple goal was relegated to the distant future when conditions might change, when Chicago might become a community instead of a collection of ethnic minorities grouped for convenience in various wards. Instead, "the Chicago instinct" remained the rule, and amid the graft and the gunplay some good was achieved. Carl Sandburg could acknowledge the city he claimed as his own was wicked, crooked, brutal, and yet boast: "Come and show me another city with lifted head singing so proud to be alive and coarse and strong and cunning."

At the time Steffens wrote, fifty thousand people were coming to Chicago each year, most of them from southern and eastern Europe. The Irish had already arrived; the blacks would come during and after World War I. "Immigrant trains" were common — hundreds of new arrivals, tied together by ropes to keep them from becoming lost, led through the streets by an agent who collected so much per head for each future citizen. They were taken to live in wooden shacks, many of them built on land cleared by the Great Fire. A Hull House report describes a typical scene:

> Little idea can be given of the filthy and rotten tene-
> ments, the dingy courts and tumbledown sheds, the
> foul stables and dilapidated outhouses, the broken
> sewer-pipes, the piles of garbage fairly alive with dis-
> eased odors, and of the numbers of children filling
> every nook, working and playing in every room, eating
> and sleeping on every windowsill, pouring in and out of
> every door, and seeming literally to pave every scrap of
> "yard." In one block the writer numbered over
> seventy-five children in the open street.

One area, mentioned by the Hull House researcher, was said to house nineteen thousand people whose only bathing facility was the polluted river.

In such a city of immigrants one can easily understand why reformers despaired of immediate good government and why a poet could be proud of its vitality. Before a municipal government could maintain law and justice, its people had to learn what the words meant. Yet, one might add, how could they ever learn when corruption was accepted as a way of life? Over several decades, literally millions of Chicagoans grew up knowing no other way. Indeed, they assumed *their* way was the *normal* way and those who said otherwise were but hypocrites. Those who knew otherwise, the educated and the wealthy, found room to profit in the status quo, and the reformers grew resigned to what some called "working within the system" and what, as the years passed, became known as "working with the machine."

It is ironic, perhaps, but not really surprising, that the Voters League of Steffens' time endorsed in 1900 a young, wealthy Republican to oppose "Candyman" Gunther in the Second Ward. The league considered its candidate a bit stupid but, on the whole, harmless; the same could not be said of Gunther. Better a zero than a minus, the leaders believed. Their candidate ran with league backing, won, and thus began a career that even for Chicago became notorious. The young man's name was William Hale Thompson and in time he made alliance with gangsters Johnny Torrio and Al Capone. In the heady "America First" days that followed the defeat of President Wilson's dream, he won the applause of voters of German descent by promising to punch King George of England in the nose if for any reason that personage should set foot in Chicago. Outrageous, flamboyant, ridiculous, corrupt — those were the words for Thompson, but he won a unique place in the hearts of millions of citizens.

"Big Bill the Builder," as Thompson advertised himself, ruled Chicago with help from the Mob from 1915 to 1923 when, confronted with a coalition of outraged liberals and practical politicians, he withdrew from a third race. It was time to let the reformers try and fail, whereupon he would come back stronger than before.

This decision forced Torrio to move his headquarters from Chicago to the suburb of Cicero where he located at the Hawthorne Inn. But even in corrupt Cicero where, according to legend, gunsmoke was the prevailing odor, the winds of change were blowing. When the 1924 spring elections came along, Capone, the action man, was forced to take strong measures to ensure the return to office of cooperative officials. A few horrified citizens appealed to a Cook County judge for aid in maintaining the sanctity of the ballot — an indication of some progress, this — and a small army of deputized policemen, detectives, and motorcycle cops was sent to the rescue. A pitched battle resulted. Frank Capone was killed and his brother, Scarface Al, was seen running down an alley as the gangsters dispersed. Yet it was a classic case of winning a battle and losing a war, for when the votes were counted that night the pro-Capone politicians were still firmly in control of the town.

In Chicago, meanwhile, the new mayor was William E. Dever, a former judge and a respected one. The situation was too serious, he decided, for wheeling and dealing according to tradition. The advent of Prohibition and the rise of powerful gangs to exploit the national thirst had created a crisis situation that Mayor Dever believed required direct action. Naming a new police chief, he ordered him to enforce the anti-liquor laws, and Chief Morgan A. Collins tried to do so. He was more successful in an attack on commercialized vice: prostitution and bookie joints. Gambling almost ceased inside Chicago, and the brothels that had existed before the Everleigh sisters became famous, disappeared. They had but moved to the suburbs, of course, where they remained within easy reach of the Model T. Business everywhere benefited by automobiles, good roads, telephones, and other modern wonders, and illicit business was no exception.

Beer, of course, remained the principal source of income for Capone — boss now after a failure to unify Chicago crime caused Torrio to quit in disgust — and for Capone's rivals. Withdrawal to Cicero did not mean the beer trucks didn't keep the central city's thousands of speakeasies supplied, and that gang wars didn't litter the streets with bodies, for the rank and file cop was still corrupt, and the citizen looked on beer as a symbol of personal freedom.

The mayor knew the political risk. "People tell me I'm wrecking a promising political career, but it can't be helped," he said to the press.

Amid the violence, Dever pushed reforms. He encouraged Dr. Herman N. Bundesen, a nationally known health authority, to do something about purifying the milk supply. Additional recreational centers were built. The Board of Education was reorganized and enjoyed a brief period of freedom from politics. Finally, the mayor tried to interest his citizens in the finer things of life: music, literature, art. A civic commission was appointed to study the problem.

It was all for naught, of course. Late in 1926, "Big Bill" became bored with "laboring as a private citizen for all of the people," and announced he would run once more. Easily winning the Republican nomination, he boasted:

"I'm wetter than the Atlantic Ocean. When I'm elected we'll not only reopen places those people have closed, but we'll open ten thousand new ones."

All gangsters, at least, could unite behind such a man, and they supplied cash and muscle as needed. In April, 1927, Thompson won by more than 83,000 votes. He was almost sixty, a giant, fat clown who, somehow, still possessed ability to please the ignorant laborer and charm society women on Chicago's Gold Coast. Of his defeated rival, folks spoke with some regret: "He was so straight he leaned over backward." What's more, and therein was the real problem, "he would not compromise."

To prove the good old days were back, Thompson fired Police Chief Collins and replaced him with a former chief who had once admitted: "Sixty per cent of my police are in the bootleg business." And Capone moved back into the city.

The story of the next four years has been told many times and need not be elaborated here. It was a wide open era, exceeding the worst excesses of the past. The reformers, disillusioned as always to discover that good intentions had been insufficient, were helpless. Too many citizens considered that "life, liberty, and the pursuit of happiness" meant they had a constitutional right to drink what, when, and where they pleased, and to visit a bookie or a brothel on the same basis. That politicians were collecting millions in graft, and gangsters were making millions by openly violating any law they pleased, all meant very little. Indeed, as Chicago became a byword for lawlessness, that old municipal pride intensified.

The plight of the reformers was well illustrated as the 1928 general election approached. Frank Loesch, head of the Chicago Crime Commission and a seventy-five-year-old veteran of many civic causes, went hat in hand to Capone at his plush new headquarters in the Hotel Lexington. Please, he asked, help us give Chicago a violence-free, honest election. What, if anything, Capone demanded in return, Loesch never said, but the deal was made and Chicago had its most peaceful election in many a year. Perhaps the only reward Capone wanted was the boost to the ego this classic example of "the Chicago instinct" provided.

With the economic crash of 1929 and the onset of the Great Depression, prospects for continued Republican rule in Chicago and in the country began to dim. Thanks to Thompson's extravagances and the dreary years of graft, the city was near bankruptcy. Citizens who had admired Thompson's excesses and accepted the graft as normal, now began to worry. There developed no concerted drive to "throw the rascals out," but a-time-for-a-change mood could be detected. Anton Joseph Cermak, who had just purchased the Democrat Party leadership with money supplied by an ex-convict, Moe Rosenberg, was ready to take advantage of the opportunity. He had been preparing for a long time.

At age one, Cermak was brought to America in 1874 from the part of Europe then known as Bohemia and today as Czechoslovakia. The family settled near Chicago, moving around as jobs in the coal mines of the area became available. The boy spent approximately three years in elementary schools, and at age thirteen became a mule driver in the pits. A brawler, he also demonstrated leadership qualities. When the mule-skinners decided to ask for a raise, he acted as spokesman and was fired instantly. Shortly thereafter, he boarded a passing freight to Chicago and found a job on the horse cars in the Czech neighborhood of Pilsen. Soon he became the leader of the local ethnic gang, his fighting ability and his capacity for liquor combining to win the respect of other young toughs. It also brought him to the attention of the local precinct boss who was always seeking to recruit youths who could hold the rank and file in line.

Suddenly Cermak was in politics, and he liked it. Meanwhile, he needed a business and a wife. Acquiring a horse and wagon, he became a wood hauler, one always willing to add a personal touch such as lighting fires on the Jewish Sabbath. Within two years he was able to marry and within four he was able to build his wife a house. Mary, a seamstress with even less education than her husband, felt her place was in that house, and there for the most part she stayed.

A hard worker, Cermak achieved wealth in business while climbing steadily upward in politics and in government. Much of his success, however, can be attributed to the fact that the Czechs had increasing political impact. By 1920 their number was estimated in Chicago and adjoining areas of Cook County at 200,000. By virtue of being available at the right time and place, Cermak became their first leader. He rose steadily: the state legislature, alderman from Lawndale, and, of course, precinct captain. George Brennan, leader of the Democrats, played off one ethnic group against another and concentrated power in the Irish. Cermak didn't object — he had friends among the Irish and also among the Jews. Eventually he would form a coalition of various ethnic groups, but that day was still to come.

The Jews of North Lawndale and Douglas Park grew into the largest Jewish ghetto in the country. Kosher markets drew Jews from all over the city each Thursday night, and scores of synagogues were needed to attend the needs of local citizens. Politically, they were largely controlled by Moe Rosenberg and Jacob Arvey, who in the best tradition of the times, supplied everything from noodles to shoes on Jewish holidays.

Cermak allied himself with these men, and with Jacob Lindheimer and Henry Horner, whose real name was Levy. (Horner's parents divorced when he was five, a rare occurrence among Jews of the period, and when his mother went home to her mother, Hannah Horner, the grandmother accepted them only on condition they call themselves Horner. No action was taken to legalize the change, however.) Jacob Lindheimer, a German Jew who was Marje Everett's grandfather, operated a saloon near the stockyards and got into politics through friendship with the Irish of the area who patronized his joint. Before long he was managing the county treasurer's office for Paddy Carr, an important politician of the day. It was there he met Horner, a bright young attorney with an interest in politics and some promising connections.

Although Lindheimer had a son, Ben, only two years younger than Horner, he unofficially adopted Horner and pushed his career steadily upward. Perhaps he recognized that Ben was a born businessman who would be able to use politicians but could not be one. Possibly another reason Horner became almost a member of the family was his friendship, if that is the word, with Lindheimer's married daughter, Maude. A strong woman like Horner's grandmother, she was also pretty and exciting. Her pet name for Horner was Hanky-Panky. Earlier he had been engaged to, and in love with, a wealthy Jewish girl, but had broken the engagement to please his mother. After his mother's death, however, it was Maude's marriage that kept him an increasingly lonely bachelor.

Another political ally of Cermak was Otto Kerner, Sr., son of a Czech cabinetmaker. He became a precinct captain for Cermak, who rewarded him in the usual way by pushing him upward to alderman and then circuit judge. Ultimately he would become wealthy and respectable, thanks largely to Cermak, and would be appointed to an appellate court seat on the federal bench.

Another factor in Cermak's rise was the liquor problem. Long before prohibition became law and smuggling became a big business across the lakes from Canada, Chicago had wrestled with the issue. In 1906 the Democratic mayor, Edward Dunne, was blamed as election day neared for not enforcing the 1 A.M. closing laws for saloons. He reacted by ordering the law enforced, and thus outraged many of his supporters among the ethnic groups. They got together to form The United Societies for Local Self-Government, and Cermak emerged as secretary, the all-powerful job. That made him spokesman for the "Dripping Wet" and gave him an almost unlimited expense account. Brewers and distillers provided cash as needed and asked no accounting. He was able to bribe legislators in behalf of the society, and promote his own career as well.

Equally important, Cermak was able to make alliance with underworld leaders. At that period, white slavery was the big racket in Chicago. Many an immigrant came to America alone, hoping to make enough money to send for his family later. Meanwhile, he craved sex. To supply the demand, an elaborate organization was set up to recruit young girls just off the ships or farms. Some went willingly, lured by promises of high pay. Others were virtually held prisoner and raped repeatedly until they became docile. The customer, ironically, wanted a prostitute who spoke his language and resembled his absent wife, so girls of all ethnic backgrounds were needed. It was a shocking situation but local politicians considered it necessary and perhaps natural, given the second-rate position of women in general. Action finally came on the national level with the passage of the Mann Act forbidding the transportation of women across state lines for immoral purposes.

The blacks, late arrivals in Chicago, were convenient targets of prejudice for other ethnic groups. *Everyone* could feel superior to the sons of slaves. It was no accident that the first big race riot in midcentury America came in June, 1951, when a Negro bus driver tried to move into Cicero. That suburb, which as late as 1963 was being described as "a walled city of the syndicate," reacted furiously. Three days of rioting followed and five companies of National Guardsmen were necessary to restore order, but the Mob won. The bus driver took his family elsewhere.

Presumably, Cermak would have made a deal with blacks if they had been, as they are today, an important political factor. Meantime, he would even deal with Republicans. In 1909, he supported William Lorimer, "the blond boss" of the west side, when the legislature elected Lorimer to the Senate of the United States. Cermak and other Democrats were accused of accepting bribes. Ultimately the Senate expelled Lorimer, but Cermak was officially cleared. The stink lingered on, but the folks who lived near the stockyards were accustomed to foul odors. Certainly it wouldn't be the last time a politician of one party made a deal with a leader of another in Cook County.

In 1921, George E. Brennan, an Irish leader who had lost a leg in those same coal mines Cermak worked as a boy, got control of the Democratic organization by entering his own slate of candidates for local office. Cermak was slated as the candidate for president of the Board of Commissioners of Cook County. The Brennan slate made a clean sweep of the primary, and won most offices in the general election. Cermak was one of the winners but his task was formidable: eight of the fifteen commissioners were Republicans. He solved the problem by "buying" one of the Republicans who was on the verge of bankruptcy.

During Mayor Dever's attempts at reform, Cermak played it cool. He made no open break with Brennan and the Democrats, but he gave secret support to the Republicans. Obviously, he recognized that Dever, wet or dry, was an obstacle to his own ambitions. And in 1926, with Thompson making his bid for a return to power, Cermak stabbed Dever in the back. The move won him new friends among the Irish and vindicated him in the eyes of those ethnic groups who wanted no restriction on their right to drink.

Cermak had given some thought to opposing Dever in the primary and then taking on Thompson himself, but Brennan discouraged it and Cermak sensed his time hadn't come. Moreover, he developed a larger ambition: to be governor. The streets had hardly been swept clean after Thompson's victory when a boom began for Cermak to run for governor in 1928. Unfortunately he became seriously ill in September, and left town for Hot Springs, Arkansas — that tiny spa to which so many politicians and gangsters were attracted. When he returned early in 1928, Brennan had made other arrangements. He did, however, agree to slate Cermak for United States senator. Unhappy, Cermak went along with the party, and he and the rest of the Democrats were overwhelmed in Herbert Hoover's landslide that buried Al Smith.

Still, the campaign was profitable in a political sense. The man from Bohemia proved his vote-getting ability. In Cook County alone he polled 133,000 more votes than Al Smith, and in Chicago he won by 77,000 while Smith was losing by 21,000. Immediately, his friends began booming him for mayor in 1931, and he called in his closest advisers and began making plans. This was no longer a problem since Boss Brennan died in August, 1928, leaving the post of party leader open.

As John Dienhart, a reporter close to Cermak, put it: "Cermak raised the money and bought the organization."

Where did he get the money? From that old crook Moe Rosenberg. The story did not come out until 1934 when Rosenberg was indicted on income-tax evasion charges, and confessed that in 1929-30 he had distributed almost $500,000 for Cermak's use. Part of it went to pay off $200,000 in debts the Democrats owed, and the rest went to various politicians whose support was needed. Allegedly, Cermak retained $90,000 for himself. Arvey got $12,000. The rest got anywhere from $6,000 to $1,000, depending on their price. Those paid included Irishmen, Italians, Czechs, Scandinavians, Poles, Jews, and — showing how times were changing — blacks.

Where did Rosenberg get all that cash?

Samuel Insull was responsible. An Englishman by birth, Insull came to Chicago and acquired a monopoly over electricity, gas, and the transit system. He bought politicians right and left, and Cermak was no exception. Indeed, it was Cermak who suggested the Rosenberg Iron and Metal Company be set up, and arranged with Insull for it to receive 90 per cent of all utility scrap in Cook County as well as all the scrap of the Illinois Bell Telephone Company. It was from the profits these monopolies made possible that the payoff money was derived.

By 1931 Cermak and his allies were ready, and they won by a majority of 194,267 — until then the greatest majority ever polled in a race for mayor of Chicago. Big Bill wasn't just beaten, he was humiliated. And the Chicago Machine, that coalition of ethnic groups, was firmly established. At the time of this writing, it is still operating smoothly.

Cermak took charge of a bankrupt city in May, 1931, with conditions getting worse each passing day. After first consolidating his power in Chicago and Cook County, he began looking for help to ease the financial crisis. The big problem was Chicago's lack of home rule. Almost every financial decision had to be approved by the state government, and it was in Republican hands. Coming up in 1932, however, was an opportunity to remedy that situation. Voters would not only be electing a new president, but in Illinois they would be voting for a governor, a new legislature, and other state offices. The mayor's seat was hardly warm before Cermak told his friends that he would run for governor. His reasoning was simple: "Why should I stay mayor when I can run the city from Springfield?"

It wasn't quite that simple, however. In his campaign against Thompson he had won Irish support by promising to back one of their number, Mike Igoe, for governor in 1932, and Igoe was eager to run. Another complication was a promise made to Ben Lindheimer to slate Henry Horner, the protégé of Ben's father.

Back in 1914, Jacob Lindheimer had arranged for Horner to be elected judge of the Probate Court of Cook County. It was politically a most important job. Horner made final decisions on estates totaling hundreds of millions each year, and in the process became acquainted with the rich and powerful, about whom he learned many family secrets. After seventeen years, however, it was time to move up if ever he was to do so.

Jacob, almost blind in his last years, died in 1928, but before doing so called his family together and asked them to carry out his plans and remain friends. They agreed to have dinner together once a month, and to help Horner, now almost fifty and virtually a member of the family.

Ben quickly stepped into his father's shoes as a behind-the-scenes political manipulator, and it was he who rallied the so-called Standard Club Crowd — all Jews of German descent — to Cermak's side in his battle with Big Bill. Now with 1932 coming up fast, they wanted their reward, a Jew elected governor of Illinois.

Cermak, his own ambition demanding its chance, hesitated as long as possible, but Igoe forced his hand by announcing he would run in the primary with or without the organization's approval. That meant the Irish vote would be lost, and chances were good the Jews would join the Irish if Horner wasn't slated. Horner, meanwhile, had won some Irish support in addition to the money and votes Lindheimer could muster: men like Pat Nash.

Horner helped Cermak off the hook by saying he had "no ambition to become a political leader." This the mayor interpreted to mean that Horner would be largely a figurehead, taking orders from the boss back in Chicago. Instead of running Chicago from Springfield, Cermak decided, he would run Springfield from Chicago. He then proceeded to balance out the ticket with men of German, Irish, and Czech descent. The Czech was Otto Kerner, Sr., candidate for attorney general.

Horner's victory was assured when Bruce Campbell, a popular downstate Democrat, made it a three-man race. Campbell and Igoe canceled each other out in the south, while Chicago and Cook County piled up an unbeatable margin for the Horner ticket. Moe Rosenberg proved he had not lost his old ability to get out the Jewish vote in the Twenty-fourth Ward. There Horner tallied 15,614 to 241 for Igoe and 17 for Campbell. It was a great achievement but a tougher test lay ahead in the general election.

Traditionally downstate Illinois was, and remains, Republican. One area is called Egypt, presumably because its leading city is named Cairo and because the fertile land reminded some Bible student of the soil-restoring qualities of the Nile. Much of Southern Illinois was settled by transplanted Scotch-Irish from the mountains of the Blue Ridge. A hardy, independent people, much given to violence, they had little in common with the ethnic blocs of Chicago. Indeed, in 1923, the Ku Klux Klan took over law-enforcement duties, allegedly to do battle with Italian-American bootleggers of East St. Louis. That city had a reputation comparable to Chicago for gangland violence and served St. Louis much as, on occasion, Cicero served Chicago. So different were the two sections that an effort was made in 1927 to create two states, North Illinois and South Illinois.

Selling a Jew as governor in the downstate area was no easy task, but Ben Lindheimer as campaign manager did an efficient job. He was the first to use billboards effectively. Barbecues brought out thousands to get free food and to see a Jew. Many were impressed with what they saw.

The campaign wasn't half over when, abruptly, the Insull financial empire collapsed. At one point its worth had been estimated at $3 billion, but fraud and reckless expansion caused it at last to topple. Insull fled to Greece, was later extradited and put on trial for embezzlement. To no one's surprise, he was acquitted. Nevertheless, the Insull collapse hurt Chicago's financial institutions badly and contributed to the general depression. It also meant that Rosenberg would no longer have large hunks of cash with which to buy politicians on behalf of future Cermaks and Horners, but perhaps that wouldn't be necessary.

Illinois went Democrat in 1932, only the third time since the Civil War that it had done so. Roosevelt carried the state by 550,000 votes, and Horner won by 650,000. Democrats captured the legislature and all state offices. Otto Kerner, Sr., became attorney general. In effect, although Horner was governor, Cermak was boss of Illinois.

Ben Lindheimer, who had shared with his family the $600,000 estate left by his father, was rewarded by Horner with the chairmanship of the commerce commission, a powerful post indeed. Lindheimer had become rich through real estate deals, and he would get richer. Joseph Knight, only twenty-one but a tireless worker in the campaign, was appointed an assistant commerce commissioner under Lindheimer. He would be heard from again as he grew older. There were some Horner appointments that displeased Cermak, but on the whole the two men got along. Rumors that Cermak might be appointed secretary of commerce by President Roosevelt pleased some of the disgruntled, but others pointed out the Boss was now so strong he could run Chicago and Illinois from Washington. In any case, Cermak wanted to have a voice when federal jobs were handed out. To get it he went to Miami where on February 15, 1933, the president-elect was scheduled to end a yachting trip.

A huge crowd gathered in Bayfront Park at the foot of Flagler Street where a makeshift grandstand had been erected. Roosevelt rode up in an open car and made a short speech. Spotting Cermak, he motioned the mayor to come to the car. The two men talked briefly. Abruptly shots rang out. Cermak and several others were hit, but the president-elect was untouched. His car started up, then stopped. Cermak was lifted inside where, cradled in Roosevelt's arms, he was driven to a hospital. Nineteen days later he died of complications.

The debate began before his death: were the bullets fired by

Guiseppe Zangara aimed at Roosevelt or Cermak? Was Zangara an unlikely assassin hired by Chicago gangsters who feared Cermak would upset the balance of power in the underworld? Or was Zangara a mentally sick nut who wanted a place in history as the man who killed a president-elect? Whatever the answers, little time was permitted for investigation. Before Cermak died, Zangara was tried and sentenced to eighty years in prison. Three days after Cermak died, he was tried again for murder. The trial took one day. He was sentenced to die. No appeals were made. Two weeks after Cermak's death he sat down in the electric chair and shouted "push the button." Someone did, and a lot of answers died with him.

Chicago's gangsters had taught the city how to make a funeral into a pageant, so Boss Cermak was given a "sendoff" spectacular enough to satisfy a Capone. The procession moved from City Hall to Chicago Stadium and thence to the Bohemian National Cemetery. The floor of the stadium was arranged with flowers to form a giant cross. Hundreds of thousands watched or took part in the march.

In death much is forgiven — and a lot is soon forgotten. The eulogies were many and laudatory. Clarence Darrow, however, tried to put the late Boss into better perspective: "On the whole," he said, "he was a pretty good man." And after much debate about a monument, the aldermen changed the name of Twenty-second Street to Cermak Road. Perhaps logically, it was the main artery connecting Chicago to gangster-controlled Cicero and was called the Street of Whores.

Governor Horner delivered the principal eulogy at Cermak's funeral, but he made no effort to fill the two empty chairs Cermak left: party boss in Cook County and Chicago mayor. The nuts and bolts of party organization had no appeal for Horner who, as governor, had enough problems to worry about at a time when banks were failing and the nation as well as the state seemed on the edge of financial anarchy. Instead of going to the expense of holding a special election, the legislature passed, and Horner signed, a bill giving the Chicago City Council power to select a successor to Cermak. With Patrick A. Nash, Cermak's county chairman, pulling the strings, Edward J. Kelly was elected.

That Kelly was chief engineer of the sanitary district and Nash was in the sewer contracting business may have been coincidence. More important, perhaps, was the fact that Nash was a breeder of

thoroughbred horses — an improver of the breed — and Ben Lindheimer, Marje Everett's father, had ambitions to become a racetrack
owner. Before anything could be done about that, however, both Kelly
and Nash had to settle their tax problems with the suddenly potent
Bureau of Internal Revenue — the agency that had sent Capone to
prison. Governor Horner visited Washington on behalf of the new
bosses and perhaps prevented their indictment. Kelly settled up by
paying $105,000. Nash got clipped for a bit more: $175,000.

With that out of the way, Lindheimer's dreams got attention.
Parimutuel wagering had been legal in Illinois since 1927, but the state
was satisfied with a flat license fee from operating tracks. No effort was
made to regulate the betting. Consequently, mobsters were largely in
control and public confidence in racing was low. Lindheimer had faith
that if the right image could be created, the betting "handle" could be
increased many times. In 1933, therefore, he arranged for the creation
of the Illinois Racing Commission. Its first act was to bar "persons
engaged in illegal business, bookmakers, and any other type of unde-
sirables" from owning and/or operating a racetrack. That gave Lindheimer the opportunity he wanted — the only question was when to
use it.

Meanwhile, the Kelly-Nash combination began to improve the
machine Cermak had constructed, giving it more horsepower and
mobility. In successive elections it won by larger margins than ever,
and soon it was time to think about getting a new and more cooperative
governor. To replace Horner would require Lindheimer's active assistance, and before pledging it, "Little Ben" — as Kelly called him —
wanted his racetrack.

Jack Lynch, a notorious gambler allegedly worth $10 million, was
the power at Washington Park. Back in 1931, he had made headlines by
getting himself kidnapped by other gangsters and paying a $50,000
ransom. He had been on good terms with Capone and such Capone
lieutenants as Jake "Greasy Thumb" Guzik, but essentially he was
independent. Much of his wealth came from the General News
Bureau, the wire service founded by Mont Tennes. Lynch owned forty
per cent, but he was fighting to retain that piece of the action with
Moses Annenberg, who wanted the whole thing. The wire service
supplied racing data to handbooks, and was immensely profitable.
Annenberg, who got his start fighting for Hearst newspapers in the
bitter circulation wars earlier in the century, was manager of General

News. Yet he had founded a rival, the Nationwide News Service, and was driving General News out of business. Lynch considered that a conflict of interest, and filed suit. Annenberg countered that since the wire service to handbooks was illegal, the court had no jurisdiction. Chicago newspapers reported the affair somewhat gleefully, and suddenly Lynch was reminded of the rule forbidding persons engaged in illegal business to own or operate racetracks.

Mayor Kelly suggested to Lynch that he should make the best deal possible with Lindheimer and get out before he was thrown out. So Lindheimer "bought" control of Washington Park in February, 1935, paying three cents each for 150,000 shares. Even for Chicago, that was a pretty good deal.

Lindheimer, however, wasn't ready to take command of the track. He needed to remain chairman of the Illinois Commerce Commission just a little longer. Another scheme helpful to the betting business was scheduled for action, and he wanted to be in a position to influence his close friend, Governor Horner, to accept it. Lynch, meanwhile, bowed to Annenberg and sold his stock in General News. Frank "the Enforcer" Nitti acted as broker. Allegedly Lynch collected a cool million from Annenberg for the stock and Nitti got $100,000 for his services. Annenberg went on to build a fantastic racing empire that supplied every bookie and bettor in the country. The Internal Revenue agents couldn't even estimate how wealthy he was, but they sent him to prison for tax evasion and the judge fined him $8,000,000. Some three decades later, however, President Richard Nixon appointed his son, Walter, to be ambassador to England. Lynch died before that happened — in 1945, in Miami. His estate was estimated at $25,000.

The new scheme Lindheimer had devised was a bill to legalize 2,500 handbooks in Chicago. The excuse for such a law was the need for new revenue to pay teachers and police. Each book would be licensed and operate much as a tavern. It sounded good, but much more was involved. Organized-crime leaders had consulted and concluded that gambling offered cash profits equal to the millions made in liquor. The urge to gamble was just as strong as the urge to drink and could be cultivated by making bookies respectable citizens. Of course, a lot would depend on who controlled — or, at least, was allied with — City Hall. Since Capone's departure to federal prison, however, the Outfit, as it was known, had achieved a degree of unity and such men as Nitti felt strong enough to control all ambitious independents.

Lindheimer thought he could control Horner despite an early statement by the governor that he didn't approve of legalized gambling. Properly greased, the bill easily passed both houses of the legislature. Attorney General Otto Kerner, Sr., announced the bill was constitutional. From "Egypt," however, where lived the descendants of men who had fought at King's Mountain and founded such states as Tennessee and Kentucky, came a roar of outrage. The Protestants of the area lived up to their name.

The governor certainly realized that to defy the Chicago Machine would be to risk political suicide. He weighed the consequences so long that it seemed as if perhaps he intended to let the bill become law without his signature. A coward's way out, perhaps, but an expedient one. Not so. Horner had his faults, perhaps, but cowardice wasn't one of them. Four hours before the deadline he vetoed the bill. One paragraph in his veto message shows plainly he understood that more was at stake than the bill authorized:

> It is readily admitted that the desire to gamble is found in most persons — perhaps in some form and to some extent in all persons. Its prevalence, however, does not stamp it as a virtue. Nor do I concede that public and commercialized gambling cannot largely be suppressed, even if it cannot be entirely eradicated. Because there are violations of a law, it does not follow that the law should be repealed. If there is any justification in legalized bookmaking, *there is equal justification in legalizing all other forms of public gambling now prohibited.* [Emphasis added.]

Kelly had sent a message to the governor warning that if Horner vetoed the bookie bill, he would veto the governor's chances for a second term in office. It was no idle threat. He passed the word to Lindheimer, who was willing enough to dump the man who had been almost a brother to him. Yet he wanted something in return: Arlington Park, another racetrack. Kelly agreed, but suggested that the deal would have to wait until they were finished with Horner. The break became official on February 11, 1936, when Lindheimer resigned from Horner's cabinet, effective May 1. Horace Lindheimer, Ben's brother, was brought into line with the promise he would be slated as county treasurer in the upcoming elections. Only Maude, Horner's old and dearest friend, stuck with Father Jacob's protégé.

Dr. Herman Bundesen, the man who had once done so much to purify milk and improve health under Mayor Dever, was slated by Kelly to succeed Horner. John Stelle, a legendary political figure from downstate, was named to run for lieutenant governor. Incumbent Otto Kerner, Sr., agreed to seek reelection as attorney general on Kelly's slate. Several other incumbents were won over. All in all, the prospects looked bleak for the second Jewish governor in American history. (The first was David Emanuel of Georgia a century before.) He still had hopes, however, that President Roosevelt would support him. Instead, the White House offered him a federal judgeship and a future shot at the Supreme Court.

It was a dirty campaign. Most of the wealthy Standard Club Jews put their money behind Horner despite the defection of the Lindheimers. To Jake Arvey, whose ancestors came from Eastern Europe, went the job of converting the West Side Jews of similar background who, four years earlier, had considered Horner a hero. Arvey has told of being halted on the steps of a synagogue on primary election day by an old man with a long beard. The man said: "You did a terrible thing. You made me vote against Henry Horner, our Henry Horner, today."

Kelly had a simpler task. In speech after speech he thundered: "God deliver us from this lily-white governor, this self-styled reformer, who is against betting and against everything a liberal man wants or likes."

That argument carried weight in Chicago, but it made Horner popular downstate. Arvey's ward voted as he desired, but the total vote in Cook County for Bundesen was less than half what Kelly expected. Certainly it wasn't enough to offset Horner's landslide downstate where he carried every county. Others on his slate were not so fortunate. John Stelle, the Chicago Machine candidate, won nomination for lieutenant governor, and Kerner was renominated as attorney general.

The Roosevelt sweep in the general election guaranteed Horner's victory over the Republicans. Yet in winning a battle, he lost the war. Instead of feeling refreshed and vindicated by the mandate of people who trusted him, he became bitter and vain. Virtue, he decided, had not triumphed but practical politics instead. The tactics he had once deplored he began to enjoy. Immediately after the general election he began trying to get rid of Otto Kerner, Sr., one of those who had betrayed him. It took some doing, but finally Kerner was appointed an appellate court judge and Horner was able to name his own man attorney general. A similar effort to get Lieutenant Governor Stelle out of office failed. The men remained bitter rivals.

Two years later Horner suffered a stroke just before the 1938 elections. The thought of Stelle taking over as governor was the one thing that kept him alive. He went to Florida to recuperate, leaving trusted aides "to keep an eye on Stelle." Angry feelings developed between the two groups. Horner returned some months later and officially resumed his duties, but his health continued to decline. A "bedside cabinet" took over, concealing the truth from the public and from Stelle. Still the vultures gathered, and the mansion became a combination hospital and poker casino. In his lucid moments, Horner refused to quit and turn the state over to Stelle. Finally, however, he accepted as fact the impossibility of his running for a third term.

Kelly, the old enemy, was invited to the mansion. Horner got out of bed to greet him. The two men decided to slate Judge Kerner for governor in 1940. Kerner turned it down on grounds of health. He, too, had a heart condition. The next choice was Harry Hershey, a mine company attorney and state Democratic chairman. He accepted. The weeping governor promised to see that he was elected. Stelle announced he would form a rebel slate. The Republicans nominated Dwight Green, a United States Attorney who helped convict Capone of income tax evasion.

The end came on October 6, 1940. Henry Horner, a man who had wanted to be a good governor and found it impossible, died in agony ninety-nine days before the end of his second term. Stelle took over, and the lights never dimmed in the mansion until the next governor was inaugurated. It was, perhaps, the longest and most expensive party in American history. Stelle found time, however, to appoint Hubert E. Howard, a Lindheimer buddy, to the state racing board.

Meanwhile, on April 16, 1940, the *Daily Racing Form* announced that Arlington Park had been sold to a group "consisting of Ben F. Lindheimer, majority stockholder of Washington Park; John D. Allen, vice president of Brinks & Company; John G. McCarthy, president of the Chicago Board of Trade; Modie Spiegel, chairman of the board of Spiegel, Inc.; Daniel F. Rice, grain broker; Ralph Atlass, director of Chicago radio stations WJJD and WIND and others."

Marjorie Lindheimer, Ben's adopted daughter, a tall, gangling teenager, was delighted. She just loved horses and racing and manipulating politicians, and she learned as much as she could about these adult things. Some day the knowledge would be useful. Horner's failure proved once more the validity of the "Chicago instinct," and within that concept was ample opportunity to make reformers pay dearly for progress, real or imagined.

3

The Entrepreneur

Why would Ben Lindheimer, the new owner of a major racetrack, favor legalizing handbooks in Chicago? Surely if the average bettor could legally drop off his wager with his friendly neighborhood bookie, he would have no particular interest in trekking out to Washington Park to see the nags run. Even the illegal books were efficient, thanks to Moe Annenberg, in obtaining fast race results, and some offered facilities equal to the best clubhouse. Moreover, a large book would accept bets on every race in the country, something even Lindheimer's tracks didn't do.

All of which was true, but before there can be bets taken there has to be a race to bet on and that usually requires a track. Equally important, there has to be a universal method of fixing the odds. Otherwise each bookie would have to be a handicapper. Thanks to the parimutuel system, legalized in Illinois in 1927, the track served as final arbiter, and bookies paid "track odds." Under the parimutuel system (a corruption of the Paris Mutual betting system devised in France) all money bet on a race goes into a pool. The odds on each horse are determined by the amount bet on that horse in the race. A heavy favorite, receiving the bulk of the action, would carry very low odds whereas a longshot which received very little support might pay off at 100 to 1 if, by hook or crook, it managed to win. The operator of the system, in this case the track owner, automatically took a percentage off the top, so the track made money regardless of the outcome of the race. Today, of course, the state also takes a percentage off the top, but in Illinois in 1935 that idea had not occurred to anyone. Because of this oversight, if that's what it was, there was no state supervision of the betting, and the track operator was free to do all sorts of wondrous things.

26

And nothing was more wondrous than "come-back money."
Then and now a bookie often finds he has accepted more bets on a horse than he can afford to pay if the horse wins. He can either "lay off" part of the bets to another bookie, or he can send it to the track to be bet through the parimutuel system, thus lowering the odds on the horse to a level he can handle. Officially the practice is frowned upon, but, in the absence of supervision, it was a gold mine for Lindheimer at Washington Park.

Certain big bookies such as "Greasy Thumb" Guzik sent their come-back money out to Lindheimer. He, or his representative, held it. The sleeper might go off at 10 to 1. If it lost, then Lindheimer simply put the money in his pocket. If the horse won he quickly dumped the money in the mutuel pool, and the *final* payoff odds flashed on the tote board would reflect the post-race bet and come down to perhaps 8 to 5, thus saving the bookie from financial disaster.

In the five years before the laws were tightened in 1940, Washington Park became notorious as the come-back money track, and it was estimated by people in a position to know that Lindheimer handled a million dollars a week in come-back money.

Legalizing Chicago books might have increased the number of bettors and thus the amount of come-back money to drop into the parimutuel pool or one's pockets, as the outcome of each race indicated. This increase would have more than compensated for any drop in attendance by bettors at the track.

That, at least, was the theory. Since Horner vetoed the bookie bill, its validity wasn't tested. The illegal books continued to operate more or less openly, and the total handle increased steadily. Lindheimer, however, made one mistake. He gave stock to Mayor Kelly, but he neglected John Stelle, the downstate power. In 1941, Stelle marshaled his forces and rewrote the Illinois Horse Racing Act. The new law increased the power of the Racing Board, as it was now called, and directed the state to levy a tax on the parimutuel handle for the first time. In the nineteen years before Lindheimer's death, the state collected $195,379,314.00, and, of that, Lindheimer tracks paid approximately half.

With each annual report of the Racing Board, Stelle would note the tax extracted from Lindheimer and make pious public pronouncement: "He who has light in his own clean breast may sit in the midst of darkness and enjoy bright day."

Perhaps not everyone understood his comment, but odds are that Lindheimer did. Yet he could not have blamed himself overmuch for the failure to keep Stelle happy. The parimutuel tax would have been imposed sooner or later since other states were doing it and obtaining important revenue. Indeed, the taxes thus acquired became in time a type of insurance for the racing industry. Legislators are still warned today to do nothing to hurt racing because a large hunk of state revenue depends upon the industry remaining healthy. The racing industry does what it can in every way it can to see that friendly officials fill key jobs on local and state levels. Lindheimer, with his experience in public office ranging from membership on the park board to commerce commission chairman, to say nothing of his successful management of Horner's first campaign, understood the relationship of racing to politics better than most men.

It is possible that Lindheimer would not have become so obsessed with building a racing empire if he had enjoyed a happy home life similar to what he had known as a boy. Unfortunately he and his wife, Vera, were childless. They adopted three children: Walter, Patricia, and Marjorie, but this valiant effort to create a family was not altogether successful. Patricia, pretty and petite, enjoyed parties and popularity. Marjorie, tall and coltish, adored her foster father. Walter was completely uninterested in racing. Conflicts developed and, according to the Grand Jury testimony of attorney George J. Schaller, Mrs. Lindheimer "had a problem with alcohol."

In any event, Marjorie became Lindheimer's pet, was permitted to accompany him everywhere, and sit in on his conferences with trainers, lawyers, and politicians. She was only fourteen in 1935 when he acquired Washington Park, but she had some knowledge of the role of gambler Jack Lynch. On May 22, 1961, she wrote to Daniel F. Rice, one of her father's business associates, who was trying to collect $10,000 from Lindheimer's estate. In that letter she naively or not made a very amusing comment:

"Unfortunately, the $10,000 advance made by you to Dad remained on his books without anyone of us in the family having personal knowledge of the circumstances. While I was working for Dad at that time, I was not aware of the details of this particular matter, other than to know that *Jack Lynch had tremendous financial problems and that Dad was trying to assist him.*" (Emphasis added.)

By April, 1940, when Arlington Park was acquired, Marje, as the press and the racing industry knew her, had become an official assistant to Lindheimer. The announcement of the change in ownership made no mention of the fact that with 80,000 shares, Lindheimer had controlling interest, or that the shares had cost him four cents each.

If the price was cheap, Lindheimer more than made up for it by spending a young fortune improving his two tracks. He poured millions into them, doing everything possible to make them beautiful and luxurious. Until his entry into the field, racing in Illinois had been more or less on the county-fair style, attracting neither the best horses nor the so-called best people. The new image he gave the tracks put them on a par with the best in the country, and produced such profits it was even possible to erase Washington Park's reputation as a come-back money track.

Goodwill was created by this devotion to quality, but he was not content. There was always in his private office a box filled with currency — big bills — and over the years he ladled out large sums to people whose goodwill he wanted to ensure. They ranged from politicians to businessmen, from society figures to sportswriters and editors. Sometimes the payoffs were called "loans," but repayment was never expected. Meticulous records of this Currency Box Account were maintained, and over the years the total came to more than $750,000. You can buy a lot of goodwill in Chicago for that kind of pre-inflation money.

Once he had Arlington and Washington Parks well established, Lindheimer looked around for new worlds to conquer. Lincoln Fields, an old and not very prosperous track, caught his eye, but upon consideration he decided the time was not yet right to make his move. Instead, he ventured far afield to a new city and another sport.

On October 24, 1945, the formation was announced of a corporation to operate a professional football team in Los Angeles as part of the newly organized All-America Football Conference. As usual, Lindheimer did not take top billing. That honor went to Don Ameche, the actor. Listed ahead of Lindheimer as stockholders were Bing Crosby and Pat O'Brien, and Louis B. Mayer, head of Metro-Goldwyn-Mayer Studios. Also on the list was Daniel F. Rice, an investment genius and oft-time Lindheimer business associate. In reality, Lindheimer was majority stockholder and boss. He also became chairman of the conference's executive committee, and in that capacity fought desperately to keep the league alive.

As usual, Marje was there with the action. Sportswriters reported she often sat on the bench during the Los Angeles Dons' home games, and even took a hand in making player deals. Some of the coaches objected to her presence, but could do little about it.

The conference was ahead of its time, and encountered rough going from the beginning. College football was still king, and the T-formation was little known. Games were played for four years before the conference disbanded in 1951. Lindheimer used the funds of his racing corporations for his quarterback sneak into pro football, and he charged his losses to those same corporations despite some questions from dissident stockholders and the Internal Revenue Service. Presumably he could have continued to do so as long as racing remained profitable. He later maintained the league might have survived if a severe heart attack had not put him out of action in August, 1949.

Perhaps so, but the opportunity he had been wanting developed at Lincoln Fields and he turned back to racing with renewed enthusiasm. Seemingly the only obstacle to his plans was a Racing Board member named Miller.

William Stephen Miller was born in Crawfordsville, Indiana, a small town about fifty miles northwest of Indianapolis. His father operated a small plumbing and heating company. His mother died when he was eight. The father packed him off to a strict Catholic school where the boy took pleasure in confiding to his diary his few rebellions. He recorded an unauthorized trip to town to pick up a love letter for a seminarian in return for help with an essay on *Gulliver's Travels*. The theme proved too good; one of the prefects suspected collusion. Unlocking Miller's desk, he read the diary. The boy was eventually expelled at Christmas. A priest back home got him readmitted and he was punished by being forced to march back and forth in front of the Administration Building during his recreation hours until Easter.

Miller grew up into a tall, well-proportioned heavyweight with dark wavy hair and blue-gray eyes. In time he cultivated a small mustache that added distinction as it turned silver over the years. His first job was driving a delivery wagon for his father. Intelligent and ambitious, he won a scholarship to tiny Wabash College and fell in love with Catherine Gerlach, a petite and lovely young lady who attended St. Mary's College of Notre Dame. Catherine was impressed with the affable young man, yet she was practical and in no hurry to marry. Bill kept scratching, and ultimately won another scholarship to Notre Dame's law school.

A year later he set out with a friend for California where they hoped to practice law. In Chicago they stopped to eat, and Miller picked up a newspaper to look at the want ads. A LaSalle Street firm needed two salesmen. The friends decided to apply, and got the jobs. Soon Miller was selling school equipment. The following year, 1923, he married Catherine.

Miller was a natural salesman, using reason and logic to persuade, and Chicago in the twenties was an interesting place to learn about the relation of politics and business. He made friends easily and developed a slow charm that concealed a quick mind and an instinct for business. He began selling church furniture and was so successful he received a bonus of $14,000. Trying to impress his father, he showed the check to the old man.

"You're not worth it," was the response.

After the death at birth of a daughter, the couple adopted a daughter. In time she provided two grandchildren who, thanks to a combination of circumstances, were virtually raised by the Millers.

Came the depression and in 1932 Miller's employer went out of business leaving two orders unfilled. The astute salesman took them to a competitor, got himself a job and a challenge to find a depression-proof object to manufacture. Miller immediately drove to Washington, D.C., and asked Senator Bob LaFollette, Jr., one question: When would the Volstead Act be repealed? LaFollette gave him a pretty good estimate. Hurrying home, Miller talked his new boss into manufacturing saloon-type bars. When April 7, 1933, arrived and "real beer" brought celebrations from coast to coast, handsome bars were on display in sales windows on the corner of LaSalle Street and Wacker Drive. They were in instant demand, and soon orders were pouring in from as far away as Texas. Business boomed again on December 5, 1933, when the 18th Amendment was officially repealed and hard liquor became legal.

With his profits, Miller soon took over the J. E. Porter Company in Ottawa, Illinois, and began to manufacture playground and gymnasium equipment. Ultimately he expanded to include equipment for child care centers and home ice cream freezers. In a few years he was a millionaire and chairman of the board of the Ottawa National Bank. Back in Crawfordsville, where nothing much had happened since the National Archery Association was organized there in 1879, he was regarded with awe.

It was young Joe Knight, protégé of Lindheimer *and* Horner, who first interested Miller in politics. Nominally a Republican, Miller allowed the twenty-six-year-old Knight to persuade him to support Governor Horner in his 1936 campaign for re-election. In 1940, following Horner's death, Knight and Miller teamed up to support the man Boss Kelly had promised Horner would be slated to succeed him: Harry Hershey, the state Democratic chairman.

Hershey made the mistake, however, of vowing to suppress illegal gambling if elected. At that time an estimated five thousand bookies operated in Cook County and paid more than $350,000 a week for the privilege. Kelly had no intention of cutting off such revenue, and rumor spread as the campaign progressed that he had made a secret deal with the Republican nominee, Dwight H. Green.

Miller decided to find out for himself if the rumors were true. Green had attended Miller's alma mater, Wabash College, but the two men had not seen each other for years. By dropping a few hints in the right place, Miller received an invitation to have a reunion with Green. The invitation came from Irwin N. Walker, vice president of the Chicago Board of Education and an intimate friend of Mayor Kelly. The meeting took place on September 13, 1940, in the Congress Hotel suite of Edward J. Fleming. Another close friend of Kelly, Fleming was also a director of Lincoln Fields Racing Association.

Miller handed over a prepared check made out to the "Dwight H. Green Campaign Committee" for $1,000. The check was cashed by the treasurer of Green's campaign committee, and Miller kept the canceled instrument when it was returned to him as a bit of evidence of Kelly's duplicity. The treasurer, Gilbert Keebler, invited Miller to participate in state business following Green's election. All that was required was a ten per cent payoff to the campaign committee on all business handled. Miller said he declined in disgust, and actively opposed Green when the Republican was re-elected in 1944. He found it amusing, however, to learn that Fleming, a Democrat, was also doublecrossed by Governor Green. Instead of permitting Fleming to name the majority of members of the Racing Board, as he had promised, Green gave that privilege to Lindheimer, who, in anticipation, had the foresight to employ the *Chicago Tribune*'s law firm which routinely supported Republicans.

Chicago ran wide open in the forties. With Kelly at City Hall and Green at Springfield party labels were unimportant. Unlike Cermak, Kelly concluded that Cook County was all he could handle, and this conviction grew following the death in 1943 of his partner in bossism, Pat Nash. When the late Jake Arvey returned from the war in 1945, Kelly promptly re-nicknamed him Jack and turned over the chairmanship of the organization to him.

Arvey was not without opposition. While he had been overseas during the war with a National Guard unit, an Irishman, tough John Duffy, had become a political power. Luckily he wasn't ready yet and Arvey was permitted the luxury of making one mistake. In 1946 he slated Richard J. Daley, then holding two jobs as a state senator and chief deputy Cook County comptroller, to run for sheriff of Cook County.

A mistake? Not necessarily. While sheriffs traditionally got rich in the job, they became so tarnished in the process as to destroy their political careers. In slating Daley, Arvey may have hoped to eliminate a future rival. His mistake then was in letting him lose.

Duffy was elated, but decided to wait another year when Kelly would be up for re-election before making his move. Everyone knew that Kelly, sick, old, and incapable, wouldn't be given the opportunity. Arvey, recognizing realities, carried the message personally to the mayor. He then surprised everyone, including Duffy, by announcing that Martin Kennelly would be the Democratic candidate. Distinguished in appearance, Kennelly looked good, like a mayor should. Moreover, he had been identified as a fund raiser for the Red Cross and other good causes. In short, he presented quite a contrast to Kelly, and Arvey sensed this was what the voters wanted. He was correct: in February, 1947, Kennelly defeated his Republican opposition by more than 250,000 votes.

Everyone regarded Arvey with some awe. Not only had he elected a mayor, but that mayor was a figurehead. Once again Chicago had a single boss. If anyone had any doubts, Kennelly put them to rest shortly after the election. Asked by a reporter what he thought of the crime syndicate, the new mayor replied: "Crime syndicate? I don't know about any syndicate. Isn't that man Capone supposed to be dead?"

As a matter of fact, Scarface Al had died a few days before the election. Yet the syndicate that bore his name was stronger than it had ever been in Capone's glory years; gambling and prostitution proved more profitable than bootleg booze.

Duffy, while not displeased to have power concentrated in the hands of the party chairman, bided his time. Coming up in 1948 was the national election, and everyone knew President Truman would be booted out of the White House by Tom Dewey. Let Arvey buck the Republican tide and elect a U. S. senator and governor in Illinois. His failure was inevitable, Duffy decided, and most organization leaders agreed.

Meanwhile, the office of United States Attorney for Northern Illinois became vacant. Daley, restless and looking for a secure post from which to ride out the troubled waters ahead, made his bid for the job. Arvey rejected him and recommended instead the appointment of a clean young attorney with a famous name: Otto Kerner, Jr. The fact that the young man was married to the daughter of the late Boss Cermak may have had something to do with the decision. More important, perhaps, was the political influence his father, now a federal appellate court judge, had in party ranks. Compared to Kerner and his background, Daley was a pushy latecomer who needed to be discouraged, not helped.

Despite the pessimism of the professionals about the 1948 outlook, Paul H. Douglas, a college professor, began campaigning early in 1947 for the Senate. Late in the year, friends of Adlai Stevenson announced he would run for the same office. Possessed of a famous name in Illinois, Stevenson was best remembered for his work in 1940 when he led the Committee to Defend America by Aiding the Allies. In a city where Big Bill Thompson's promise to punch King George's nose was still fondly recalled, and the powerful *Chicago Tribune* was strictly isolationist, Stevenson's crusade marked him as a brave man. During the war he had worked in the State Department, and more recently, with the United Nations.

When Stephen A. Mitchell, a friend of Cardinal Stritch, led a delegation of Stevenson supporters to Jake Arvey's office one rainy afternoon, the politician received them warmly. Looking at the names of "Adlai's amateurs," he commented, "This is a new list. I don't remember seeing any of these names on a political committee before."

Exactly when Arvey decided that it would be better to sacrifice two outsiders in 1948 than to hurt the careers of organization men, is uncertain, but once the decision was made, he tried to make it appear both sensible and sincere. Douglas, he decreed, would be the candidate for the Senate in opposition to Republican C. Wayland Brooks, a hero of World War I. During World War II, the fifty-one-year-old Douglas had enlisted in the Marines and come home a hero. Let the younger veteran oppose the older one. Stevenson, he decided, would run for governor against the incumbent Dwight Green. A downstater, Stevenson would balance the ticket and perhaps even carry his home town of Bloomington. Having thus acted professionally enough, the boss told the candidates they were on their own financially. The machine would back them in Chicago with votes, but its money it would not waste.

Upon learning of this, Miller and Knight, those two veterans of past campaigns against Green, offered their services, and began raising money. Edward Fleming, director of Lincoln Fields and a pro-Green man in 1940, as Miller knew, was impressed with Stevenson and not only contributed to his campaign but bet on his victory as well. Ben Lindheimer, who usually contributed to both parties when the issue was in doubt, sent over a contribution via ex-Mayor Kelly. Playing it safe, Kelly demanded a receipt on the ground that "Ben might think I didn't give the money to you."

By later standards, the campaign was cheap. It took only $135,000 to elect Stevenson in those pre-television days. Even so, the campaign ended in a deficit. Post-election contributions more than covered it, however, and Miller eventually got back the money he lent the campaign. He didn't get it, however, until similar loans by relatives of Stevenson were paid off first.

Arvey remained unconvinced that the amateurs had a chance and turned down a last minute request for money to finance a radio appeal by Stevenson. The *Tribune* was equally convinced it was to be a Republican sweep, and carried its famous headline election night announcing a Dewey victory over Truman.

Truman carried the state by 33,612 votes. Stevenson carried it by 572,067 votes, and Douglas won by almost as much. Next to *Tribune* publisher Robert R. McCormick, the most surprised man in Chicago was Jake Arvey. This despite the fact that he had assigned one of his own men, Mike Howlett, to accompany the candidate everywhere and keep his feet on the ground if possible. Howlett, who looked like a Chicago politician, made quite a contrast to the fastidious Stevenson. The two men ended up disliking each other intensely.

Miller was offered the post of state revenue director as a reward for his services. He turned it down, saying his personal affairs demanded too much of his time. Stevenson then gave it to Richard Daley, pleasing both Daley and Arvey at the same time. Daley served a year, and quit to become clerk of Cook County when the incumbent dropped dead. It was an important post for a man aiming ultimately at the mayor's office.

Later, Stevenson offered Miller the job of state purchasing agent, but Miller rejected it for the same reason as before. It was a fulltime job and he was too busy selling ice cream freezers to take it.

Stevenson, meanwhile, appointed a new Racing Board, the first in eight years. Chairman Stuyvesant Peabody, Jr., was considered an Arvey man. Bernard J. Fallon and Frank E. Warton were classed as Lindheimer men. Ben's contribution had paid off. Racing was of no particular concern to the new governor until his executive secretary, James W. Mulroy, became involved in what Stephen Mitchell later called "a somewhat malodorous racetrack stock deal" and, although protesting he had done nothing unusual or illegal, resigned. Paul Powell, a downstate political power in the legislature, was also involved, receiving harness-race stock for ten cents a share. Like Mulroy, he saw no harm in such bargains, but he didn't resign. Apparently, the voters were not very shocked either for they later elected Powell secretary of state.

Meanwhile, the Kefauver Committee came to town to investigate crime and corruption. Senator Kefauver had presidential ambitions, and that posed certain problems. Police Captain Daniel Gilbert had been slated to run for Cook County sheriff, so the committee listened to him in closed session. An enterprising reporter got copies of the testimony and splashed Gilbert's admissions that he had made a fortune in gambling on the front page of the *Sun-Times*. Gilbert became instantly famous as "the richest cop in the world," and five days later he was overwhelmed at the polls. The scandal also carried to defeat Senator Scott Lucas and brought gravel-voiced Everett Dirksen to Washington in his place. Arvey was humiliated and Stevenson decided that racing needed a tighter rein. As if to underscore that thought, ex-cop Gilbert went to work for Ben Lindheimer as chief of security at Arlington and Washington Parks. Why waste a good cop?

Arvey was blamed for the Gilbert fiasco — along with Kefauver, of course — and some politicians felt he might not survive as Boss. Lindheimer didn't agree, or perhaps he felt that Arvey would remain a man of importance if not of decision. In any case, he was still worth influencing.

On October 31, 1950, he offered Arvey an option on 3,000 shares of Arlington common stock and 3,000 shares of Washington Park common stock. The price was $8 a share for Arlington and $8.50 for Washington, for a combined total of $49,500. The option was to be returned to Marje, who was getting another lesson in how to influence politicians.

Six months later the option was renewed on the same terms for another six months, and when that expired it was renewed yet again — this time for two years. By then the stock had increased in value to such an extent that Arvey was able to exercise his option and immediately make a nice profit. In the interval, of course, it was to his interest to see that nothing happened to Lindheimer's empire to depress the value of its stock. When one remembers the days of Big Bill Thompson and Cermak, the day of bribes openly given and taken, it is possible to detect progress of a sort in Chicago: the boys were becoming a bit sophisticated.

How much Governor Stevenson knew or even suspected about the relation of politics to racing is uncertain, but in the fall of 1951 William S. Miller visited Europe to study the various racing systems. The study-tour came after Bernard Fallon proved he was indeed Lindheimer's man by resigning from the Racing Board to become president of Washington Park. On April 27, Miller was appointed to replace him. His tour of Europe followed. The minutes of the Racing Board note that some of his "suggested innovations" brought back from Europe "were to be submitted for national consideration" at the next meeting of the National Association of State Racing Commissioners. Miller instantly became known as "the governor's man," it being apparent to all that Stevenson had decided he needed someone he could trust to keep an eye on racing.

The appointment was well timed. Lindheimer, ably assisted by his adopted daughter Marje, was about to lose Lincoln Fields as a tenant — and that meant trouble for someone.

Matt Winn of Churchill Downs fame, the man who made parimutuel machines popular, built Lincoln Fields near the town of Crete, and was very proud of his achievement. It was, he wrote, "the dream come true of a racetrack, perfect in all its appointments." The track opened in 1926 and was an immediate success, so much so that the legislature legalized parimutuel wagering in Illinois the following year. In 1947, Winn was getting old so he reluctantly sold the track to a group headed by Edward Fleming, who had been a stockholder and director from the beginning. Fleming died in 1949, but his trustees continued the operation.

But on November 19, 1952, the last official meeting of the Adlai Stevenson-appointed Racing Board, a pronouncement relating to 1954 racing dates contained this demanding and authoritative statement:

> The board recommends that any future application of the Lincoln Fields Racing Association be declined unless that association operates at its own facility.

Republican William G. Stratton was elected governor of Illinois in November, 1952, and he was not only significantly unhurried about replacing Stevenson's Racing Board but also significantly silent about the Stevenson board's decision to require modernization of Lincoln Fields.

In actuality, the track at Crete of which Matt Winn had been so proud was abandoned in 1943, and other Racing Boards, supported by bought-and-paid-for crazyquilt patterns of opinion from the attorney general's office, had permitted Lincoln Fields to run its racing days at other racetracks for eleven previous years. However, no such opinion ever completely ignored the statutory requirement that an applicant have a plant suitable for racing at the time of allocation of racing dates. The Stevenson-appointed Racing Board decided, therefore, to enforce the law on this point, and the trustees of the Fleming estate hurried to spend funds from the estate and from bank loans to make Lincoln Fields suitable for racing in the spring of 1954.

The return to its own reconstructed plant at Crete for its 1954 meeting of thirty days (May 20–June 22) was not a success. On Memorial Day, Monday, May 31, most of the 30,000 in attendance waded in water ankle high and hundreds of automobiles were mired in mud hubcap deep. Some of Ed Fleming's heirs were outraged and went to court to force the sale of Lincoln Fields so that the estate could be finally settled. The court agreed and directed the trustees to find a buyer.

Ben Lindheimer had had Lincoln Fields as a tenant from 1948 through 1951. He was well aware of this desirable avenue of profit so he decided to round out his empire at this crucial period with the track that Matt Winn built. It was March 17, 1955, when the sale of Lincoln Fields was announced. A new corporation, the Balmoral Jockey Club, Inc., headed by President Hubert Howard, Lindheimer's man, had paid $3,100,000 for the property. Lindheimer's name wasn't mentioned, but the new corporation asked the Racing Board for permission to hold a thirty-day race meet at Washington Park. A special meeting of the Racing Board was called to consider the application. Miller couldn't be present, but he outlined his views in a letter.

He wrote in part:

> From what has appeared in the public press, and has been talked about generally in racing circles, one would have to be very naive indeed to fail to conclude that Mr. Benjamin Lindheimer is the man behind the purchase of Lincoln Fields and the plan to operate the meeting dates allotted to that track at Washington Park.
>
> This board in the best interest of the sport of thoroughbred racing cannot permit a monopoly to be created in the Chicago area. Such a monopoly would be an evil to which this board cannot close its eyes. At present, Mr. Lindheimer operates Arlington Park and Washington Park to which the board has allotted the most favorable and desirable racing dates. As a member of the Illinois Racing Board, I am unalterably opposed to increasing his operation to a third racing meeting. That, in my opinion, would violate the letter and spirit of the Illinois Racing Act.
>
> I strongly urge that when the board hears this matter, it conduct a thorough examination and investigation of who is the real purchaser of Lincoln Fields.

The makeup of the Racing Board in 1955 had changed little since Miller's appointment. Adlai Stevenson in 1952 gave up the governorship to run a gallant if hopeless race against Dwight Eisenhower. Republican William G. Stratton succeeded him as governor and reappointed Miller and Warton to the Racing Board, but replaced Peabody as chairman with Paul Serdar, a horse and mink breeder of Antioch. Serdar was appointed at the special request of James Simpson, Jr., scion of a famous Chicago-area family and former assistant coordinator of law-enforcement agencies as well as Republican state central committeeman of the 10th District, consisting of Cook and Lake Counties, Illinois.

It was Serdar who ignored Miller's letter of protest at the special meeting of the Racing Board. He did so after Joseph Zoline, attorney for the applicants, assured the board that Lindheimer's interest in the deal "was nominal" and amounted to "less than five per cent of the stock." The applicants of record, Hubert Howard, Herbert Herff, and a friend of Serdar, Russell Reineman, pledged they would provide the $2,300,000 price of the track.

"I think that Mr. Lindheimer is being more than generous and liberal in this arrangement with Balmoral," said Chairman Serdar. "There has been some concern expressed by various interests in racing relative to the fact that a monopoly is being created in Illinois as a result of one man operating three tracks. I think the evidence presented here today indicates that not to be true."

Cheers! The application was granted — but it returned to haunt them.

The truth was that eleven days before the special meeting, Lindheimer used his two racetrack corporations to provide the $300,000 needed to bind the purchase agreement with the owners of Lincoln Fields. On April 13, he lent $700,000 more, the total secured by Balmoral debentures. By May 24, through the use of nominees, he controlled 58 per cent of the stock of Balmoral. By the end of 1957 his nominees — including his physician, his attorney, his caterer, and son-in-law — owned 75 per cent of the stock. Arlington and Washington Parks showed up holding the largest blocks of stock, and there was something called the Arlington-Washington-Balmoral Trust as well, but Lindheimer voted it all.

It was done very neatly. Howard and Reineman had publicly subscribed to large amounts of stock in addition to the small amounts they actually purchased. At the right moment they assigned their subscriptions — actually the right to buy stock reserved for them — to

Arlington and Washington Parks. Reineman said later he did this because Lindheimer assured him the stock would be resold to racing-stable owners and solid businessmen, thus putting Balmoral on a broader foundation.

Balmoral raced at Washington Park in 1955, and paid a rent of $139,146.32 for the privilege. Next year the rent went up a bit to $287,146.06, and in 1957 it reached $336,274.08. For the period 1955 through 1966, rent payments by Balmoral to Lindheimer totaled $4,440,920.50.

Two years after Serdar ignored Miller's protests and gave Lindheimer what he wanted, there was a strange reversal of attitudes on the part of the Racing Board members. Abruptly, Serdar discovered that Lindheimer did, in fact, have a near monopoly, and he demanded it be broken up. Neither Miller nor Warton was consulted by Serdar in advance, and each ended up supporting Lindheimer.

Miller's switch began when he received a call from Weymouth Kirkland of the prestigious law firm that represented the *Chicago Tribune*. The attorney was a living legend, and when he asked Miller to come to see him about an important matter the man from Crawfordsville was glad to go. Kirkland, who also represented Lindheimer, was very frank. His conversation as recalled later by Miller went about like this:

"I'm going to confide certain facts about Ben Lindheimer and you will wonder why you, the minority member on the Illinois Racing Board, were chosen to hear them instead of Chairman Serdar or Frank Warton. Governor Stratton has told me that you have brains, substance, and guts, and that he depends on you for direction in thoroughbred racing. After observing your performance, I not only agree with Bill Stratton but I ask you to help me solve some serious problems. Ben Lindheimer and his stockholders could lose some money if we don't come up with a solution, but the sport of racing and the State of Illinois — which I think means a lot to you and me — could lose much more than money.

"Goddamnit, you were prudent when you surmised for the public record that Lindheimer instead of Reineman and Nathenson actually bought Lincoln Fields. Let's for the moment say he did. Then let's consider the alternatives. You know and I know that Charley Aaron, the trustee of the Ed Fleming estate, wanted out of the horse racing business. Moreover, the court told him to sell. Charley could either sell to a Ben Lindheimer-controlled group or to a questionable and financially unreliable assortment of characters. I say Charley's choice was the best for his client and for racing in Illinois.

"I realize you do not agree. May I, therefore, ask a favor? Please meet with my associate, Dudley Jessup, and our client, Ben Lindheimer. Satisfy yourself as to their sincerity of purpose. Ask them anything you please. If you are still against Ben after that, tell him so. If you are not, I'll say that you and Ben, working together, can make Illinois racing second to none in America or the world."

It was a challenge Miller could not refuse. For the first time since his appointment to the Racing Board he met with Lindheimer. Attorney Jessup was present. Lindheimer was very frank, admitting that Balmoral's profits had been used to retire its debts instead of being used to make the Crete track operational as the Racing Board had demanded. He agreed, however, that Washington and Arlington Parks would defer payments on the mortgage and debentures they held. Finally, he argued that a ninety-seven-day coordinated program was in the best interests of racing. Miller left the meeting convinced that Kirkland was right.

At the Racing Board hearing on November 18, 1957, Reineman — now in revolt — asked permission to hold Balmoral's thirty-day meeting at Hawthorne. Serdar approved. Miller read into the record a long statement noting that Balmoral had adopted no plan of improvement and was using its profits to pay its debts. "We find," said Miller, "to our chagrin and amazement that even the water tower at Balmoral's Crete plant still has the name *Lincoln Fields* on it."

Nevertheless, and because of this failure, Miller continued, Balmoral "cannot be competitive at its Crete plant." Rather than force it to race there, Miller added, he would favor denying it any racing dates and equitably distributing the dates to the other tracks. On the other hand, he added, the board shouldn't let Balmoral race at Washington or Arlington unless the corporations controlling those parks waived all payments and permitted Balmoral's 1958 profits to be "reserved without exception for the rehabilitation of the Crete, Illinois, plant."

If this could be arranged, Miller concluded, he would recommend that Balmoral race at Washington Park in 1958 and that the schedules of the three racing corporations be reshuffled to permit forty-eight continuous days of racing at Washington and forty-nine continuous days at Arlington.

The board voted two to one, Serdar dissenting, to reject Reineman's application for racing at Hawthorne. A week later, the majority stockholders representing Lindheimer presented a new application based on the formula Miller had demanded, and it was approved. Racing continued at Washington Park. Reineman's faction appealed, but the Illinois Supreme Court ultimately upheld the board's two-to-one decision. Balmoral's surplus cash piled up, and by 1961 it totaled more than a million dollars.

The strange relationship that began that day in 1957 between Miller and Lindheimer continued and deepened. Miller, who since his appointment by Stevenson had been seeking to improve Illinois racing, concluded that Lindheimer, his empire established, was attempting to do the same thing if not for the same reasons. Kirkland was right; what was good for racing by 1958, was good for Lindheimer. A successful horse breeder-owner in his own right, Miller had learned enough about politics and racing to comprehend that perfection couldn't be achieved overnight. It came, instead, step by step, deal by deal, as the political situation permitted.

In short, Miller found himself the spiritual heir of those long-dead reformers of Lincoln Steffens' time. "The Chicago instinct" had reasserted itself, and a no longer naive Miller was willing to forget the methods used by Lindheimer to become king of the sport of kings in Chicago, and accept at face value his future good intentions. In defense of this decision, Miller was later to state:

> The record is completely clear that Illinois thoroughbred racing reached its highest peak of public acceptance and quality under Ben Lindheimer.

If it is difficult to understand why Miller found it expedient to work with Lindheimer, it is easy to see how the son of Jacob, the saloon-keeper, grew to value the country boy from Indiana. Miller, a self-made millionaire genuinely interested in racing, needed no help from politicians and had no compulsion to emulate a famous political fixer who had maintained, "You never get enough." Indeed, Miller liked to quote Isadora Duncan: "It's easy to be virtuous if you never have occasion to be otherwise." In Lindheimer's experience Miller was unique, a man to trust and to confide the most personal family problems. And, as previously noted, the family had problems.

Marje, the only one of the three adopted children to like racing, had gained a reputation for toughness. A former special agent in charge of the Chicago office of the FBI and a former director of Arlington-Washington Park, said of her at this time, "She is the sort of person who would relish the chance to cut off your balls and throw them in your face."

Yet Marje had apparently put her emotional life in order. In 1957, at the age of thirty-six, she married a man twenty-five years her senior. Her husband, the late Webb Everett, began as a jockey's valet and worked his way up to become a stockholder in Hollywood Park and a part owner and director of racing at Golden Gate Fields in San Francisco. He remained in that post after the marriage and Marje continued to work with her father as vice president of the Chicago tracks. Webb died in September, 1977. The marriage was childless. Marje acquired a dog named Biff, a fat boxer who became her constant companion. When he became old she employed a registered nurse to care for Biff, and when he died friends as far away as California were notified of funeral arrangements. The dog was buried outside Marje's bedroom at Arlington Park. A banquet hall at the park's hotel was named The Biff Room in memoriam.

The political situation in Chicago had also achieved stability. Thanks to the unexpected death in an automobile accident of a rival, Richard Daley became chairman of Cook County Democrats on July 21, 1953. He immediately set his sights on the mayor's chair still occupied by the silver-haired Kennelly. For reasons no one could fathom, the mild-mannered mayor had attempted to give thousands of city employees civil service status, thus freeing them from dependence on ward bosses. Such a move threatened the very existence of the machine Cermak had built, and enraged all the little bosses as well as Daley, who really didn't need any reasons but wanted an excuse. Rep. William Levi Dawson, boss of the black ghetto, supplied another. Back when Kefauver was in town, his committee disclosed that syndicate bosses Tony Accardo and Jake Guzik received $278,000 in 1949 as their share of the numbers racket in Dawson's district. Kennelly, embarrassed, had ordered a crackdown on numbers while blandly ignoring all the rackets running in the white sections of the city. Dawson considered that unfair, and Dawson was important. When votes were needed he could get them.

So it was in December, 1954, Mayor Kennelly — although an announced candidate for re-election — was unceremoniously dumped by the Democratic Central Committee chaired by Daley. A few days later Daley was slated. The mayor ran anyway, and was supported by the city's three newspapers and alleged civic leaders, but in the February primary Daley won by 100,064 votes. Most of his majority came from Dawson's wards and those controlled by the syndicate. The so-called good citizen simply stayed home that day. On April 5, 1955, Daley defeated the Republican candidate, 708,222 to 581,255.

Once again the offices of chairman and mayor were combined. Realists such as Alderman Charles Weber had no doubts as to what would happen. "This Daley," said Weber, "he's going to be one tough sonofabitch."

William Miller wasn't worried. He had been on a friendly basis with Daley since that enterprising politician worked for Adlai Stevenson in 1948. Things would quickly settle down, he predicted.

He was right. Soon Daley was being proclaimed by his sycophants as The Greatest Mayor in the World, and no one was disagreeing very loudly. In 1956, Stevenson tilted at windmills once again, and once again lost graciously. Governor Stratton, despite a local scandal which sent state auditor Orville Hodge to prison, won re-election. Daley began looking ahead to 1960 when Eisenhower would be off the national ticket and, he hoped, his friend and fellow Catholic, John F. Kennedy, would be on it.

On May 28, 1960, William Miller received a telephone call from Lindheimer in Beverly Hills where he had spent the winter. The old man sounded strangely weary as he asked Miller to do him a special favor by coming to California to see him as quickly as possible. Knowing that Lindheimer had been in ill health, Miller agreed, but not even the need for speed would make him fly. He arrived two days later by train.

The two men talked alone for many hours. Lindheimer disclosed he had hired Sidney Korshak, an alleged labor-relations expert who got his start with the Capone Mob, to head off a strike threatening at Washington Park where the Balmoral meet was being run. A strike was the last thing Lindheimer was worried about, however. He knew he was near death and he was worried about his family and his racing empire. Jacob Lindheimer had asked his children to dine once a month with their mother after his death, but Ben knew there was no point in making an appeal for unity to his adopted children.

Miller gave his word to the dying man that he would do his utmost to keep the racing empire in the family. Both knew that meant working with Marje, and each realized the relationship could be difficult. To provide his friend with a weapon, Lindheimer gave Miller a letter Marje had written. The father had intercepted it. The letter was pathetic: a lonely woman crying out for love. Miller was authorized to show it to Marje if it became necessary to prove he was acting with Ben's blessing, but, despite great provocation, he never used it. Indeed, he tended to regard the entire interview with Lindheimer as being in the nature of a confessional, something not to be talked about to others. A practicing Catholic was Miller, despite that episode in his youth when his diary was used to incriminate him.

Miller returned to Chicago by train. He was hardly back when on the night of June 5, 1960, Lindheimer died. A heart attack was blamed. The body was shipped to Chicago for burial, and Marje flew in to attend to arrangements. Miller met her at the airport and asked her to schedule a meeting of the family at Washington Park after the funeral.

An era had ended.

The new one would see Ben Lindheimer's fondest hopes and worst fears realized.

James Thompson, a man who would have much to do with future events, was placidly teaching at Northwestern University. He had been admitted to the Illinois bar only the year before.

I got it [racing stock] and I don't intend for nobody to get it away from me.

PAUL POWELL
June 27, 1961

4

The Queen

It was June 9, 1960, and they were burying old Ben Lindheimer.

The rich and the powerful were at Rosehill Cemetery that morning as tradition required. Always when one of their number crossed the Finish Line, his peers paid respect. Mayor Daley led the honorary pallbearers. "Chicago has lost a great citizen," he told the press, "and I've lost a great personal friend."

Other honorary pallbearers included Republican Senate Leader Arthur Bidwill; Edwin L. Weisl, attorney and investment counselor for, among others, Lyndon B. Johnson; Robert E. Strauss, bank president; Ralph Atlass, radio executive; and William S. Miller, banker, businessman, member of the Illinois Racing Board, and the last of those to talk with Lindheimer before his death.

Miller was thinking about that last conversation and of the promises he had made to help the Lindheimer family retain control of Ben's racing empire. It wouldn't be easy. Already Strauss had taken advantage of the opportunity to ask Miller to call him later that day. The American National Bank of Chicago was deeply involved in Lindheimer's financial affairs and Strauss was obviously worried about the future.

Looking around the respectful mourners, Miller sorted through the gangsters gone respectable, the politicians who considered graft a natural right, and the "sportsmen" who found racing a boost to the ego. Well, at least one exception was present. Standing next to Mayor Daley was Otto Kerner, Jr., the Mr. Clean of Illinois politics. His father had helped organize Chicago's political machine and turned down a chance to be governor in favor of a seat on the federal appellate court bench. His father-in-law had been Anton "Boss" Cermak, the man who put the machine together. Briefly, Miller wondered about young Kerner's motives in marrying Helena. She was older than he, and had a daughter by a previous marriage which had ended in divorce. Was it love or the political advantage that attracted the ambitious young man? Both perhaps. Born to wealth and status, the youth had been educated at Trinity College, Cambridge, and at Northwestern University Law School. After distinguished service in World War II — as a Major General — he returned home to enter politics. Political doors opened easily. For seven years he served as U. S. Attorney for the Northern District of Illinois, and for the past six years he had been Cook County judge with control over election machinery. Now he was moving up — slated by Daley to be the Democratic candidate for governor.

Even as Miller gazed, Daley, looking like an oversized leprechaun, left Kerner's side and strolled casually toward Miller. He paused only long enough to mutter that a problem had come up and he'd be calling Miller soon to arrange a chat. Well, even at a funeral, some men look ahead.

Strauss was certainly doing so when, as promised, Miller called him that afternoon. Knowing how much Ben had trusted the Racing Board member, Strauss had no qualms about discussing the estate. The trustees of that estate, he said, consisted of five entities: the widow, Vera Lindheimer; three children, Walter, Patricia, and Marjorie; and Strauss' bank. In any action to be taken regarding the estate, a numerical majority was necessary, but the bank had to be one of the majority. In other words, the bank had veto power.

Fair enough, Miller decided.

The big problem insofar as the bank was concerned, Strauss continued, was the nature of the racing business. He was aware of some of the problems: racing date applications, hearings, sale of concessions, size of the purses, etc., and he, frankly, didn't relish the thought of the bank's involvement in such matters.

Or in certain other matters, thought Miller.

Moreover, said the banker, he seriously doubted the Lindheimer family would stick together and try to operate the tracks. So, all things considered, what would Miller — and the other members of the Racing Board — think of a sale of Lindheimer's stock to a corporation outside Illinois? Strauss said he had made some inquiries and thought there would be no great difficulty in arranging such a sale.

That was exactly what Lindheimer had been worrying about in the hours before his death, but Miller said nothing of this to the banker. The king was dead so what did his wishes matter to a bank with investments to protect? Outwardly affable, Miller promised to study the situation, consult with the family, and call Strauss later. The out-of-state corporation mentioned by Strauss as a possible buyer had organized-crime connections, but neither Miller nor Strauss knew it. Miller's reaction was largely instinctive, and reflected Ben Lindheimer's views.

The meeting at Washington Park a few days later seemed to confirm Strauss' opinion of the family, but Miller did his best. Without mentioning Strauss' sales idea, he told them of his opposition to out-of-state, conglomerate-type owners of racetracks. To have the public confidence, to prosper, a track needed to be identified with respected citizens within a state. Ben, he emphasized, wanted the family to operate the tracks, and out of respect for Ben he would do whatever he could to assist.

It was a teary affair. Mrs. Lindheimer took Miller to one side and told him bluntly she did not understand Marje and neither she nor Ben liked Webb Everett, the older man Marje had married. To be in business with them was unthinkable. What's more, her son, Walter, shared her desire to be out of this "dirty business."

Patricia — Mrs. Perry Steiner — declined to take a position. She wasn't very interested in racing, she confessed, but she respected her father's wishes. She wanted to think about it awhile.

Marje let everyone have his say before putting her sentiments on the line: "I've never wanted anything more in my life than to be able to continue my father's racing interests."

Suddenly Miller felt sorry for her — pathetic yet resolute, desolate and alone. For the strong-willed Marje, always so self-reliant and aggressive, it was a unique situation; she had aroused sympathy in a man. Having done so, she knew how to exploit it.

"I felt compelled to help her," said Miller later. First he sent her to Strauss at American National. If those talks proved unsatisfactory, as he rather expected they would, she should come back to Miller and, together, they would figure out the next move.

Meanwhile, from Marje's puzzled mother came a handwritten note:

My dear Bill Miller —
There was respectful affection
between you and Ben.
So it has been said.
So let it be written.
I too have it for you,
So have mine —
God Bless —
                    Vera Burnstine Lindheimer

Right after Miller's meeting with the heirs, Mayor Daley called to invite Miller to have breakfast with him and Kerner at the Morrison Hotel headquarters of the Democratic Party on the day following. It was the first time Miller had met Cermak's son-in-law, and he was glad to have the opportunity. Years later, upon looking back, he was to ponder the coincidence of being drawn so abruptly into the affairs of Marje Lindheimer and Otto Kerner at almost the same time. Like a Grecian tragedy, the threads were being spun that would inevitably bring those three center stage in desperate climax.

Daley, of course, wanted something. Kerner's campaign needed "seed money" to finance newspaper and radio advertising. Would Miller help? Of course. He would supply $120,000 in U. S. Government treasury bills to serve as collateral for a loan to Kerner by the Continental Illinois National Bank. In the course of the conversation, Miller's nine years on the Racing Board and his international reputation were duly commented upon by Daley and acknowledged by the candidate. Enough said.

Long before the election that fall, Kerner repaid the money he had borrowed, and Miller's collateral was returned. It had been a favor, nothing more, a favor a hundred men in Chicago would have been eager to supply if asked. Indeed, Miller felt a bit flattered to have been selected. He could not know, of course, that the day would come when that favor would be pictured by prosecutors as virtually a bribe to ensure his reappointment to the Racing Board from whence he could manipulate events to steal part of the Lindheimer racing empire from Marje Everett.

Marje, meanwhile, had come back to Miller for help, her conferences with Strauss having proved fruitless. She was determined to buy control of her father's empire despite the fact that she was already indebted to it for almost $35,000 she had borrowed in 1958 and as late as May 4, 1960. The estate when filed for probate was valued at $8 million. Lindheimer's will left one-third to his widow, and two-ninths each to the three children. Walter Lindheimer was designated executor, proof enough that Ben didn't consider Marje his successor.

One problem confronting the heirs was what to do about Lindheimer's secret Currency Box Account. The ledger, in which he had kept a record of all transactions, showed "Notes and Accounts Receivable, 12/31/59: $927,824.98." Quite a sum, but it was not filed with Probate Court. Marje, taking charge, slipped the ledger from the vault at Arlington Park, sealed it in heavy paper, marked the wrapper "Confidential Papers of M.L.E.," and delivered it to Miller's office at 664 North Michigan Avenue for "temporary" safekeeping. Unaware of its contents, Miller put it in his vault and forgot about it for eleven years.

In the belief that ownership by Marje would be preferable to an out-of-state corporation, Miller at the suggestion of his bankers caused Marje to retain an independent accounting firm to prepare a detailed feasibility plan by which she might get control. The first step required that she pay $100,000 as earnest money. To get it, Miller took her to his bank and cosigned her note.

When she continued to call him daily as new problems arose he advised her to hire an expert attorney on a fulltime basis. Selected was Joseph Zoline, who had helped Marje's father put together the complex deal that got him Lincoln Fields under its new name of Balmoral. Zoline was known to the other heirs and trusted.

Zoline took the job, after making his own deal with Marje. He persuaded Vera Lindheimer and Walter to sell their stock for less than $4 million, thus giving Marje control. And he created a complicated merger of Arlington and Washington Park into a new corporation: Chicago Thoroughbred Enterprises, Inc., or CTE, with Marjorie Everett the principal stockholder. In January, 1961, the First National Bank of Chicago lent $1 million to Marje personally and $6.6 million to her corporation, CTE. As collateral, Zoline was required to pledge all the racetrack stock he and she owned in CTE and Balmoral, and some Marje owned in Hialeah at Miami.

Marje was deeply in debt but as far as the public knew she was "the Queen of Illinois Racing." The queen did not always appear to be regal.

She paid little attention to clothes on working days, often appearing at the office in casual dress and tennis shoes. Although she didn't smoke or drink, she had a fondness for steak tartare, chocolate cokes, and hot fudge sundaes, none of which did her complexion or her figure much good. She was capable of turning on the charm at will when someone had something she wanted, and just as capable of humiliating someone else for reasons known only to her ego. Employees walked carefully around her — more than one had been fired on the spot when he happened along at a time she wanted to exercise her authority. The color green was a pet hate — she simply couldn't stand it. Decorating at the tracks was done in carnival manner, using every color but green in strange combinations. Red dominated at Arlington Park where she entertained in what formerly was the Post and Paddock Club. The exclusive club had occupied a two-story building next to the Club House. One of the members was that powerful individual, Attorney Kirkland. Marje waited until his death and then, without consulting other members, moved it inside the Club House. Thereupon she made the nineteen-room "cottage" her private home. Her parties there became famous, attended eagerly by politicians, movie stars, and other celebrities. The expense was, after all, tax-deductible, and the place had a certain charm. It might have looked less businesslike if Marje had not replaced as many green lawns as she could with asphalt, and ordered all the trees cut down. Still, when the food and booze are on the house, one can overlook a lot of parking lots. "Marje's Inn" became famous.

Despite her shortage of cash — some detractors said her dislike of green stemmed from the fact it reminded her of all the money she didn't have — Marje was able to find $45,000, in the fall of 1960, to contribute to candidate Kerner. She gave the money to Miller to pass on, and he turned it over to Theodore J. Isaacs, Kerner's campaign manager. Only as an afterthought did he ask for a receipt. His confidential secretary, Miss Faith McInturf, routinely filed it away, and ultimately it proved useful.

Mayor Daley has been given credit, and justly so, for giving Kennedy a majority of 456,312 votes in Chicago in the November elections. It was an incredible performance even if one assumes there was fraud involved. Moreover, he announced the vote early, contrary to the usual practice of holding back until the Republican area downstate reported, and the news certainly had an effect in the west where polls were still open. Yet without the huge majority Kerner piled up statewide, it is doubtful that Daley's best effort would have been sufficient. Certainly, Nixon blamed Kerner as well as Daley, but there didn't seem to be much he could do about it then.

Once in office, Kerner named Ted Isaacs, his former campaign manager, director of revenue. Joe Knight, that partner in lost causes with Miller, became, first, assistant director and, a year later, director of the Department of Financial Institutions. Miller was reappointed to the IRB for the fourth consecutive term, and named chairman. Other IRB members were Donald M. McKellar and Ernest S. Marsh. It was necessary for McKellar to sell his stock in Arlington Park to accept the appointment. Under Ben he had been a director, and was on good terms with Marje. A wealthy man, he was executive vice president of foreign affairs at the publishing empire known as Field Enterprises. Marsh, the other commissioner, was a friend of Marje's husband, Webb Everett. He was president of the Santa Fe Railroad, which owned the land under Golden Gate Fields where Everett was a principal stockholder. Shortly after Marsh's appointment to the IRB, Marje hired his son, Larry, to an executive position at Arlington Park despite a complete lack of experience. If Mrs. Everett anticipated no difficulties with the Racing Board, she had good reason. Even without Miller, *she had control.*

Attendance at thoroughbred tracks in Illinois reached 3,079,130 in 1961, a new record. Revenue to the state also hit a new high of $15,745,978.31. Impressive, yes, but far from reassuring to Marje who was in hock up to her neck, or to Miller who had pledged her dying father he would help the Lindheimer empire survive. The combined annual net income of Arlington and Washington Parks for the years 1958 through 1960 averaged $652,000, barely enough to service the debt Marje had assumed. She was treading water desperately, barely able to keep her head above it. Additional revenue was needed badly.

One problem was solved easily. Until 1961, inadequate roads served Arlington Park but in July of that year Marje told her bankers that a six-lane highway would be built to allow patrons to travel the thirty miles from Chicago without hitting a single red light. Apparently William J. Mortimer, Cook County highway superintendent, sponsored the project after being allowed to make $90,000 buying and selling racetrack stock. When the road was completed, he resigned to become a consultant for Marje at $25,000 a year.

A big help, but a drop in the Lake Michigan of Marje's financial woes. The only answer, it appeared, was a *new* source of revenue.

The First National Bank of Chicago's eight-page digest of attorney Zoline's loan application made January 16, 1961, on behalf of CTE, contained this statement: "Consideration is being given to the possibility of harness racing at Washington Park and this may add $200,000 to $300,000 in earnings annually." The bank added that "an outlay for lighting equipment would be needed." Actually, the entire park would need rebuilding: the track shortened, the grandstand enclosed, and other major alterations required, but Zoline was astute enough not to mention them. One bridge at a time was his policy.

Marje turned to her father's friend for advice. Miller approved. (Harness racing at the time was regulated by a separate body over which he had no authority.) There was no harness racing to the south near Washington Park, an area easily accessible to two million fans. Only on the west side was there competition. William H. Johnston, who dominated the sport there, agreed that, as in other forms of gambling, the more opportunities to bet the more bettors, so he supplied guidelines and cost figures. Washington Park could be quickly but not cheaply converted to harness racing and the thoroughbred or "flat" racing formerly held there could be shifted to Arlington Park. The additional funds from harness racing would make more secure the thoroughbred industry which was Miller's concern. At least that was his rationalization although later he was to say, "my good intentions were scarcely equal to my bad judgment" in allowing himself to become so deeply involved in Marje's affairs.

The problem, as usual, was money. It was necessary to convert Washington into a harness-racing track. Zoline went back to the First National and struck out. A bank memo of June 2, 1961, contained a suggestion that Zoline ask the Racing Board to release Lindheimer's successor from his pledge to use Balmoral's cash to rehabilitate the track at Crete. Zoline, who had taken part in arranging that compromise, countered by suggesting the First National make a first mortgage on the Balmoral property. Twenty-one days later the bank refused on the grounds the track was not being used for racing, and it repeated its suggestion that Zoline "clear with the Racing Board the use of Balmoral funds to retire debentures and mortgages."

Stalemate! Zoline felt honor-bound to observe the pledge he had helped Lindheimer make. This led to a bitter dispute with Marje and it became apparent to her she needed an attorney with *clout*. Getting rid of Zoline would not be easy since he owned 500 shares of CTE stock. He remained as her attorney until March, 1962, but in the meantime Marje retained William J. Lynch.

A swinging, red-faced bachelor, Lynch was locally famous for his love of liquor and his friendship with Mayor Daley. The two had grown up together in the Bridgeport section, and they had practiced law together before Daley moved to City Hall. A third law partner was George Schaller. Daley's friendship was of tremendous value, especially to a lawyer who was not especially remarkable for his legal abilities. (A few years later, after Daley's influence had made Lynch a federal judge, the Chicago Council of Lawyers rated the city's thirteen sitting federal judges. Lynch was listed in tenth place, just ahead of Julius J. Hoffman of "Chicago Seven" fame.)

It was *clout*, not legal ability, Marje needed, however, so while Zoline handled routine details and worked out the deal that would let him sell his stock for $1.1 million and depart, Lynch found a way to get Balmoral's cash into action.

On November 27, 1961, a special meeting of Balmoral directors was held and Webb Everett reported he "was advised" the Racing Board no longer believed the funds had to be restricted as previously. He did not identify for the record the source of his advice, and there is no record that anyone connected with the board told Everett anything to that effect. Miller is emphatic today, and so is Dan Shannon, then secretary of the board, that no one to their knowledge, either officially or unofficially, told Everett or anyone else the funds were free. There seems no question that *clout* was at work, ignoring rules made for those without influence in high places. As a precaution, however, the application for Balmoral's racing dates in 1962 showed the money was still in Balmoral's coffers as of the certified audit for the period ending on December 30, 1960.

Delighted by Everett's announcement, the Balmoral board adopted resolutions to redeem the debentures and retire the mortgage notes. Zoline announced he had been negotiating with the bank for an unsecured loan and it was then and there decided that Balmoral would borrow $600,000.

According to the First National's records, the Everetts visited the bank on December 22, 1961, and reached agreement with bank officials on every point including the new loan. Yet it was decided to wait until "around January 15, 1962" to consummate the transactions. The delay meant that, in the normal course of events, the financial deals would not be included in the annual audit for 1961, and, in fact, would not reach the Racing Board until applications for 1964 racing dates were filed in October, 1963. Much could happen in two years — and it did. For one thing, Ernst & Ernst, the CPA firm used by Balmoral and CTE, proved conscientious, and in its audit for the period ended December 31, 1961, looked ahead and made mention of "mortgage notes and debentures retired on January 15, 1962." That meant the Racing Board would get the news a year earlier than planned — in October, 1962.

A danger signal, and from it stemmed the Kerner case. Meanwhile, however, the shareholders of CTE met on April 24, 1962, to legalize retroactively the actions already taken by the directors. Only three appeared: Mr. and Mrs. Everett and an employee, Sidney G. Karras. Lynch, serving as chairman, made the first order of business a motion to increase the number of directors from five to seven. All agreed, and Lynch and his partner, Schaller, were added to the board, thus assuring Marje of a majority. The business of Balmoral and its funds, as well as the new loan, was discussed, and "on motion duly made, seconded, and unanimously carried, the actions of the officers, directors, and executive committee during the fiscal year 1961 were ratified and approved."

Webb Everett was voted a salary of $15,000 a year, plus expenses; Lynch, as executive vice presient, was given a $10,000 salary, and the law firm of Lynch, Schaller & Reilly was retained "as legal counsel for the corporation." Not mentioned was the fact that the CTE increased Balmoral's rent for racing at Arlington from $279,000 to a huge $488,000.

The thought of what Miller might do upon learning that Balmoral had been looted and Lindheimer's promise broken, worried Marje, and even as efforts went forward to appease greedy politicians on the legislative level, Marje set out to get "a handle" on the chairman. Obviously, the one sure way was to go to his boss. If she could win the favor of Governor Kerner, she would have nothing to fear — or so she assumed — from Miller.

The key to Kerner was Isaacs, who would eventually be called "the bungling bagman." He would also be indicted in a scandal involving a printing company in which he had an interest. Marje began her court-ship in 1962 by paying Isaacs $5,000 for nonexistent envelopes. It was something of a test, and Isaacs passed. A Chicago native, he had been practicing law since 1934, and, of course, had managed Kerner's 1960 campaign. Shortly after that election, his law firm was retained to settle Ben Lindheimer's estate. Since Marje was the only heir in town, it was easy to develop a social relationship. Isaacs' job as Illinois director of revenue didn't impair his usefulness one bit. Friendship between the Isaacs and the Everetts blossomed.

Contractors friendly to Isaacs were awarded considerable business at Arlington and Washington. One such contractor allegedly over-charged, causing Marje to ask Miller for help in a letter dated October 29, 1963. She noted in passing, "I knew of your interest in assisting Ted in this request, and I, too, had the same interest because of the friendship that we both have for Ted and the knowledge of his sincer-ity."

In March, 1962, Marje allegedly set aside stock for Isaacs and Kerner. As Isaacs told it years later, "She said they would be a good investment. Following all the good work we had done in the Lind-heimer estate, she had an interest in our working with her. The shares were estimated at that time to be worth $1,000 each. I promised to pay $50,000, for them when I could pick them up and I offered to make that payment in July of 1966 together with our two checks for interest in the amount of $4,479. . . ." Miller wasn't told about this "understanding" with Isaacs until late in 1962.

Meanwhile, Marje wondered about Kerner's attitude. She had contributed, via Miller, $45,000 to his campaign in 1960, certainly a large enough gift to merit acknowledgment, but from Springfield there was silence. Kerner had not returned the cash but neither had he displayed any appreciation.

On June 28, 1962, Marje wrote a formal invitation asking the governor to appear at Arlington Park on September 8 and present the winner of the Arlington–Washington Futurity with a trophy. (A *futur-ity* is a race for two-year-olds that are usually nominated for the race before they are born.) Marje hoped that ultimately this race would achieve the prestige of the Kentucky Derby or the Preakness. In her letter she told Kerner, "This will be the richest race ever run anywhere. We feel it extremely appropriate that you as governor of the state make this presentation." She also promised "to give a luncheon in your honor," if Governor and Mrs. Kerner would show up.

Kerner's reply, dated July 11, 1962, was addressed to "Dear Mrs. Everett," and it was almost curt: "I am sorry that prior commitments for that date will prevent me from accepting this honor and will also preclude our accepting your very gracious invitation to luncheon."

Isaacs received an invitation to another event at about the same time. His reply on July 5, 1962, was addressed to "Dear Marje," and was signed "Ted." While he too turned down the invitation because he was leaving for military duty next day "in the woods of Minnesota," he promised to bring his wife and "come out and visit with you" on his return. Meanwhile:

"As to the box seats that you so graciously sent to me, I am trying to make arrangements to have my friend and friends of people like Crowdus Baker make use of these facilities during my absence."

"My friend" meant Otto Kerner. Crowdus Baker was president of Sears, Roebuck & Company. Isaacs was cultivating Baker, and it paid off in 1963 when his law firm was retained by Sears at $15,000 per year to act "specifically in the area of taxes" affecting Sears' property in Cook County. Baker was appointed to the Racing Board in 1965 by Kerner.

Quite a contrast to Kerner's aloof rejection was this letter of Isaacs; but, of course, it was Kerner's "untouchable" image that made such an aide as Isaacs necessary in the first place. He had conveyed Marje's stock offer and been told by Kerner to handle it in any way he saw fit.

It was sometime in October, 1962, when Miller first learned of Marje's tender of stock to the governor and Isaacs the previous March. She called as she did every day, and after some discussion of pending problems she casually mentioned she had "set aside" some stock for Isaacs and Kerner. She neglected to note that all her stock was held by her bank as collateral for the millions lent to her.

Supposing she had just recently made the offer, Miller asked, "Did you talk to Kerner about it?"

"No," admitted Mrs. Everett.

"Have you talked to Bill Lynch?"

Once more the reply was negative. She had not discussed the deal with her very influential attorney.

"Well, I intend to talk to Lynch," said Miller, and he did as quickly as he could reach him. Lynch was surprised, or a good actor. "How in hell," he asked, "does she know that Kerner wants her stock?"

Miller hung up the telephone in a state of shock, the history of Ben Lindheimer's unfulfilled promises of stock to John Stelle and others filling his thoughts. Was Marje up to Ben's old tricks? If so, it was a dangerous game, as Ben discovered. And Lynch had a point: how would Marje's offer sit with Mr. Clean? Miller knew the governor well enough to know the man enjoyed, believed in, lived the legend that he was above the battle, untainted and untaintable. He might very well consider the stock an attempt to bribe him, regardless of how carefully Isaacs presented it. There were rumors about Isaacs, but where Kerner was concerned Miller tended to discount them. One thing was certain, if Kerner did consider the stock an insult, he could destroy Marje's racing empire with nothing more than a statement to the press. No official action would be needed, although he could act if necessary. He had forced Republican Paul Serdar to resign from the Racing Board by promising to fire him if he did not. And if Marje fell, the racing industry Miller had tried for eleven years to upgrade would be seriously hurt. On top of everything else, he was still cosigner of her $100,000 note, and $100,000 was still an important bundle of money. Unsure as to what he should do, Miller finally called Marje back and suggested she "hold up this stock thing until you hear from me."

Marje agreed, but as the days passed and the time for the Racing Board to approve racing dates for 1963 approached, she became impatient. On November 8 she again called Miller. They talked about several new problems including a libel suit she had decided to file against the *New York Post*. Then she made a suggestion: since Miller was scheduled to see Kerner the next day, would he feel the governor out about the stock? She had received no word from him independent of Isaacs, and she couldn't help wondering.

Miller agreed. If Kerner appeared annoyed, perhaps he could convince him that Marje meant no harm and certainly no insult to a man of integrity. But he wasn't going to raise the subject without something in writing to substantiate the deal. Would Marje send him a memo outlining her promises to Isaacs and he would take it from there?

A few hours later a messenger delivered two notes from Marje to Miller's apartment. The memo about the stock was in Marje's handwriting: at least she had sense enough not to dictate it. On the stationery of Washington Park–Arlington Park, she had written:

Dear W S
The following memo is to
confirm our telephone conversation
of today.
At your earlier suggestion we
have been holding:
For O.K.
25 shares of C.T.E. common $25,000
10,000 shares of W.P.T.A. common $10,000
For T.I.
5 shares of C.T.E. common $ 5,000
2,000 shares of W.P.T.A. common $ 2,000
We did not issue the above as you
had suggested that I hold this stock
until we received further instructions
from you.
For your further information you
will recall that the common stock
of C.T.E. at the time of merger
had a value of $1,000 a share.
I shall be pleased to either
issue the above stock or hold it —
or handle it in any manner you
suggest.
Kindest personal regards,
Marje
November 8, 1962

The second note was typewritten and noted that Marje was leaving at noon that day for New York. It told where she could be reached "in case you need me."

Miller assumed the occasion for the New York trip was the libel suit Marje had filed against sports columnist Milton Gross and his newspaper. Gross had written some unkind things about Marje when he happened to be present at Arlington Park when Marje intervened while track stewards were debating a foul claim lodged after a race. She had retained Ed Weisl, a powerful New York attorney and a director of CTE, to prosecute the $2 million suit, but it was actually Mrs. Weisl she was going to see. The lady was about to have surgery for cancer.

Ultimately, after Marje cooled off, the suit was dismissed for lack of prosecution.

Next day Miller went to Springfield, prepared, he thought, for anything. Isaacs sat in on the meeting which was held in the governor's private office, a large room with a desk in a far corner where people could talk in privacy. He began by discussing various racing problems including some difficulty Marje was having with Health Department officials. The governor seemed to be listening, and he commented that Marje, of course, would have to obey the law like anyone else. The libel suit was mentioned, and Miller predicted it wouldn't amount to much. Finally, he said, that "out of a desire to be kind" Marje had set aside stock for Kerner and Isaacs. He read from the note she had sent him.

The patrician face of Otto Kerner, Jr., did not change expression. He nodded:

"That's very kind of Marje," he said.

Slowly, Miller released his breath.

Much later, Miller learned that Isaacs and Kerner had agreed to buy stock — but not in the amounts listed by Marje in her memo — *long before he was told about it.* Only then did he realize that her suggestion he "feel out" Kerner was her way of letting him, the chairman of the Illinois Racing Board, know just prior to the annual allocation of racing dates that she was no longer dependent upon him. *She had his boss now.*

Consequently, he did not suppose that he had offered a bribe to Kerner. He had told Kerner nothing the governor did not already know. So little did the episode impress himself, he filed Marje's notes under "1962 Miscellaneous" and forgot about them.

Later he was to say he was naive where Marje was concerned. Perhaps, but he was not so naive as to be unable to recognize that a potentially dangerous situation was developing. In addition to offering stock to the governor, Marje's new attorneys had handed it out wholesale to legislators.

Lynch and Schaller incorporated the Washington Park Trotting Association on November 13, 1961, and received forty-two racing days from September 3 to October 20 from the Illinois Harness Racing Commission. The news came on Thanksgiving Day, and by a coincidence Mr. and Mrs. Paul Powell were guests of the Everetts that day at their Arlington Park residence.

Powell was essential to the success of the new WPTA. The downstate politician was speaker of the house and a power in the harness-racing business. His help would be needed in gaining the cooperation of John Stelle, who disliked the name Lindheimer because he felt that "Little Ben" had doublecrossed him.

Early in 1961, Miller arranged a meeting in Springfield at the St. Nicholas Hotel. Ironically, the suite assigned them had been the home of State Auditor Orville Hodge until his conviction on embezzlement charges, but perhaps it seemed familiar to Powell and Stelle. Also in attendance were Schaefer O'Neill, a former state senator, and Bill Johnston, Sr., of Sportsman's Park. Marje, as presented by Miller, turned on the charm, and Miller assured the downstaters that Lindheimer's daughter could be trusted to conduct harness racing on the highest standards.

"Those present had a big financial investment in the industry, as well as political power," said Miller. "They would have been stupid not to try to be friends. That was the sole purpose of the meeting and that purpose was accomplished."

Attorney Lynch would carry on. Marje kept her hand in, however, especially in dealing with Powell. Soon he was writing to "Dear Margie" and signing himself "Paul." In one letter he told her she had made "a great hit" with the legislators. "If we are going ahead with plans as previously discussed, we need to be properly organized," he concluded.

Those plans amounted to what one government agent later called "the biggest bribe in Illinois history." Key legislators were to be issued 49 per cent of the new Washington Park Trotting Association. They would pay nothing. Later, after any needed legislation was passed and racing dates received, their stock would be bought back at a handsome profit. No one would know about the wheeling and dealing, of course, for officially and superficially, all the stock would be owned by outstanding citizens of good reputation.

Officially, the original 98,000 shares of WPTA stock went to Webb Everett, Charles Wacker III, Ralph Atlass, William Lynch, George Schaller, Harold Anderson, Lawrence Marsh, and Henry D. Williams. Three of them — Lynch, Schaller, and Williams — were attorneys for the Everetts. Webb put up $100,000 to capitalize the new corporation and held 25,000 shares. Lynch was ahead with 30,000 shares, and he put up no money.

Selected to receive stock at $1 a share some time in the immediate future were Democrat Powell, speaker of the house in 1961; Republican John Lewis, speaker in 1963; Democrat George Dunne, majority leader, 1961; Republican William Pollack, minority leader, 1961; Democrat Clyde Choate, majority whip, 1961; Republican Robert McCloskey, minority whip, 1961; Democrat Clyde Lee, in 1961 chairman of the House Agriculture Committee, the body that handled most racing legislation; Republican Arthur Bidwill, president pro tempore of the Senate in 1961 and 1963; and, finally, three members of the Senate Executive Committee, the group that handled racing legislation in the upper chamber: Democrats Paul Ziegler and A. L. Cronin, and Republican Everett Peters.

Payoff came on July 1, 1964. Lynch, Atlass, Wacker, and Schaller had their names on various stock certificates issued on that date, but the actual owners were the politicians. Beginning May 12, 1967, and continuing to October 29, 1970, the WPTA or Chicago Thoroughbred Enterprises — Marje's holding company — bought back the stock. Prices varied from $3 to $10 a share, depending on the circumstances and the current power of the individual, but everyone made a profit. The record, according to IRS reports:

Powell, $35,000; Choate, $35,000; Dunne, $20,000; Wm. Murphy, $35,000; Lewis, $15,000; McCloskey, $10,000; Pollack, $35,000; Bidwill, $72,000; Mertyce Fagot (now Mrs. John P. Meyer), $5,000; Ziegler, $18,000; Peters, $10,000; Cronin, $22,500; and Lee, $28,000.

In addition, Bidwill had an extra 12,000 shares which he made available to his son, Neal, and Neal's nominee, Peter Biggam. Neal Bidwill made a profit of $20,000 and another $63,000 rolled in via Biggam's name. Cronin, likewise, shared the loot, allowing his law partner, John J. Kennelly, an additional 2,500 shares on which he made a profit of $22,500. It should be noted that Ziegler, Biggam, and Cronin waited until 1970 to sell, and arranged for attorney Arthur Susman to handle it. Susman got the highest price, $10 per share, for his clients, and deducted fifty cents per share as his commission.

In total: 97,000 shares of stock were "sold" in 1964 to the politicians at $1 a share. They were later "bought" back for a total of $543,000, leaving the legislators with a combined profit of $446,000.

Was it worth it?

In the summer of 1962, Washington Park Trotting Association entered into a longterm lease with Marje's CTE for rental of the racing plant at Washington Park. The rent was to be two per cent of the gross mutuel handle. In the seven years, 1962 through 1968, the rent totaled $3,675,068.40.

In those same seven years, the net profit of WPTA after paying the rent was $1,275,504.34. The book value per share increased from sixty-eight cents in 1963 to $8.80 at the end of 1968. No stock or cash dividends were paid during the period.

And, all this time the stock certificates remained in the hands of Marje's attorneys, those ex-partners of Mayor Daley, Lynch and Schaller.

The original blue-ribbon stockholders didn't do so badly either. They sold their stock purchased in 1962 for $1 a share back to CTE in September, 1966, for $5 a share except Wacker, who got $8. Lynch made a profit of $120,000; Wacker, $105,000; Schaller, $44,000; Atlass and Anderson, $20,000 each; Marsh and Williams, $4,000 each; and Webb Everett got back $100,000 in addition to the $100,000 he had originally advanced to WPTA.

As far as the Internal Revenue Service could discover, Miller didn't make a penny despite all his aid to Marje. That fact, however, didn't prevent him from being labeled the *mastermind* when, later, a scapegoat was needed. Contrast this with Lynch's profits. In addition to everything else, Lynch was "sold" 150 shares of CTE stock. His total profit on all his dealings with Marje was almost $2,000,000. To top it off, Mayor Daley arranged for Lyndon Johnson to appoint him to the federal bench. Bidwill, a Republican, was cut in on other deals and cleaned up some $1,600,000. Then there was James Leo Hayes, a former director of Washington Park. When Governor Kerner appointed him in 1961 to the Harness Racing Commission, he received CTE stock on December 2, 1961. On December 22, 1961, he signed the order granting 1962 racing dates to WPTA. Later he was rewarded with other stock. His total take was estimated at $600,000. The fact that it was against the law to own racing stock while a member of the Harness Racing Commission seemed to have escaped the attention of all law-enforcement agencies, then and later.

While Miller wasn't aware as 1962 drew to a close which legislator or businessman got what, he was very unhappy about the stock offer to Kerner. Ironically, Marje's reasons for making the offer and for letting the IRB chairman know about it at the time her racing applications for

1963 would reveal the fast shuffle at Balmoral, were unjustified. The Racing Board staff, which routinely processed the dozens of applications, made no report of the contents of the annual audit, and Miller and his colleagues remained in ignorance of what their files contained. If Marje assumed that her stock offer to the governor was responsible for the silence about Balmoral, she was mistaken.

Basically, Miller was disillusioned. In the spirit of the old reformers, and in fulfillment of his promise to Lindheimer, he had tried to help both Marje and the racing industry. On the surface, he had succeeded. There had been improvements and growth, and if there was dry rot beneath, it wasn't visible. With things finally calm, why not get out? Get out while he could in honor and some pride? The only problem was to find a suitable excuse for quitting, a reason that would seem natural.

He began looking for the reason. Unfortunately for him, it was already too late.

A city is not builded in a day.

VACHEL LINDSAY, 1908

5
The Chairman

The racing episode which led to Mrs. Everett filing a libel suit against the *New York Post* occurred on August 22, 1962, during the running of the Futurity Trials. Jockey Robert Nono aboard *Petro Tim* filed a foul claim against Jockey Willie Shoemaker, who rode *Candy Spots* to victory. Shoemaker was a friend of Marje, and his horse was owned by another friend of hers, Rex Ellsworth.

The stewards retired to a private room to view the film of the race and determine if Nono's claim was valid. While they were watching, Marje called to complain about the delay and to indicate her belief that Shoemaker had done nothing wrong. In the racing world, such intervention by the owner of the track is considered a breach of ethics. The stewards disallowed Nono's claim, but one of them immediately resigned his post in protest.

It was very embarrassing to Miller, who was vice president of the National Association of Racing Commissioners, and Marje's subsequent action in filing a libel suit did nothing to improve his mood. It darkened more when his friend Daniel F. Rice followed up his verbal disapproval of Marje's action at the Futurity Trials and her operation of Chicago Thoroughbred Enterprises, with action. Rice had been dissatisfied for some time. As early as June 16, 1962, Miller had written to attorney Lynch:

> I know you feel as I do that Dan Rice is a decent and superior gentleman. Also, he is a friend worth having and worth keeping. I urge you to spare no effort in proving to him that Chicago Thoroughbred is worthy of his trust and active support.

This Lynch failed to do. In September, 1962, Rice confronted

66

Marje with an offer to buy her interest in CTE or to sell his shares worth $609,375. Chicago businessman Modie Spiegel agreed to buy Rice's common stock, and Marje borrowed money from her bank to buy his preferred stock. Rice retained 3,500 shares of Balmoral Jockey Club stock.

Topping this was Marje's later revelation she was holding stock for Governor Kerner and Kerner's acceptance of the situation. Miller began thinking it would be nice to get a long way from Chicago. He had relatives in the tiny duchy of Luxembourg of whom he was fond. It might be fun, he decided, to be named U. S. ambassador to that country and no questions would be asked.

In 1960, Miller had been a delegate-at-large to the Democratic convention that nominated John Kennedy. His influence among downstate delegates had been so helpful the candidate personally invited Miller to meet his father, Joseph Kennedy, the driving force in that family.

If Mayor Daley, the dispenser of patronage in the Chicago area, would give his okay, President Kennedy would grant any reasonable request Miller might make. Early in March he discussed it with Daley, who seemed willing. Miller was encouraged enough to write to his relatives in Luxembourg about the prospects. Five days later, however, on March 18, 1963, the answer came from Daley's former law partner, attorney Lynch. It was a turndown. Illinois needed Miller more than the State Department, Lynch said. Problems were piling up — for Marje.

Fifteen dissident stockholders had filed suit against CTE, and several others were threatening to do so. They were bitter. How bitter was discovered some years later by a special agent of the Internal Revenue Department who interviewed one of them, an attorney named I. J. Berkson. The agent's handwritten notes include these statements:

> He bought his stock from Ben Lindheimer 20 or 30 yrs. ago. He and Lindheimer were very good friends.
> He sold his stock back to Marje Everett after the reorganization [the formation of CTE] because he disliked her intensely and didn't want to be associated with her any more. He described her as a "ruthless bitch."

He never attended any stockholders meetings, but claims that Lynch ran the corporation & was Marje's "clout."

Lynch asked for help. Rice was still angry, he said, and was now demanding arrangements be made to buy back his Balmoral stock. Unhappily, CTE was short of cash and faced with a huge capital deficiency.

Instead of getting free of Marje and her financial problems, Miller found himself becoming more deeply involved. At Lynch's urgent request, he agreed to lend Lynch $122,500, with which to buy Rice's Balmoral stock. As collateral he was given that stock. The loan was to be repaid in six months but it wasn't until November 28, 1964, that Miller got his money back. Later, the charge was made that Miller "always wanted to gain control of Balmoral." If so, he missed a good opportunity to begin obtaining that control when the loan to Lynch became delinquent. Moreover, he was still guaranteeing that $100,000 note Marje obtained in 1960. His promises to the dying Lindheimer were making him more and more a captive of circumstances over which neither he nor Marje's bank had very much control. The very future of racing was at stake, and Miller loved the so-called sport.

An inter-office memo of the First National Bank of Chicago on July 24, 1963, listed that capital deficiency mentioned by Lynch as amounting to $626,000. Apparently, the bank was startled enough to try to do something. Another bank memo dated August 29, 1963, stated:

> Mrs. Everett and Senator Lynch were in yesterday to discuss compliance with our directive regarding "excessive outlays for capital expenditures and proposed amendments to the loan agreement. . . ." Mrs. Everett was obviously not aware that the company's undertakings were so great and it was clear there was no control over them. Actually much of the work was done without written contracts. The board established a policy under which all future capital expenditures of $25,000 or more will require prior board approval. Senator Lynch suggested the possible sale of Balmoral stock and the application of the proceeds to the loan. The bank felt this was premature.

The bank could issue directives; Miller could not. Far from having "life or death powers" as Marje claimed later, the chairman had only one vote of three on the IRB, and while he had personal prestige it had to be carefully used. There was enough doubt circulating already that any action by Miller would but confirm the worst fears. It was the Racing Board's duty to keep the industry *looking* respectable, not to expose it. The hope was still what it had been in 1900: ultimately conditions might improve to the point where graft and politics could be eliminated from racing, but not just yet. While waiting you worked with the system and tried to hold things together as best you might.

Troubled, but not despairing, Miller went to Springfield in June to ask the advice of Paul Powell, the powerful downstate politician who had been wheeling and dealing in racing stock for decades. Powell could understand why Miller wanted out, but, on the other hand, he didn't want Marje and her enterprise harmed. Just recently he had found her another tenant, the Egyptian Trotting Association, for Washington Park. He felt that Miller's resignation would be detrimental to the Kerner administration as well as to racing unless it was clearly a shift of jobs. An Illinois Crime Commission had just been authorized — a reaction to Robert Kennedy's "war on crime." Why not move over to it as the first step toward freedom?

Miller was willing. On July 1, 1963, Powell wrote to Governor Kerner recommending Miller for membership on the commission. Apparently Kerner was happy with his Racing Board chairman, for on July 19, one of his assistants, William Chamberlain, wrote to Powell and promised only "to keep your letter in our pending file for reference and consideration by the governor when these members are being finally determined."

Nothing more was heard on the subject. And as the complaints continued, Miller cracked the whip just a little. In letters dated August 5, 1963, to Lynch and Webb Everett, he reported that longtime Balmoral stockholder Hubert Howard was unhappy "about certain of the acts and practices of the present officers and directors of that corporation." He added:

"In my desire to save Illinois racing from unfavorable and undeserved publicity, I have volunteered, unofficially and temporarily, my services in this matter. If a proper and amicable disposition cannot be reached within a reasonable period of time, I will necessarily abandon my unofficial position."

He then made seven "unofficial" demands for various records including "copies of the Balmoral Corporation minutes for each directors' meeting held six months prior to April 30, 1962, and all meetings subsequent to that date."

When Lynch examined Howard's written complaint, he exclaimed, "My God! I couldn't win this lawsuit even with a crooked judge."

A few days later Miller and Lynch met with Howard. Lynch agreed to buy Howard's Balmoral shares, as well as the shares of some of his friends who also wanted out, at Howard's price of $40 a share. That was almost twice the book value of the stock, an indication if nothing else that Howard held all the aces. Once again Miller had kept the lid on by acting unofficially, but nothing changed. The pot kept bubbling.

As part of his investigation, Miller asked Marje for information about the status of her corporations. His notes of that July 19, 1963, meeting later became a government exhibit as part of an effort to prove a conspiracy. Actually, they prove just the opposite. Marje, as the record today shows, did not tell the chairman the whole truth about her stock dealings with politicians and others. It is now obvious she used her father's friend as needed, but she did not confide her secrets to him.

Meanwhile, he became more and more involved. He helped Marje organize still another corporation to become a tenant of Washington Park and thus provide another jet of cash to steady her shaky empire. Chicago Harness Racing, Inc. proved just as profitable as WPTA, and it enabled Marje to make new friends. One such was Joe Knight, Kerner's director of the Department of Financial Institutions. Apparently feeling neglected, he told Miller in 1962 and again the following year that he wanted to own racetrack stock like every other self-respecting politician in the state. Miller passed the second request on to Marje, and she arranged through Ralph Atlass for Knight to buy 50,000 shares of Chicago Harness at forty cents per share. By coincidence, at the same time she helped a Democrat, she permitted Republican Senator Bidwill to buy an equal amount at the same price. No one could accuse the Queen of Illinois Racing of playing favorites where politics was concerned.

The nature of friendship being what it is, Miller could not simply convey a request and then wash his hands of the details. It was April 21, 1964, when Atlass notified Miller that Knight's stock was ready and payment was in order. Miller was at his oceanside home in Golden Beach, Florida, at the time, so he called Miss McInturf, his confidential secretary and business associate, and instructed her to issue a $20,000 check that day to Atlass. The check was marked "Loan." The stock certificate wasn't delivered until later. When at last it arrived, Knight didn't have $20,000 available. At his suggestion, the shares were deposited in a brokerage concern with the solid-sounding name of Sincere & Company. Another sixteen months passed before — on August 9, 1966 — Knight paid in his money to Sincere, and Sincere returned Miller's $20,000.

Of such patient friendships are theories of conspiracy made. Had Miller wanted to own Chicago Harness stock in 1963, he could have bought all he wanted in his own name. He was not then a member of the Harness Racing Commission which regulated that part of the industry, so there was no legal restriction preventing him from open ownership. Like the modern gangster interested in acquiring a gambling casino, the politicians of Illinois tried to use everyone's money but their own when making bargain purchases of stock. The Knight purchase was not the first time Miller was used by his friends, and it wasn't the last time as he tried to keep racing as clean as conditions permitted.

The next crisis concerned Modie Spiegel, president of Chicago Harness. Spiegel's father, who built the giant mail-order house bearing his name, had lent respectability to Ben Lindheimer, and the son had done the same for Marje. The new trotting association had just finished its first meet, when Spiegel at last rebelled. In a letter to Mrs. Everett, copies of which went to Lynch and Miller, Spiegel said he had "as tactfully as I know how, pinpointed the many evidences I have felt of either your irritation, dissatisfaction or indifference toward me." He, like Rice and Howard before him, demanded that Marje buy him out.

Again Miller the peacemaker stepped in. He persuaded Spiegel to stay with Chicago Harness after William Brady of Corn Products agreed to buy Spiegel's stock in Chicago Thoroughbred Enterprises. A showdown was postponed, yet trouble continued. When Chicago Harness was formed a Voting Trust had been set up by Lynch at Marje's instructions. It was patterned after a similar trust created for WPTA, and Spiegel and his attorney, Al Bell, were named as two of the three trustees, giving them control. When Spiegel became disenchanted,

Marje told Lynch to dissolve the trust, putting power back in the hands of the stockholders where she had a majority. Spiegel declined to go along with the idea. Lynch was forced to show *his* muscle. If Spiegel didn't cooperate, he suggested, he might find the garbage of the Spiegel Company uncollected for a while. Other, unspecified things might happen as well. Racing for Spiegel was essentially a hobby. Rather than allow it to harm his business, he reluctantly backed down. Mayor Daley's ex-partner had too much influence at City Hall to justify taking unnecessary risks. A better opportunity would come along sooner or later.

On November 22, 1963, President Kennedy was killed in Dallas. Lyndon Johnson was not popular with Mayor Daley, yet both men were professionals and put aside their feelings as the 1964 elections approached. Daley had been re-elected the year before, and he was anxious to demonstrate his power by helping Governor Kerner win a second term.

Marje was also eager to see Kerner re-elected. Early in the campaign she sent a package to Miller's office. He found it on his desk upon returning from lunch. At that moment Marje called. She wanted him to open the package and count the contents. Miller obeyed.

"Thirty thousand dollars," he reported.

"Oh," said Mrs. Everett. "I made a mistake. Will you please put half of it in one package and the rest in another. I'll have one picked up and I'd appreciate it if you'd see the other is given to the governor."

Miller did as requested, then called the Chicago office of Kerner for an appointment. On that day there was no one else present. "I have a package here from Marje," said Miller, handing it over.

"That's very nice," said Kerner, and he put it unopened into a desk drawer.

Later Marje contributed five checks, each for $5,000, making her total $40,000 for the campaign. In five years she had invested $85,000 in Kerner, and had promised him valuable stock as well. Did she get value received? Miller could only assume she was satisfied.

In the middle of the campaign — *scandal*. Ted Isaacs, who had resigned in 1963 as revenue director after a newspaper exposé, was indicted on thirty-six counts of conspiracy, collusion to rig bidding on state contracts, conflict of interest, and official misconduct. The specifics involved a printing company doing business with the state.

While protesting innocence, Isaacs took "leave of absence" from managing Kerner's re-election bid, so the affair wouldn't damage Kerner's image as Mr. Clean. Isaacs had been involved in other scandals, and such things were more or less expected of him. A year later the charges were quashed on the ground the indictment wasn't specific. The state appealed. The Illinois Supreme Court concurred. It then became necessary to set up a special commission to hear charges of impropriety against two of the Supreme Court justices who had voted to quash. The men had received stock in a bank Isaacs helped organize. The two justices resigned. And so it went; Isaacs was home free.

Kerner was re-elected by a large majority, not as huge as in 1960, but respectable enough. On the national level Johnson smashed Barry Goldwater's dream of returning the country to the nineteenth century. Encouraged by this defeat of the right wing, figuring their time had come, various minority groups joined with idealistic college students to demand immediate reform.

Governor Kerner had his problems, and one of them was Maywood Park. It was owned by the Galt family (the same people who developed Galt Ocean Mile north of Fort Lauderdale) and its inadequate facilities had been leased to the Maywood Park Trotting Association. Allegedly, the association had some shadowy link to organized crime. The state occasionally lost money at Maywood because it did not have an all-weather track and could not operate when the weather was bad.

The governor called in Thomas C. Bradley, chairman of the Harness Racing Commission since 1961. He had known Kerner for years, yet when appointed he went to Mayor Daley to give thanks. Daley obviously didn't have anything to do with the decision so he recommended the new chairman consult with Miller to learn about his new duties. "Prior to my appointment I had never seen a harness race and had been to the thoroughbred track only occasionally," Bradley later stated.

At that May meeting in 1964, Kerner was very critical of Maywood Park's facilities and management's failure to improve them. Bradley was astonished when Kerner ordered him to cancel Maywood's racing days and give them to the two other harness tracks in the area: Washington Park and Sportsman's Park. He refused.

"Well, now, Tom," said Kerner, "this is an order."

Bradley disobeyed it. When some new construction was completed at Maywood, the Harness Commission voted to let MPTA keep its usual dates in 1964. Several months passed and suddenly Kerner called to demand Bradley's resignation. Bradley at first refused, but after a few days when he realized the governor meant business, he did write a letter of resignation.

This left harness racing in Illinois in a state of crisis. The second board member, James Hayes, was in a Houston hospital for open-heart surgery. The third member, Walter Murphy, reported he was unable to get Hayes to accept the racing-date schedule he had worked out. Under the law, a two-member approval was required. Kerner called Hayes in his hospital room and ordered him to accept the dates. Hayes told his wife about the call and she was later to remember it to Kerner's great discomfort. The harness schedule was approved.

Was this dispute simply the excuse to propose the consolidation of the two regulatory bodies, or did the interests of efficiency and economy prompt it? Later on darker motives would be suggested.

The record shows that on August 6, 1965, an executive session of the Racing Board was called to order in its offices at 160 North LaSalle Street. Chairman Miller "stated that the board had been reconstituted as of August 1, 1965, by order of Gov. Otto Kerner, to include seven members, and also to encompass the responsibilities of the Illinois Harness Racing Commission." Crowdus Baker of Sears, Roebuck was one of the new members.

Miller had been named chairman of the combined boards. All rules and regulations previously adopted by the Harness Commission were formally adopted by the Racing Board and Ernest Marsh was asked to begin a study looking toward their revision. Roy Tuchbreiter was requested to review all the applications and financial statements filed by the harness associations in order to advise the board as to their plants and financial structures.

(Tuchbreiter was president and chief executive officer of a large insurance company, and was an intimate friend of Marje's attorney, William Lynch. Indeed, it was Lynch who had sponsored his appointment to the IRB. Mayor Daley's old law partners also rendered professional services to a bank which Tuchbreiter founded.)

If it was a coup, it was done quietly and efficiently. Miller, whose ego warred constantly with his Catholic conscience and smalltown common sense, was at once proud and appalled. He had new power, new prestige, but his chances of breaking away seemed more remote than ever. He told himself that with his new power, he could act more efficiently to achieve stability and thus reach the point where his services as a mediator would not be needed. In his long tenure he had achieved a national reputation and was serving as president of the National Association of State Racing Commissioners. Just as Kerner enjoyed his almost legendary image for honesty, so Miller took pleasure in the name he had won in racing circles for innovation and integrity. As his final contribution he was working hard on *The Racing Commissioners' Manual*, an idea he conceived and, as executive editor, carried to completion in 1966. Miller wrote part of it, and found experts to contribute specialized knowledge in various fields. He began Chapter One with this statement which certainly reflected his own experience:

> A commissioner should be on the side of the sport of racing — and to the sport, everything is subordinate including the state, the racing associations, the owners, the trainers, the jockeys, etc. This is not to say that a commissioner and the various constituent parts of racing should be inharmoniously related. In fact we serve the sport best when we strive to make each segment strong; and in the synchronizing of these segments, we must leave a tension — a delicately precise line of demarcation — between us.

On November 17, 1965, Miller found much of which to be proud. He told his board:

> Our mutuel handle at the thoroughbred tracks in the season of 1960 was $212,000,000; in 1965 it will be over $285,000,000, an increase of 34.4 per cent. Our total attendance at the thoroughbred tracks in the 1960 season was 2,827,324; in 1965 it will be over 3,500,000, an increase of 24 per cent. . . . Our mutuel handle at the harness meetings in the season of 1960 was $60,900,000; in 1965 it will exceed $167,000,000, an increase of over 174 per cent. Our total harness racing attendance in 1960 was 1,100,000; in 1965 it will exceed 2,800,000, an increase of 150 per cent.

Grounds for complacency, perhaps, but in Illinois racing a new crisis was always just around the corner. In January, 1966, it appeared in the person of Ted Isaacs. Despite the scandals in which he had been involved, he still retained the friendship of Governor Kerner. Perhaps Kerner was looking ahead to an early appointment to the federal bench, and wanted to get his affairs in order. Or perhaps Isaacs was hungry. In any case, he came to Miller to remind him that Marje had never followed through on her promise of racetrack stock.

"Those people can either do it or forget it," said Isaacs. "The old man and I are irritated."

This was the type of situation Miller had expected, and dreaded, remembering how Ben Lindheimer's empty promises to John Stelle had made a bitter enemy out of that downstate power. He called Marje at once, telling her that having made the promise she should now deliver. She agreed, and began making arrangements. How complicated those arrangements were can only be guessed at, but evidence eventually developed to indicate they were complex indeed.

On February 8, 1966, Marje's secretary wrote as follows to "the Honorable William J. Lynch," Marje's influential attorney:

> Enclosed are the following stock
> certificates of CTE:
> No. CS 160 dated February 8, 1966
> for 25 shares issued in the name of
> Marjorie L. Everett.
> No. CS 159 dated February 8, 1966
> for 25 shares issued in the name of
> Marjorie L. Everett.
> Inasmuch as Mary Carroll is on
> vacation, would you kindly ask Mr.
> Schaller to sign these two certificates?
> Sincerely yours,

At the bottom of the formal letter appeared a note in Marje's handwriting:

> These certificates have been endorsed by me and I
> believe you said you would guarantee my signature.
> Thanks. Marje

Months went by, however, before delivery was made. When Miller told Lynch once more that Isaacs was becoming impatient, Lynch gave him Marje's memo to prove she was acting in good faith.

That action was at last impending is reflected by a bank memo written by Senior Vice President Rudy Palluck of the First National Bank of Chicago. Written on August 8, 1966, the memo noted that "Mrs. Everett also reported that she will sell fifty shares of CTE common and immediately reacquire such shares in exchange for her 10,820 shares of Balmoral stock having a present value of about $30. Marje said she held the above shares of CTE subject to an option letter based on the original issue price of $1,000 per share and the exchange for her Balmoral stock will clear the obligation."

Did the bank, which had a first and second lien on Marje's CTE stock, know what Marje planned to do with the fifty shares she was, in effect, borrowing from the bank? It seems unlikely bank officials would accept at face value the story of the option letter, or would otherwise cooperate without a better understanding of the importance of the transaction. Not everything is spelled out — even in internal bank memos.

The actual transfer of the stock was a complex affair, partly because of the desire to keep Kerner's name out of it and partly because of a cash shortage. That old campaigner and longtime friend of both Kerner and Miller, Joe Knight, was recruited. Knight had an apartment in the Seneca Hotel near Miller's office, and he was always dropping in to entertain the staff with "homespun stories."

Knight had been a stockholder in Miller's J. E. Porter Company, which had recently been sold, and so had Miller's secretary, Faith McInturf. Knight knew that the sale had been immensely profitable and that Miss McInturf had at least $300,000 to invest. So, as the first step in the complicated exchange, he borrowed $40,000 from her.

Miss McInturf knew Knight was a solid businessman, and saw the loan as a chance to get better interest on her money than her savings account was providing. It was a business deal, pure and simple, made largely because of convenience. Had anyone told Miller's confidential secretary that she would some day be indicted because of that loan, she would have laughed out loud.

Knight took the $40,000 from McInturf and lent it to Isaacs and Kerner, although Kerner's name wasn't mentioned in the papers. Thus the stage was set for the next act of the drama which took place on August 10, 1966, at Miller's office on North Michigan. Present, in addition to Miller, were Knight, Isaacs, and — representing Marje Everett — attorney George Schaller.

The attorney delivered CTE stock certificates 159 and 160, both good for twenty-five shares issued to Marje. She had endorsed them and Schaller, as she had requested, formally guaranteed her signature.

Isaacs presented two checks drawn on his own account in payment, the bulk of the money borrowed from Miss McInturf, and the rest from Isaacs' savings. One check was for the principal, $50,000, and the second was for interest, $8,958. Upon leaving the meeting, Schaller sent both checks to Marje along with a letter suggesting the money be "forwarded to the First National Bank of Chicago as a payment on your personal loan."

It was all very correct — until Marje started revising the facts to get Miller into trouble.

Isaacs held the stock certificates for a few seconds and then gave them to Knight to serve as collateral until he could repay the $40,000 he had borrowed from that gentleman, who, of course, had borrowed it from Faith McInturf. In other words, the forty grand had gone from McInturf to Knight to Isaacs — who added $18,958 more — to Schaller to Marje to the bank.

After Schaller and Isaacs left the office, Knight gave the two stock certificates to Miss McInturf to hold as collateral for her loan to him. Miss McInturf waited until Knight was gone to give them to Miller to keep for her in a safe place. Meanwhile, arrangements had to be made to repay the loans so that the stock could be sold or exchanged.

On August 17, 1966, one week after the stock transfer in Miller's office, Knight sold the 28,000 shares of CHR that he had obtained to Kerner and Isaacs for the same forty cents per share they cost in 1964. The two buyers paid $5,600 each, but left the stock in Knight's name as their nominee. His health was so bad that Knight took the precaution of asking Schaller to serve as nominee for Kerner and Isaacs, and the attorney — with permission from Marje — did so.

Largely because Knight's health *was* bad, the complicated deal continued at a leisurely pace. On November 16, 1966, Isaacs gave Knight permission to substitute 10,000 shares of Balmoral stock worth $30 each for the fifty shares of CTE stock. This, of course, was to enable Marje to keep her promise to the bank to reacquire the CTE stock. It also provided an additional layer of insulation to protect the governor and Marje.

Ready cash was still a problem, but it was eased when Chicago Harness paid a dividend in February, 1967. By a coincidence, it came to $5,600, half the original purchase price Kerner-Isaacs had paid. Schaller, as nominee, forwarded the money after being told by Knight to send it "to the true owners." The bargain became sweeter.

On May 12, 1967, the hitherto agreed exchange of Balmoral stock for the CTE stock was finally made, although the CTE stock certificates remained in the custody of Miller, who was holding them for his secretary. Knight, however, was at last moving to wind up the deal. On May 25, 1967, he directed Schaller to sell for $2 a share the 28,000 shares of CHR stock he was holding as nominee for Kerner and Isaacs, and to send him the $56,000. They brought in two checks of $28,000 each. This was for bookkeeping convenience since, officially, he had been acting for two men.

From the $56,000 total, Knight deducted the $40,000 he had "lent" Isaacs, and took out another $2,000 in interest. Left was $14,000, so he sent checks of $7,000 each to Kerner and Isaacs, and shuffled up to Miller's office to give Faith the $40,000 he had borrowed from her. Plus $1,642.48 in interest as her profit, of course.

Meanwhile, Isaacs and Schaller had been engaged in a bit of intrigue themselves. Deciding in 1966 that some documentation might be useful for tax purposes, Isaacs arranged to have a promissory note prepared. It was for $50,000, at five per cent interest, and was payable to Marje. In return, Schaller dictated a letter for Marje to sign. It read:

> Dear Ted:
> This will confirm that I have purchased for you and paid for on behalf of yourself and/or your nominees fifty (50) shares of Chicago Thoroughbred Enterprises, Inc., at the issuing price of $1,000 per share. According to our understanding, I will hold these shares in my possession as collateral for your note to me of this date for $50,000.00 bearing interest at the rate of 5% per year (simple interest), with the further understanding that your note will be paid on or before November 15, 1966.
> Kindest personal regards,
> Very truly yours,
> Mrs. Webb A. Everett

There was only one thing wrong with Isaacs' note and Marje's letter: both were backdated from 1966 to November 12, 1962. Later, Mrs. Everett became quite confused. She told an IRS agent auditing her 1966 returns that it was written in 1962. In a January, 1971, affidavit which was the basis of the indictment against Kerner, et al., she swore it was 1962. And in her Grand Jury testimony on July 15, 1971, she swore it was 1962.

The government believed her, and it was not until Miller told the prosecutors the truth that they began checking. Isaacs and Schaller reluctantly confirmed the backdating, but insisted there was nothing illegal about it. (Several years later, one of President Nixon's "experts" went to prison for backdating documents to give Nixon a tax break.) It proved rather embarrassing to a lot of people, but Schaller was in an especially awkward position. It turned out he and his partner Lynch had done some backdating for their own benefit. They bought 5,000 shares of WPTA stock at $1 a share from Webb Everett in 1966, and backdated documents to make it appear the sale took place in April, 1962. The stock was sold in 1967 for $5 a share, making a neat profit for Mayor Daley's ex-partners of $20,000.

Mrs. Everett didn't object to the deal, she said, because she considered the profits as added compensation for services rendered her corporations. Lynch, of course, served as nominee for WPTA stock owned by those so-essential politicians such as Powell, Choate, Dunne, Murphy, Lewis, and McCloskey, and Schaller acted as a nominee for Clyde Lee. For these services they were permitted to buy 26,000 shares at $1 a share in 1962, in addition to the 5,000 they picked up four years later and backdated.

Both men were further rewarded by being elevated to the bench, but for that they thanked Daley rather than Marje.

The final act came some ten months later when Knight sold the 10,000 shares of Balmoral stock — which he had exchanged for Marje's CTE stock — back to the Balmoral Jockey Club for $300,000. Endorsing it, he took the check to Isaacs, who took it to the Civic Center Bank and deposited it into four new accounts — two for Kerner, two for Isaacs. The bank, according to federal investigators, "made none of the usual entries and documentation," not even requiring Isaacs to endorse it.

At last the big deal that started in 1962 was finished. Out of its complications the U. S. government would weave a magnificent conspiracy theory and produce a drama that held Chicago agog for years. Somehow, however, the search for truth became instead a selective process to find those facts and allegations which best would achieve the goal of "getting Otto."

It is interesting to note that Knight, the self-styled banker in the deal, made a profit of exactly $357.52. That was all he had left after paying interest and principal on the money he borrowed from Miss McInturf to lend to Isaacs. Small recompense indeed for the humiliation of being indicted while dying of cancer.

Miller, of course, didn't receive a cent. Long before the deal was completely consummated, he was striving desperately to avert still another scandal. This time it was Charles Wacker III, a member of Marje's "blue ribbon" group whose names had been used to give Washington Park Trotting Association an aura of respectability.

Wacker was technically president of WPTA, but gradually it dawned on him that he lacked the powers of a president. He became concerned about conflicts of interests between the WPTA and its landlord, CTE: directors in one owned stock in the other; the same attorneys were used by both corporations; the same accountants were used. He had difficulty getting facts and figures when he wanted them. And now, Mrs. Everett was demanding the original ten-year lease of Washington Park's racing facilities be replaced with another one which would give CTE a much higher rent.

Even worse, from Wacker's view, was his growing suspicion that he and his fellow businessmen had been used as fronts and did not own all the stock listed in their names. In early June of 1966 he went to the offices of Schaller, Reilly & Daley to demand some answers.

(Bill Lynch had just been appointed to the federal bench, and his old law firm had replaced him with Mayor Daley's son, Michael. This shift made Schaller the attorney Marje relied upon for matters involving politicians and influential businessmen. Ultimately Schaller would be named to the Cook County bench and the firm would be reorganized again.) Wasting no words, Wacker demanded to know exactly who his fellow stockholders in WPTA were. Schaller quickly compiled a list. Wacker was shocked to discover he was the nominee for 49,000 shares owned by the Republican Majority Leader, Art Bidwill, and for 7,000 shares owned by Rep. William Pollack, the Republican Minority Leader. Schaller left no doubt that the stock had been distributed on a bipartisan basis. Paul Powell, he noted, was now secretary of state of Illinois.

Wacker compared notes with his Chicago Harness counterpart, Modie Spiegel, and then called Racing Board Chairman William Miller for an appointment. Al Bell went along with them. Spiegel and Wacker recited their complaints, stated they were utterly opposed to the new lease Marje wanted, and produced their bomb — the list Schaller had prepared of participating politicians.

This, the three respectables said, was the final straw. They wanted nothing more to do with either the WPTA or CHR or Marje Everett. If their own holdings were not repurchased immediately, they would expose the entire mess to whatever agency would listen.

Miller, the mediator, could only agree with them. He gave his personal assurance that he would insist their stock be bought up, and he pledged to do everything in his power to clean up the situation and get the politicians out. As usual, he was effective. The men trusted him and left his office with their pride soothed.

Hardly were they out the door when Miller got on the phone to Powell and set up a meeting in Powell's suite at the Conrad Hilton. Outlining the problem, Miller advised the politician to "tell your people to get out before Wacker blows the lid off." Powell agreed to get busy the same day. Next the chairman met with Marje. After briefing her, he gave her an official order:

"Get those politicians out of these racing organizations."

For once, Marje didn't argue. Businessman and politician alike were paid off with handsome profits at a cost in excess of $1.5 million. Wacker, Bell, and Spiegel got the highest price of anyone for Marje feared them the most. It took a lot of juggling to find the cash and when it was done CTE ended up owning almost all of WPTA, and Balmoral had most of CHR. This posed a new problem: Illinois law prohibited one group or organization from owning two harness associations. Schaller and Webb Everett solved the problem by forming a new corporation, Illinois Racing Enterprises (IRE), and bought up most of Balmoral's CHR stock. With racing applications pending, however, the arrangement was kept quiet. Even the Balmoral stockholders knew nothing about the buying or the sale of Chicago Harness.

Surveying the scene, Miller decided he could now quit the Racing Board. Things had calmed. The year 1966, while a hectic one for Miller, had been profitable for Illinois. New records had been set. The state had received $35,561,116.62, an increase of $5,059,687.39 over the record year of 1965. A total of 6,506,379 horse fans, both thoroughbred and harness, wagered $491,301,900. The thoroughbred season lasted 307 days, the harness meets took 321 days. Obviously, the limits of expansion were near. Moreover, the dissidents were satisfied and most of the politicians were out of racing. On the face of things, it appeared that Miller's optimism had been justified and he had indeed conned his ship through shoals and reefs into peaceful waters. So why not quit before a new squall broke as, inevitably, one would?

During more than fifteen years on the Illinois Racing Board, Miller had helped others get rich, but had declined all suggestions he use his position for personal gain. Racing, however, had become part of his life, and he considered he had many good years left. So when Webb Everett invited him to share ownership of IRE after his resignation, Miller was interested. Joe Knight, George Schaller, and Bailey Howard — the latter a publishing executive — were interested in becoming stockholders as well. But the First National Bank of Chicago declined to finance the new proposal because only Miller had cash to invest, so they dropped out.

On April 17, 1967, Miller resigned. In his letter to Governor Kerner, he noted that "We now have racing practically every day or night of the year except Sundays and this means continuous, every-day supervisory service on the part of the chairman. Regretfully, I cannot conform to that kind of condition now, and it would be unfair to you, to racing, and to the people of Illinois to pretend otherwise."

Kerner, accepting the resignation, praised Miller's work highly, then added, "I do hope that your severance from the Racing Board, however, will not remove your interest from government in Illinois. It is not often that we find dedicated citizens of your quality willing to give your time and your talent for the benefit of the state."

Newspapers were unanimous in praising Miller's long career. Typical was the comment of David Condon in the *Chicago Tribune*:

> You name it in racing, and Miller did it. Oh, no, we never saw him up on a horse heading down the home stretch, but that's because he no longer can make 110 pounds.
> The gentleman served Illinois racing well. He de-

serves semiretirement. Meanwhile, he will be available when sound counsel is needed in a growing sport.

By unanimous vote, the Illinois Senate adopted a resolution "commending and congratulating" Miller. Among other achievements with which he was credited, the Senate noted his "successful efforts to eliminate the hoodlum element from our tracks."

Similar praise came from the National Association of State Racing Commissioners, and it was followed up in June when at a special luncheon at Arlington Park the NASRC presented a plaque to Miller. In accepting it, Miller, "this erudite and articulate man," noted that his position had not been a salaried one. "However," he added, "even in this day and age in which so much is measured on a purely monetary basis, I can truly say that I am drenched with riches — the riches provided by my friends assembled here."

Among those so assembled were Mr. and Mrs. Webb Everett.

In the years to come, the bitter years and the serene, that luncheon at Arlington assumed the misty character of a half-remembered dream. Looking backward, the ex-chairman could conclude that despite naiveté and a touch of egocentrism he had been, during those dangerous years of power, "in God's pocket."

> *Power breeds arrogance, and arrogance, of course, breeds corruption, and there has been too much of both in Chicago.*
>
> VIRGIL PETERSON
> Chicago Crime Commission

6
The Probe

William S. Miller and his wife, Catherine, paid $626,537.67 in federal income taxes for the year 1965, having disposed of their controlling interest in The J. E. Porter Company in Ottawa.

Various sound business reasons dictated the sale despite the fact that Miller had to pay a whopping accumulated earnings tax on top of his income tax. He was later to point out that had he been interested in buying racing stock, it would have been easy — and far more profitable — to have used his company's surplus cash to do so prior to the 1965 sale. Still, he emerged a millionaire and it is certain the money had much to do with his decision to quit the Illinois Racing Board and invest in a track of his own in 1967.

Early in January, Miller and Webb Everett conferred with one of Everett's tax attorneys, Henry D. Williams, who lived on Miami Beach and practiced law in Miami. For many years Williams had been consulted by Marje Everett and had served as a stockholder and director of Chicago Thoroughbred Enterprises.

Webb Everett formed IRE — Illinois Racing Enterprises — and bought control for that corporation of Chicago Harness Racing. Miller became interested in buying control of CHR, but there were sticky legal problems to be settled so Williams was consulted.

The attorney studied the matter and ultimately advised Everett to drop the project. Ownership of CHR stock would cause tax problems for the Everetts, he said, since IRE could be considered a personal holding company. In addition, as noted, Illinois law prohibited an entity from owning more than one harness racing association, and Marje already had WPTA.

On the other hand, Williams saw no reason why Miller should not proceed without Webb. He advised, however, that he buy the assets of IRE — the CHR stock — rather than the stock of IRE itself. It was, as he put it later, cleaner to keep away from IRE which, "by reason of rules of attribution, might be considered part of all these other corporations."

It was the Everetts' attorney talking, and his advice — for which Miller paid $5,000 — made good sense to Miller. As soon as details could be worked out following his resignation from the Illinois Racing Board on April 17, he bought IRE's assets — the Chicago Harness Racing stock. IRE, having no longer any excuse for living, was dissolved.

Marje had discussed disposing of Balmoral for years as a means of reducing her personal debt at the bank. Now bank officials agreed the time had come. Miller, using CHR's surplus cash and a bank loan of $500,000, bought controlling interest in Matt Winn's old dream. Ironically, in doing so, he acquired Governor Kerner and Ted Isaacs as stockholders — the transfer of the fifty shares of CTE stock for 10,000 shares of Balmoral having just been completed. The former Racing Board chairman wasn't worried too much, however, since he was convinced both men would soon cash in their chips.

A man can find many things to worry about if he puts his mind to it, but Miller in his most pessimistic moments never considerd the possibility a day would come when he would be accused of having acquired CHR and Balmoral from the Everetts by means of extortion. Luckily for him attorney Williams had good files, a sound memory, courage and integrity.

One of Miller's first acts was to put the name *Balmoral Park* on the water tower at long last. Then he began the work of rehabilitating the neglected property to comply with Illinois law, which the previous owners had sidestepped.

Under the Everetts, Balmoral had become largely a manure pile. Literally tons upon tons of manure from the stables of Washington Park had been hauled to Crete and dumped on the acres of parking lots. Getting rid of it was an expensive proposition, but it was given top priority.

In a four-color brochure sent during the rebuilding to several
million residents of the south side of Chicago, Miller said:

"Balmoral Park will be the finest. The club house and grandstand
will be glass enclosed and heated electrically — the only such installa-
tion in the world. There will be escalator and elevator service, acres of
paved parking facilities and fine food and drink. Yes, Balmoral Park will
be truly elegant."

Miller's brochure added that

"The environment is delightful. While only minutes away from
bustling Chicago, Balmoral Park is situated in the serene countryside.
Centered in more than 1,000 acres of rolling heavily-wooded farmland.
Balmoral Park is the environment Nature intended for horses and
horsemen."

All of which cost over $5 million, more money than he personally
wanted to spend, so a new corporation was formed. The usual wealthy
friends bought stock. Marje invested in the name of her Western
Concessions, but Miller was careful to see she didn't gain control.
Problems had already developed between the two. The relation of a
tenant to Marje was quite different than had been the status of a Racing
Board chairman, Miller discovered.

The first shock came when his accountants found an unrecorded
liability of $244,000 in purse obligations charged to Chicago Harness.
Upon investigating Marje's purse policies, Miller concluded they were
designed to favor CTE and WPTA at the expense, literally, of CHR and
Balmoral. Miller formulated new guidelines, much to the displeasure
of the Queen of Illinois Racing.

An even greater shock was the discovery of the S Account.

"S" admittedly stood for Slush, and it was Marje's version of the late
Ben Lindheimer's Currency Box Account that she had learned about as
a child. She had improved upon it, in fact, having more organizations
from which to draw. Investigation revealed that CTE, WPTA, CHR,
and Balmoral were billed at frequent intervals for sums amounting to
hundreds of thousands of dollars. All went into the S Account, over
which Marje had sole control. Miller demanded that Marje justify the
charges she was making to the two corporations under his control.
Reluctantly some records were provided covering a period from October 11, 1966, through August, 1967.

During that sixteen-month period, the four companies paid

$243,829.02 into the S Account, and from it was disbursed $235,537.69. Sometimes CTE would be split into Washington Park and Arlington Park, and each would pay 20 per cent of the tribute demanded — the same basis as the three other entities. Yet again, the levy would be on a four-body basis, with CTE paying 25 per cent as a single unit.

Disbursements were diversified; they included travel expenses, charitable contributions, purchases of property and capital stock, professional fees, merchandise — and political contributions.

Checks written for political contributions were described for auditing purposes as "Nondeductible Expense." When Miss McInturf, Miller's confidential secretary, asked about the practice, she received a short note in reply:

> This is the way the information has always been given
> to accounting firms when audits are made.

For October, 1966, records found in the files of CHR show that a total of $5,214.55 was paid on demand into the S Account for the following:

3M Company — merchandise	94.55
Passionist Fathers — contribution	20.00
Nondeductible Expense	5,000.00
Columbean Fathers — contribution	100.00

Miller was curious to discover when the S Account began. The oldest records he could find showed that Balmoral's first contribution was Check 6940 dated August 25, 1962, in the amount of $5,000.00 and made payable to Account S. Chicago Harness began writing checks to Account S early in 1964. However, a check was found written to CTE on February 6, 1964, in the amount of $9,900.50 for "1963 contributions." Chicago Harness had run its first meet in 1963.

Marje wasn't very happy when Miller ordered his staff to make no payments into the S Account, but there were even bigger problems to argue about. The balance sheets of Balmoral and CHR listed $365,000 worth of equipment at cost. When after much search the equipment that could be found was located, it was in use by one of the other companies. Much of it was missing entirely. Yet even this paled into insignificance when Miller discovered that Marje had been allocating *all* of Washington Park expenditures to the tenants who ran harness races there! In addition, CHR was even charged with some of the expenses of *Arlington Park* as well. In 1966, she had charged almost a *million dollars* to her tenants: everything from telephone bills, to new roofs, to the filling in of swamp areas. Meanwhile, she had collected more than $2 million in *rent* from those same tenants.

It took a lot of book work, but Miller's accountants presented Mrs. Everett with an invoice covering all the improper charges dating back to the first of 1967. After much unpleasant discussion, Marje finally agreed to honor the invoice. She also made restitution for the missing or misappropriated equipment, but she paid only book value. Thus a fleet of fully depreciated house trailers cost her nothing. She was far from happy with her new tenant.

That displeasure increased in the spring of 1968 when CHR held its first meet under its new management at Washington Park. Miller took full control, setting purses and making all policy decisions. He followed the same practices at the Balmoral meet which was held at Arlington Park. The results were huge increases in profits over previous years. This, apparently, was more than Marje's pride could stand.

Secretly — she didn't even tell Lynch — she began negotiating with the giant conglomerate, Gulf and Western Industries, to sell her stock in CTE and WPTA. Edgar "Ned" Janotta, a man with close connections to Richard Ogilvie, the Republican candidate for governor, served as broker. Janotta was a Harvard graduate, an investment broker with William Blair & Company, and had been named one of Chicago's ten outstanding young men in 1965. His political ties also included service as treasurer of the Percy for Senator campaign of 1966, and he had been chairman of the Rumsfeld for Congress Committee the same year. Marje put him on the board of CTE and arranged for him to buy stock in her corporation. Representing the conglomerate was the ubiquitous Philip J. Levin.

Why Marje needed Janotta and paid his firm $300,000, as a finder's fee, is unclear since a director and general counsel of Gulf and Western was Edwin L. Weisl, who just happened to be a director of CTE. To the uninitiated it would seem that Weisl was capable of doing all the finding necessary, but perhaps Marje was thinking more about Janotta's political *clout* than of his abilities as an investment broker.

Mrs. Everett was not only violating her father's dying wish in attempting to sell the racing empire to an out-of-state company, she was also violating her often-expressed opposition to organized crime. For Levin, a self-made millionaire, owed much of his success to his syndicate connections. His father had been a minor loan shark in New York, but young Levin went into the real estate business and made it big rather quickly. In some law-enforcement circles he was considered a front for such shy syndicate wizards as Meyer Lansky. Much of the land he sold for huge profits was in Florida and had been purchased by syndicate figures in the decade following the collapse of the great Florida boom of the twenties.

Unlike the gangsters he allegedly represented, Levin was politically a liberal, and had helped finance John F. Kennedy's 1960 campaign. He gained national publicity in 1967 when he lost a proxy battle to take over the movie studio, Metro-Goldwyn-Mayer, but he sold his MGM stock for a $21 million profit to TIME, Inc. and Edgar Bronfman, heir to a vast bootleg-liquor fortune.

Some of that money he used to buy stock in Gulf & Western. Charles Bluhdorn, chairman of the conglomerate, put Levin on the corporation's board and appointed him head of its real estate division. It was with this division that Marje was talking. Ironically, in view of her later statements, Levin was also a friend of Sidney Korshak, the labor-relations expert with ties to the old Capone syndicate. It was Korshak who persuaded Levin to become a partner of Moe Morton in a luxury apartment-hotel in Acapulco, Mexico. Morton had strong Mob connections, and the Acapulco Towers became a syndicate hangout, or — in some circumstances — a hideout.

Gulf & Western, for that matter, was no Sunday School corporation. It had its ties to Mob figures. In addition, when Resorts International — the outfit running the Paradise Island gambling casino in Nassau harbor — tried to take over Pan American Airways, it was with the secret financial help of Gulf & Western. But we anticipate. Marje did not. Her huge debt had become too much for her. She had added to it by building Arlington Park Towers, a plush hotel near the track, and making other expensive "improvements" such as a million-dollar lighting system that was used but once. At any moment the empire might collapse. The transformation of Miller from a powerful friend to a critical tenant meant she could no longer operate in her old free-wheeling style. A sale to the conglomerate would pay her debts and make her independently wealthy. So why not?

The contract was signed on January 31, 1969. It provided that G & W would accept Marje's 2,001 shares of CTE stock — about 68 per cent — in return for $21,534,500 in convertible subordinated debentures due July 1, 1993. In addition, Marje would be employed as chief executive officer of CTE with full powers to manage the racing meets and other enterprises engaged in by CTE. For her services she was to receive $50,000 a year for ten years, and the unrestricted use of "Marje's Inn." The employment agreement spelled out the reasons: "to assure the propinquity of the employee to the scene of the performance of her duties, [and] also to cause such quarters to be utilized for promotion, entertainment and related purposes designed best to further the interests of the employer and to solicit the patronage and goodwill of persons whose patronage and goodwill are important to the continuance of the employer's business."

All costs of maintenance and any and all expenses "including without limitation the costs of repairs, food, beverage, servants and reasonable automotive transportation," were to be borne by the employer.

All in all, a good deal, and why not, since Marje's attorney, Henry Williams, drew up the contract? Perhaps Marje was justified in her announcement that "nothing will change except we'll have more resources to continue our refurbishing program at both racetracks."

She didn't know Phil Levin very well, however, nor did he know Marje. Conflict between the two aggressive personalities was almost inevitable.

Meanwhile a lot of things were changing. The Republicans took over the Governor's Mansion in Springfield and the White House in Washington. Otto Kerner, an astute observer of politics, early on realized the temper of the country was becoming hostile to the Democrats. President Johnson's failure to end the Vietnam War or cool the ghetto and the college campus cut deeply into voters' pride. Johnson's decision not to seek re-election in 1968 did not turn things around. Kerner had taken similar action earlier.

In March, 1968, he told Isaacs to sell their racetrack stock, and in May he resigned as governor to accept appointment to the same Federal Appellate Court seat his father had occupied. It was neatly done, combining the practical with the sentimental in a manner people could appreciate. It contrasted sharply with the brutal events that made 1968 a year to remember in bad dreams: the assassination of Dr.

Martin Luther King, Jr., in Memphis on April 4, an event which brought unrestrained rioting to Chicago's black slums; the execution of Robert F. Kennedy in Los Angeles on June 5, death that ended hope for millions and made Nixon's victory almost certain; and finally that wild, wild week in August when the Democrat National Convention nominated a candidate while on the streets of Chicago Daley's cops broke the heads of young demonstrators as a nation watched in horrified fascination.

The convention made Daley a household name and brought home to millions the realities of machine-politics, but, if anything, it strengthened the mayor's grip on his domain. On election day he gave Hubert H. Humphrey a plurality of 421,199 in Chicago, impressive enough, but insufficient. Nixon won the state by 130,000 votes, and easily carried Ogilvie to victory in the gubernatorial campaign as well.

The new governor named a new Racing Board and selected Alexander MacArthur, a cousin of the late General Douglas MacArthur, to be chairman. MacArthur sometimes appeared at hearings wearing cowboy boots, cowboy hat, and cowboy belt complete with holster containing sunglasses. At the slightest excuse he would declare that Ogilvie "is as square as a box" and proclaim that "we like our racing clean in Illinois."

Meanwhile, the Everett–Miller racing relationship got dirtier. When Balmoral opened its first winter harness meet in December, a license for food and beverage was denied because of unsanitary conditions. Under the contract, Western Concessions, a subsidiary of CTE, was responsible, and Marje hadn't bothered to meet county standards. As a result, the food had to be prepared in the Washington Park kitchens in another county and trucked in. Even so, it was atrocious and attendance in the dining room dropped to almost nothing. It was bad for business, but loss of customers didn't hurt Marje's feelings. She, after all, was on a straight salary.

During the Chicago Harness meet in March and April, 1969, the roof at Washington Park leaked from one end to the other. It was an unusually wet spring, and the management couldn't be persuaded to stop the leaks. An angry Miller found buckets scattered throughout the elegant Derby Room restaurant to catch the water before it could flood the floor. Customers were none too happy, and attendance fell off sharply.

The climax came in May when the Balmoral thoroughbred meet

began at Arlington Park. When Miller's staff arrived, they found the entrances to the office area locked and were forced to find makeshift headquarters. Wet paint was everywhere on opening day, and many were the complaints from patrons who rubbed against it. Toilet conditions were filthy.

Three hours before the first race on opening day, Mrs. Everett announced she wouldn't allow the electricity to be turned on for the parimutuel machines and the track cameras unless Miller paid an additional $45,000 for the rental of newly installed closed circuit televisions. No such payment was authorized under the lease, but Miller had no choice. He complained to one of Marje's attorneys who responded, "It's not right but you'd better pay the bitch."

Miller paid, and the meet went off on schedule, subject to continued harassment. After the first week, the customary between-the-races music over the loudspeaker system was eliminated. Plans to televise featured races on a local station were dropped when Marje refused permission. There were disputes over the concessions.

When at last the meet was over, Miller complained bitterly to one of Levin's attorneys who happened to be in Chicago. He passed the word to his boss. Levin was annoyed. What's more he was in a stronger position than before to take action against his annoyances. The real estate division of G & W had become a public company through a partial stock spin-off. Levin swapped his Gulf and Western stock for 31 per cent of Transnation, as the new company was called. CTE was Transnation's chief asset, and Miller represented CTE's chief tenant. If he was unhappy, Levin wanted to know why.

A meeting was set up in July at the Pierre Hotel in New York. The Pierre is for New York what the Fontainebleau is for Miami Beach. Bigshot gangsters consider it more prestigious than the Waldorf-Astoria so perhaps it is natural that both Richard M. Nixon and Philip Levin felt at home there. Levin had a large suite which served as home and office. Miller was there by invitation, accompanied by his attorney. Marje was there by command, and she brought several attorneys. Legal advice was insufficient for the occasion, however, so quickly Marje turned on the tears. She was unjustly blamed, she sobbed, by Miller's people. The attorneys looked at each other and shrugged. Miller tried not to laugh. Levin began to fidget. Finally he stood up and motioned to Miller.

"Come to my office," he said, "and we'll have a drink."

Marje, famous as a teetotaler, could not object. Inside the smaller room where Levin had his desk, the short, balding man said in a rasping voice:

"Bill Miller, if you and that dame have had a lovers' quarrel, forget I offered you a drink."

"It's no lovers' quarrel," said Miller. "I can assure you of that."

"Then she's gone bananas," said Levin. Turning to a side bar, he began to pour the Scotch. "You're my tenant and you pay me a million dollars a year. I want you to be happy."

"I want to be happy," said Miller, and on that note they had their drink.

Despite assurances from Levin that Marje would give no more trouble, friction continued. Levin moved to take away some of Marje's duties, and for that she blamed Miller while nourishing steady hatred for her boss. In the interim she began cultivating the Republicans. Janotta introduced her to George E. Mahin, Governor Ogilvie's chief aide. He declined her invitations to parties and other social affairs, but he was ready to help on a matter of business. When asked, he arranged for her to meet such diverse people as Jack Walsh, a special agent of the Internal Revenue Service's intelligence division, and Jack Clarke, a private detective. Marje excited Walsh with dark tales of untaxed skulduggery in high places, and put Clarke to work hunting dirt on Miller. He didn't find anything, but Marje got revenge anyway. The new Republican-dominated Racing Board met in November and denied Chicago Harness's application for racing dates in 1970.

Miller was crushed. Under his direction CHR had completed two successful seasons, and was in excellent shape financially. He appealed in vain, scarcely comprehending that in the new era of Nixon-Ogilvie, the rules had changed.

The denial of dates was also a body blow to Levin; it meant the loss of a valuable tenant. Becoming at last convinced that Marje was perfectly willing to cost him money in order to hurt Miller, he fired her on March 4, 1970, despite her longterm contract.

Columnist Jack Griffin, writing in the *Chicago Sun-Times*, saluted the end of a racing dynasty. He blamed a drop of almost nine per cent in the 1969 mutuel handle for Levin's decision. Of Marje, he wrote:

> There will be many who will not mourn her departure.
> She is a controversial, highly complex person who often

left resentments, sometimes bitterness, in her wake. She often said she was not running a popularity contest, but sometimes she would add wistfully that it would be nice to be liked. She could fret over a 50-cent doorknob and in the next moment be remarkably and handsomely generous, and she was a gracious hostess. Whatever else, no one ever questioned her integrity.* Marje always played from aces. She bet every pot to win, no other way, and she frequently was relentless in her determination. An associate once said of her: "All she wants out of life is her own way about everything."

Getting fired was perhaps a shock, but Mrs. Everett recovered quickly. Her attorneys filed three suits against Levin and G & W, demanding $48 million in damages and claiming fraud, conspiracy, and SEC violations. Levin countered with a libel suit for $320 million. Marje called in her favorite private eye and told him to investigate Levin. Clarke found it an easier assignment. The timing couldn't have been better.

In mid-February, top syndicate bosses held a series of conferences in Acapulco to discuss plans for legal gambling operations in Canada, Mexico, and Miami Beach. Among those registered at the Acapulco Hilton was "M. Lansky." In the room next door was Moses Polakoff, the New York lawyer who had defended Lucky Luciano in 1936. Soon agents of three nations were investigating, and abruptly on March 1, Lansky vanished. Acapulco was searched, airlines were checked, but the chairman of the board had become invisible. Three days later he flew into Miami.

Clarke, on the trail of Levin, learned about that small hotel in Acapulco, and about Moe Morton, Levin's partner in the hotel. He also picked up gossip about hoods such as Sam Giancana, the pride of Chicago, associating with Morton. Soon he had enough to turn over to the Illinois Bureau of Investigation. Agents of that agency went south of the border and there they found witnesses who testified that from March 1 to March 4, Lansky had been safely hidden in the Acapulco Towers.

Additional investigation located Alberto Batani, a friend of Morton. He revealed that Morton called him early in March and asked his help in getting Lansky out of Mexico. Batani called a friend in Mexico City

* Griffin is entitled to his opinion but he didn't have all the facts.

and arranged for tickets to be waiting there for Lansky. The gangster was then allowed to fly out of Acapulco without tickets, thus keeping his name off passenger lists. No one was checking in Mexico City, so Lansky was able to pick up his tickets and fly home where U. S. Customs agents shook him down in a vain effort to learn where he had been hiding for the previous three days. All they found were some pills for Lansky's ulcers, but the pills weren't in the proper bottles, a violation of state law. Several days later Florida Department of Law Enforcement agents arrested Lansky in his plush apartment on Miami Beach. He won a directed verdict of acquittal, and flew off to Israel to become, if possible, a citizen under the Law of the Return. Publicity made it impossible.

In Illinois, meanwhile, information about Levin's Mob connections was given the Racing Board. Levin was forced to appear at a series of hearings lasting through August. Finally, after Levin had been thoroughly embarrassed, Chairman MacArthur doffed his cowboy hat and announced that Levin's associations did not provide justification for canceling CTE's racing dates or license.

Did justice triumph? Hardly. Levin *did* have Mob connections that by the standards MacArthur had set for his board — "beyond reproach like Caesar's wife" — should have made him ineligible. Of course, by the ethical and moral rules *actually* in force in Chicago, Levin was fairly clean. That, however, was beside the point. Levin *bought* his vindication by contributing $100,000 to Chicago Republicans on August 31, 1970. When in June, 1971, the *Wall Street Journal* broke the story of the payoffs, no one could remember much about the case.

Marje's suits against Levin and Transnation were settled in June, 1971. Among other things she won substantial shares of stock in Hollywood Park near Los Angeles. They made her the single largest stockholder in that racetrack. Meantime, she moved to Scottsdale, Arizona, a suburb of Phoenix. It was there she got the news of Levin's sudden death less than two months after the suits were terminated.

Miller remained, but wheels Marje had set in motion were turning. Thanks to Mahin and Special Agent Walsh, Project CRIMP was under way. Attorney General Mitchell threw scores of investigators into the effort aimed primarily at ex-Governor Kerner, and soon rumors were finding their way into print. Walsh was rewarded for his enterprise by being promoted and transferred. Overall responsibility for the probe was given to a Justice Department team headed by Victor C.

Woerheide, a top prosecutor with a reputation for losing his briefcase and being otherwise inattentive to details. Yet he had convicted several wayward politicians and his zeal couldn't be doubted. Still, it remained essentially an IRS case, and the field investigations were headed by Special Agents Peter Stufflebeam and William Witkowski.

According to Stufflebeam, the IRS men assigned to Project CRIMP were chiefly worried that Nixon would use their findings to make a deal with Daley and thus deprive them of a chance to advance their own careers by "getting Otto's ass." Daley had made deals with Republicans before, sacrificing individual Democrats and even high offices for what he considered to be the good of the machine — and its boss.

As were most special agents of Intelligence, to say nothing of the FBI, Stufflebeam was a political conservative in theory and a political realist in practice. Under President Lyndon Johnson he worked hard on "Operation Snowball," that nationwide probe of businessmen who in the 1964 elections disguised political contributions as business expenses. As did other agents, Stufflebeam had cases ready for a grand jury when Nixon took office. Attorney General Mitchell promptly killed them, explaining the businessmen involved had promised never to do it again. The time was not far away when some agents would claim that Watergate with all its one hundred dollar bills floating about wouldn't have happened if Snowball had been allowed to roll.

Stufflebeam wasn't one of the bitter agents. To let the guilty go wasn't justice, of course, but it was sound politics and that, after all, was the name of the game. Now, as proof that over the long haul things even out, the handsome special agent was to have a shot at a bigger prize — Mr. Clean himself.

This attitude is typical of many law-enforcement officers on both state and national levels. Such men soothe ethical misgivings by assuring themselves that in the end the matter will be determined by a judge and jury. The adversary system to which attorneys pledge loyalty, assumes that if one side comes up with all the evidence it can find to show the defendant's guilt, and the other side works just as hard to prove his innocence, the truth will somehow emerge from the conflict. A case isn't assigned to a special agent until a preliminary investigation has found a strong possibility of tax fraud. It then becomes the special agent's duty to find facts to sustain that possibility. Ultimately, his career prospers according to how well he succeeds in case after case. Supervisors who have as much to gain by a successful prosecution are apt to wink at rule violations if, as a result, important information is obtained.

Somewhat the same situation exists within the prosecutor's office. The goal remains to win the big ones, and if the truth is an obstacle there are ways it can be bypassed or distorted. There's little that can be done to change this system even if someone wanted to try. Consequently one does his job as best he can, be he special agent or United States Attorney. If he's good at it, well, it becomes very much a sport comparable, perhaps, to big-game hunting. "Getting Otto's ass" was big game indeed for some of the men involved.

The investigative record reflects the conflicting aims of Marje, whose target was Miller, and of the Nixon administration, which wanted Kerner above all else. The probe of Miller began "officially" on May 8, 1970, but did not become full-scale until June 18, 1971. The stalk of Kerner began June 12, 1970, and became full-scale before the year ended.

Stufflebeam, who had interviewed Kerner during Operation Snowball, was later to maintain that if Kerner had not lied on July 15, 1970, the entire probe might have been aborted.

It was 10:30 A.M. when Stufflebeam and Special Agent Robert Campbell entered the judge's chambers high above Chicago in the new federal building. After introducing themselves and presenting identification, the special agents gave Kerner a letter informing him that he was under investigation by the Intelligence Division. The dignified judge read the letter carefully and Stufflebeam informed him of his constitutional rights.

It was a solemn moment, yet, given the judicial surroundings, there were elements of black comedy in the ritual. When the special agent asked the federal judge if he understood his constitutional rights, Kerner replied with an understandable touch of asperity, "I certainly do."

Producing copies of Kerner's tax returns for 1966, 1967, and 1968, Stufflebeam asked for an explanation of some stock transactions listed on Schedule D of the 1967 return. The judge explained he exchanged stock of "CT Co." for an equal amount dollarwise of Balmoral stock. He didn't say why the exchange was made, but he did identify both companies as being related to racetracks. CT Co. was obviously Chicago Thoroughbred Enterprises, Inc., which was usually abbreviated as CTE.

(On December 6, 1967, Isaacs had written a long letter to Miller about the stock exchange. His auditor, he explained, "claims that the exchange constituted a taxable transaction and consequently had to be reported. . . . Since I am not really cognizant of what actually went on when the switch was made, I thought it best to ask your advice. I suppose it is possible that when it came time to deliver the C.T. shares, they simply were not available and therefore a substitution had to be made. If this is the case, it might be well to check with Henry [Williams] and see if he would agree that something like this would avoid the necessity for making a return on this transaction. . . . Since our friend is most deeply concerned about this, I would certainly appreciate hearing from you as soon as possible.")

Now, thirty-one months later, Isaacs' "friend" was being questioned by special agents, and he was digging his own grave. When Stufflebeam asked him to identify a company listed on the 1967 return as "Chicago Co.," the judge replied that it was a financial institution in the Chicago area. He bought stock in it, he said, on the advice of his broker. After buying the stock, he discovered he was personally acquainted with some of the corporate officers. Calling his bluff, Campbell asked him to name the officers he knew. Kerner came up with only one, Isadore Brown, an attorney he had known for many years. As if to prove it he gave Brown's home address: 1335 North Astor, Chicago.

Unimpressed with such confident detail, Stufflebeam inquired if Chicago Co. wasn't really Chicago Harness Racing. Emphatically, the judge denied it, and thus dug himself in a little deeper.

Keeping poker faces intact, the special agents asked Kerner to explain the transaction involving CT Co. and Balmoral. In his report of the interview, the special agent gave this account of the reply:

Kerner stated that Theodore Isaacs told him that he was going to purchase some stock in this company some time in 1962 or 1963.* He asked me [Kerner] if I also wanted to buy some of this stock. I told him to go ahead and handle the transaction and to let me know what my share of the deal would cost. Some time later, Isaacs

---

* This confirms that Isaacs had told Kerner about the stock offer *before* Miller was asked by Marje to feel out Kerner about it, yet the government chose to overlook the point in building its case.

informed me of the amount of money I owed for the
stock. I paid for a portion of the stock with my own
funds and borrowed the remainder from Joseph Knight
through Theodore Isaacs. Special Agent Campbell
asked Kerner if he had any documents to support this
transaction such as a note or canceled check. Kerner
replied that he could not recall if he had given a note to
Knight but that if one had been given then probably
Isaacs would now have the document. I asked Kerner if
Isaacs would have signed a note on Kerner's behalf and
Kerner replied that this might have happened. I then
asked if he [Kerner] had that kind of relationship with
Isaacs and Kerner replied, "Yes, I would have trusted
him with my life and I would still trust him with my
life." Special Agent Campbell asked Kerner if this Mr.
Isaacs was the same Mr. Isaacs that was involved in a
scandal several years ago involving state contracts.
Kerner chided Campbell and informed him that he had
better use the term allegedly involved in a scandal
since the actual events which transpired were not
scandalous at all. Kerner went on to explain that Isaacs
was just a nice, trusting man who had done a favor by
locating a rare machine needed in the envelope business. In return for this and without Isaacs' knowledge,
this man had issued stock certificates in Isaacs' name.
However, these stock certificates remained in the
company books and were never given to Isaacs. Unfortunately, the newspapers became aware of the situation and have been tormenting Isaacs ever since.

The conversation, Stufflebeam and Campbell decided later, was
quite enlightening as far as Kerner's character was concerned. Additional questions brought out information that Mrs. Kerner's child, a
daughter, was dead; that he and his wife adopted two children who
were seniors in college; that he had no employment except his judgeship and refused to accept honorariums for speeches; that he and Mrs.
Kerner kept $5,000 in currency on hand and had done so since the
Depression when they were caught short by the banks closing; his life
insurance policies totaled $100,000; he owned only one car, a 1968
Lincoln; he did not use credit cards because he didn't believe in them;

and finally, he mowed his own grass.*

In reply to yet another question, he again insisted that the only racetrack stock he had ever owned were stocks of the "CT Co." and Balmoral. When Campbell asked if he had ever used any other person, such as his mother, as a nominee, Kerner replied stiffly, "No, I'm not in that category of a judge. Besides, I wasn't raised that way."

When the agents were leaving at 11:40 A.M., the judge said he'd like to see the investigation ended as soon as possible "so this air of suspicion could be removed."

The agents were feeling pretty good as they left the judge's chambers. It now seemed certain that theirs was an opportunity to make legal history by fashioning the first conviction against a sitting judge of the U.S. Court of Appeals. As Stufflebeam put it, "We knew we had a case."

They wasted no time. At 12:05 P.M. they were in the office of Ted Isaacs at 69 West Washington Street. Stufflebeam told him it was only fair to advise Isaacs of his rights even though he wasn't under investigation. Isaacs said he wanted to help in any way he could. He recounted the purchase of the CTE stock, but couldn't recall all the details. Asked about the purchase of Chicago Harness Racing stock, "Isaacs replied that he had made a joint purchase of this stock with another party but he could not remember if this other party was Joe Knight or Judge Kerner."

From Isaacs' office the two agents went to 141 West Jackson where accountant Ethon Hyman worked. Hyman had prepared Kerner's tax returns. According to Stufflebeam's report of the interview, "We asked Hyman if the terminology used to identify stock on Schedule D of each return was Judge Kerner's terminology or his own terminology. Specifically we wanted to know if the companies which had been abbreviated were abbreviated by Kerner or him. Hyman replied that he had obtained those abbreviations directly from Kerner and that he had abbreviated nothing on his own."

The investigation continued at a rapid pace, both in Chicago and around the country. It was September 24, 1970, however, before Stufflebeam took Witkowski to the chambers of Judge Kerner. They

---

* When Kerner died in 1976, his estate — exclusive of his wife's estate — was valued at $1,300,000.

went at Kerner's urgent invitation. As Stufflebeam reported:

Kerner stated that he had requested this meeting with us because in his words our investigations are only one-way streets; that is, we request complete information from him while we in return are not willing to furnish him with any information concerning the progress and/or allegations surrounding the investigations.

Kerner mentioned that he thought our investigation may have been politically oriented and that he felt that since he has held public office he has made political enemies who have been known to spread rumors as to his dishonesty in office. Kerner said, therefore, he has decided that he would not provide us with any more of his personal records with the exception of his monthly stock brokerage accounts which Hyman had already promised to turn over to us . . . .

During the interview, Kerner spoke for about ten minutes as to his low expenditures for personal living items, giving as examples the purchase of only two suits in the last three years and pointed out his shoes to us which he said he had purchased in either 1961 or 1962, etc. . . .

Kerner stated that he had only two transactions in Illinois race-connected companies, the same two companies discussed in our prior meeting with him — Chicago Thoroughbred Enterprises and Balmoral Jockey Club.

The fifty-minute interview ended with Kerner promising to answer any specific questions concerning any particular transactions in which he had engaged. Once more he mentioned "rumor allegations," making it clear to the special agents that he was completely in the dark as to the circumstances surrounding the probe and the role of Mrs. Everett in beginning it. Had he not repeated the lie about not owning CHR stock, his performance would have been most impressive. The agents left his office feeling a bit sorry for their target.

Why did Judge Kerner lie to the special agents? The government never figured it out. Fifteen months after the interview, a prosecution memo concluded:

The reason Kerner lied to the agents is not clear and

because of its boldness and obvious falsity is quite perplexing. The most plausible theory is that at the time of the interviews he was not aware the IRS knew of his CHR bargain purchase and thus believed he could prevent its detection by deceiving the agents. Once he had done so, he was forced to continue the lie in the second interview.

Elsewhere in the memo are listed several items considered to be "evidence of intent" on the part of Kerner. One of them is perhaps a better explanation of his reasons for lying: "His appearance of self-righteousness, indignance [sic], as well as his pompous attitude."

The far-ranging probe continued. The death of Secretary of State Paul Powell on October 10, 1970, whetted the investigators' appetites. For in the closet of Powell's hotel room in Springfield were found shoeboxes containing more than $800,000 in currency. The estate of Marje's friend was valued at $3 million, of which $1 million was in racetrack stocks. Since Powell had been on the public payroll all of his adult life, the news of his wealth shocked the press and public, and raised suspicions about politicians in general. Two of Powell's aides were soon indicted on charges of perjury, tax evasion, and bribery. Sixty boxes of records found in the home of Powell's confidential secretary and at his home in Vienna, Illinois, proved — if additional proof was needed — that Powell became wealthy and politically successful by working within a system that considered corruption to be both natural and logical. Did that make him a bad man? Perhaps not, but certainly the physical evidence indicated he was far more interested in piling up treasure in shoeboxes than in heaven.

*Any experienced prosecutor will
admit that he can indict anybody at
any time for almost anything.*

WILLIAM CAMPBELL
Federal District Court Judge

7
The Inquisitor

Marje Everett began talking to special agents late in 1969, but it was January 7, 1971, before she got around to signing an affidavit swearing to her version of the facts. By then so many investigators had been assigned "it looked like a circus," according to Stufflebeam. Project CRIMP had become a big operation.

Some of the hotshots out of Washington such as Victor Woerheide, special attorney, were eager to meet their star witness and question her. The IRS special agents delayed as long as possible, fearing with some reason that the witness wouldn't hold up very well if subjected to an objective cross-examination. When at last an interview couldn't be postponed, it was decided to hold it in Dallas. To bring Marje to Chicago would risk publicity and, equally important, it was cold in December.

The original plan was to complete the affidavit in Dallas, but this proved impossible. Too many interviewers for the witness to concentrate, perhaps. In any event, Stufflebeam and Witkowski had to fly to Arizona to get it signed in January.

The six-page statement was prepared by the special agents, based on statements Marje had given earlier. It covered events from 1960 to 1967. William S. Miller was blamed for every major decision, every overt act. Thus, according to Marje, Miller not only introduced her to Paul Powell, but it was Miller who told Powell "that common stock of the new harness racing association (WPTA) would be available to Powell and his associates in the future, if Powell would not object to the introduction of harness racing at Washington Park Race Track."

Similarly it was Miller who "suggested that we form a new company and apply for 1962 harness-race dates," and Miller who "arranged" another meeting with Powell at which time "it was agreed" that 49 per cent of the new corporation would be made available to Powell and his associates.

Turning to the Kerner case, she swore:

"In late 1962, Miller, who was chairman of the Illinois Racing Commission, came to me and said that I had a friend on the Illinois Racing Board and needed a friend in the Kerner administration. Miller said he was my friend in the Racing Commission and suggested that Theodore Isaacs would be my friend in the Kerner administration. . . . All of the various negotiations surrounding the Kerner-Isaacs stock option were done at the suggestion and with the council [sic] of Miller."

It was Miller who promised to get racing dates when Chicago Harness Racing was formed, "and it was agreed that Miller would receive a substantial block of Chicago Harness Racing stock for what he termed 'his people.' " It was Miller who dictated a $2.00 per share price for Chicago Harness stock which "I felt due to the company's earnings was below the actual value of the stock."

Finally, in 1967, Miller bought 227,500 shares of CHR stock at $2.00 per share, and CHR bought controlling interest in Balmoral Jockey Club for $30.00 a share, "thereby completing my agreement with Miller."

In other words, according to Marje, Miller was the mastermind in bribing politicians, from Powell to Kerner, and Miller ended up with control of two racing associations which he secured at bargain prices. Marje didn't explain why she felt it necessary to adopt Miller's alleged suggestions, especially after he resigned from the Racing Commission, but the affidavit conveyed the impression of a weak female in the hands of an archvillain.

In February, 1971, a special Federal Grand Jury was convened. According to an affidavit by Special Assistant U. S. Attorney Woerheide, it was "merely of an exploratory nature" and when on February 19 Miller's confidential secretary and business associate, Faith McInturf, was called before it, the government did not consider her "to be a defendant or potential defendant in connection with any matter then under investigation before the grand jury."

Woerheide's affidavit was signed in April, 1972, — after Miss McInturf's indictment.

A native of Ottawa, Illinois, Miss McInturf went to work for Miller at the J. E. Porter Company in 1936. Fresh out of high school, she displayed unusual executive ability as an aide to the purchasing agent, and when in 1939 Miller opened offices in Chicago she was put in charge. Thanks to a Miller policy of giving bonuses instead of pay increases — he remembered that $14,000 check he showed his father — Faith accumulated some surplus cash and used it to buy stock in the company. So did seven other executives and all sold at a handsome profit. She held on to hers and made over $300,000 when Miller sold out to the chairman of the board of Morton Salt Company in 1965. The fact that she was an important stockholder and a slim, attractive unmarried blonde caused some gossip about her relations with her boss, but it was unfounded. Miller, said Faith, was a man's man, and his more than fifty years of marriage proclaimed a happy union. Key people stayed with him throughout his career, becoming his friends as well as his employees, and she was one of them. He hated detail although he could spot an error in a balance sheet in an instant; she loved detail, and came in time to handle it for Miller. In business they complemented each other.

As a friend, she warned Miller against Marje, telling him that "Marje doesn't even trust her husband," but Miller treated the Queen of Racing as he might a wayward daughter. Marje could be generous and gracious one moment and treat someone "like dirt" the next.

Advised by her attorney to answer all of the Grand Jury's questions but to "qualify" when she wasn't sure, Faith was nervous when she sat down in the witness chair. Woerheide began his examination by confirming she had an attorney, Gerald Brown, waiting outside the room. He then wanted to know if the witness was aware the attorney had met with him the day before and "brought up the subject of your knowledge of your constitutional rights?"

"How do you mean that?" asked Miss McInturf.

"Did he mention to you that he had discussed this with me?"

"He mentioned that he had discussed it," replied the secretary, "but I don't know just what my rights are."

It was a plain statement, but the representative of the Justice Department didn't accept it.

"He didn't tell you what your constitutional rights are?"

"Well," said Miss McInturf, "he mentioned waiving immunity and taking the Fifth Amendment, but I didn't understand it at the time and I don't recall it."

Again, a clear statement of ignorance on the part of the witness, but instead of explaining her rights — or sending her out to her attorney for another briefing — Woerheide asked, "Well, did he tell you that you had a privilege against self-incrimination under the Fifth Amendment?"

"Yes," said Miss McInturf.

With that, Woerheide got down to business, ignoring her previous statements that she didn't know what her attorney told her and didn't know what her rights were. Was an attempt being made to take advantage of her inexperience with grand juries? The answer has to be that, according to the record, for no other witness received such treatment where constitutional rights were concerned.

The first session was devoted largely to the witness identifying various records subpoenaed by the government. She offered to return with two truckloads of additional records. Hastily, Woerheide assured her he didn't want to see everything.

On February 23, she returned and spent the afternoon identifying still more financial records belonging to Balmoral and Chicago Harness. It was on her third visit, February 25, that the U. S. Attorney began asking questions about her association with Miller which stretched back thirty years. Most of her time was spent "on the freezers and the school equipment," she said, and she really didn't know much about the racing industry. Woerheide made a valiant effort to get her to say that Ralph Atlass held 50,000 shares of CHR as a nominee for Miller. She got a measure of revenge by informing the jury that her attorney had told of talking to Woerheide about the subject matter "and this has renewed my memory or at least has reminded me of some of the things that I didn't ever know about or else I didn't know if I had known before."

She denied she had ever overheard Atlass and Miller discussing stock. Asked if Atlass borrowed money from Miller, she replied, "Well, I believe he did, since Mr. Brown has recalled my memory on that, yes."

But she didn't keep Miller's books, and the books were sometimes kept at his main office in Ottawa and sometimes at his office in Chicago, "but I don't recall at this particular time."

She knew Isaacs and Kerner, having met them "socially at the racetrack," but knew nothing of any business dealings Miller might have had with them. When Joe Knight was mentioned, however, she recalled that Knight had 10,000 shares of CHR stock available and asked her if she'd be interested. She was interested. "I had always heard that there was quite a bit of money in racing, which I think is a fallacy, but, anyway, I thought maybe it would be a good investment."

She bought the stock with a check to Sincere & Company, and she still owned it. At one time George Schaller served as her nominee, but that was arranged just in case she decided not to keep the stock. As attorney for CHR, she explained, it would be easier for him "to make up new certificates in case I wanted to dispose of it."

The examination continued with Woerheide trying unsuccessfully to pry Miller's alleged secrets from Miss McInturf. He didn't learn much when he asked how she happened to loan Knight $40,000. She replied:

"Well, I recall Mr. Knight again stopped in the office at one time and he was well aware that I had my money in a savings account and that I would like to realize more of an income or profit on that money. And he asked me whether or not I would be interested in making a loan of $40,000 to him, and I did."

No, she didn't recall if Knight told her the purpose of the loan or that it was in any way connected with Otto Kerner and Ted Isaacs. She did remember "that the rate that I was going to be paid was more than I was receiving in the savings account. And I know that Mr. Knight is a person of means and responsibility. And I was interested in the extra that I would receive on the interest."

Try as he might, the frustrated official could wring no hint of sinister conspiracy or devious manipulation from efficient Miss McInturf—all she had been interested in was making a little money. And she did. Among the records in front of her was Knight's check to her for $41,642.48.

"Did he tell you where he got the money to repay the loan that you had made to him?"

"I wouldn't have questioned that or asked him," replied the witness primly.

Woerheide had no more questions.

On March 11, 1971, the March Federal Grand Jury convened at 2 P.M. to question Knight. The once debonair bachelor had suffered a massive stroke some months before, and physical deterioration was apparent. His clothes hung loosely on his wasted frame, and he spoke as if each word required a concentrated effort. Asked about his employment, he replied:

"Since I had my stroke I am incapacitated. My memory is not good and I can't function."

The former treasurer of the Democratic Party in Illinois was living on a farm near Dow, one of several he owned. He had "abandoned" his railroad, the Jerseyville & Eastern, and his mother had died in September.

Woerheide, apparently recognizing the problem of grilling a very sick man, eased into his examination with a series of questions about various individuals. Did Knight know Isaacs, Kerner, Miller, McInturf, etc.? For how long? Under what circumstances had he met them? He had known Miller for thirty years, he said, and had owned stock in Miller's manufacturing company.

> Q. Mr. Knight, directing your attention to July of 1966, do you recall borrowing for yourself or for some other person the amount of $40,000 — do you recall that, sir?
> A. Yes.
> Q. Who did you borrow this money from?
> A. Miss McInturf.
> Q. How did you happen to borrow this $40,000?
> A. I don't recall the particulars of it.
> Q. Well, did anyone ask you to borrow that money, sir?
> A. I presume so.
> Q. Did Governor Kerner ask you to borrow the $40,000?
> A. No.
> Q. Did Ted Isaacs ask you to borrow the $40,000?
> A. He might have, but Kerner did not.
> Q. Did William S. Miller ask you to borrow the $40,000?
> A. No.
> Q. Why do you say that Miller did not?
> A. Because he didn't.
> Q. I mean to ask you why do you say that Kerner did not?
> A. Because he didn't.

Q. You remember that; well, who did ask you to borrow the $40,000, sir?
A. I don't remember.

The attempt to blame Miller having failed, the special attorney returned to Isaacs. Knight said Isaacs told him the money was to buy stock in Chicago Harness for Isaacs and Kerner. He borrowed it from Miss McInturf because "she was a very economical woman and doesn't spend her money. I figured she had it." He left the stock with her as collateral. What stock? He didn't recall. Was it CTE stock? He still didn't recall.

Woerheide turned to the purchase of Chicago Harness stock purchased by Knight, and, once again, attempted to put the responsibility on Miller.

Q. Did Mr. Miller tell you that he owned shares of Chicago Harness Racing, Inc. at this time?
A. I don't recall.
Q. Did he tell you that he had shares of CHR that were for sale?
A. I know originally I asked him if I could ever get some — or any racetrack stock for myself, for my own accounts.

The complicated exchange of CTE for Balmoral stock was covered. Knight remembered paying off Miss McInturf with money made from the sale of CHR stock, but he couldn't recall details of the other transaction. When Woerheide protested it was only three years before, Knight replied, "A lot of water has gone under the dam."

The Justice official tried to refresh Knight's memory by showing him a photograph of a check from Isaacs to Knight. Abruptly Knight refused to identify his signature on the check.

"May I inquire," he asked, "am I a witness in this case?"

Woerheide replied, "Yes, Mr. Knight, you are a witness. We conferred with your attorney and he asked the same question and I gave him the same answer."

Knight wasn't satisfied. "I am not the subject of investigation?" he demanded.

"No, sir," said the special attorney.

"I never made a penny off of any of these transactions, not a penny," said Knight.

And now Darrell McGowen, another special attorney from Justice and an aide to Woerheide, added his assurance:

"We would also like to say, Mr. Knight, that when you come in here we would like for you to feel relaxed and to level with us as best your memory will allow you to. As Mr. Woerheide has said, you are not the subject of an investigation. You don't appear that you would make a very good subject for an investigation under the circumstances. We are interested in you as a witness to give truthful testimony in this matter as best you possibly can."

Thus the lie was compounded, and a virtually dying man was deceived. For Knight was to be indicted along with Kerner, Isaacs, Miller, and McInturf. Nothing better illustrates the zeal with which Project CRIMP was conducted than this flagrant deception. Mitchell's men from Washington obviously had their instructions to do whatever was necessary in the "getting" of "Otto Kerner's ass."

Shortly after the lie was spoken, Knight said he was tired. The Justice men agreed to recess the hearing and let him return the following week. "We want you early in the morning so that you will be fresh," he was told.

"This morning I sat out there for over two hours," grumbled Knight.

"This was unfortunate," said McGowen.

A week later, on March 18, Knight returned. He had "scratched around" and found a few checks but no letters in the vault he kept in a separate building on his farm. The questioning was largely repetitious. Once again he was asked how he happened to buy stock in Chicago Harness. Once again he said he told Miller that he would like to have it. "I went to him," Knight emphasized, "he didn't come to me." Asked if he checked with others to find out what the "going price of the shares was," Knight said simply, "Well, I never trade with people unless I have faith in them. I had faith in Mr. Miller and he said that is what it was so I accepted it."

After a few more minutes of sparring, Knight was excused. As he stood up to leave, urine wet the front of his trousers. No one spoke. The foreman, a woman, looked away.

Miller appeared before the May Federal Grand Jury on the morning of May 4, 1971. Woerheide was very careful to spell out the constitutional rights of the witness, including the right to consult with his attorney, William Barnett, who was outside the room. Before the questioning could begin, Miller asked permission to make a statement.

He had planned, he said, to answer any question asked "within my area of knowledge," but a telephone call from Judge George Schaller a few days before had caused him to change his mind. (Schaller, formerly Marje Everett's attorney, had recently been appointed a circuit judge in Illinois.)

Schaller told him, Miller said, that two special agents of the IRS had visited him a few days before and informed him "that I was going to be indicted by the federal government. . . . He also informed me that neither he nor Judge Lynch could be used as government witnesses against me because he felt, and he was certain, that I had done nothing to justify any such indictment."

As a result, Miller continued, he consulted his attorney who advised him to tell the Grand Jury "that I was perfectly willing to testify, that I have nothing to hide, but if I am to appear here as a defendant or a potential defendant, I certainly should exercise my rights as a citizen. . . . I am either a witness or a defendant, isn't that true, or a potential one?"

Woerheide replied with some doubletalk. He pointed out that the special agents couldn't indict anyone; only the Grand Jury could do that. "Now we are engaged at this time," he continued, "in an inquiry that does relate to the activities of a number of people, including yourself, and of which you have perhaps as much knowledge as anyone else does. And our objective at this time is not to return an indictment against you or any other person, but to find the basis, the factual basis, for various allegations that have been made by a number of people in the past. Now these allegations relate to you and they relate to a number of other people. We have to take our information, of course, where we find it."

Technically, the special attorney was telling the truth. In reality, he was weasel-wording. The decision to indict, if at all possible, had been made. As early as July 27, 1970, the Post Office had been officially notified that a tax probe of Miller was under way and that if convicted Miller "could receive a maximum sentence of $20,000 in fines and ten years in prison." The notice was in connection with a request for a mail cover on Miller's mail at his home and offices. The request was granted, but it produced nothing of value to the investigation although the spying continued for months and set off wild rumors in Ottawa where Miller was a bank president and leading citizen.

Miller replied sharply to Woerheide's statement:

"Well, sir, the representatives of the federal government have been investigating me for well over a year and it would seem that by now, if any of the so-called allegations that you refer to have any substance, they would have found something by now."

The two agents, Stufflebeam and Witkowski, continued Miller, had been all over Florida, all over Illinois, telling people they were investigating the criminal liability of Miller and, in some cases, threatening to indict the individuals too unless they testified they gave Miller money.

"I have many instances of this," said Miller. "I have made notation of this, I have asked my attorney. I can't believe that this could happen in this country."

Woerheide made no defense. "Do you have any other comments you wish to make, sir, at this time?"

Miller made use of the opportunity. He told of an offer made to his attorney, Leo Arnstein, senior member of the internationally known law firm Arnstein, Gluck, Weitzenfeld and Minow, general counsel for such clients as Sears. Special Agents Stufflebeam and Witkowski, he said, talked to Arnstein the previous November and, according to the lawyer, offered "to make a deal."

"I said [to Arnstein], 'What do you mean, a deal?'

" 'Well, they will not indict you, or cause you to be indicted, if you will cooperate.'

"I said, 'What is meant by cooperation?'

" 'Well, if you will appear before the Grand Jury and testify that Judge Otto Kerner was the recipient of some very special favors which you were the author of.'

"I said, 'Leo, that wouldn't be the truth. I would have to commit perjury to do that.' "

Later, continued Miller, the two agents appeared at his home in Golden Beach, Florida, and asked if his attorney had told them of their proposal. He replied, he told the Grand Jury:

" 'You are not going to make me panic, you are not going to make me tell a lie simply because you are waving this indictment in front of me. I have that much faith and hope and trust, but I am willing to cooperate with you people and always have been. Why don't you go up to my lawyer and arrange to have all of these people in one room. Have them come in. Let's put everything on the table.' "

Miller paused and looked at Woerheide. "That is all I have to say. You understand my position. My lawyer tells me, 'Why should you testify before this Grand Jury if they are going to indict you?' So what can I do?"

The special attorney from Washington assured the witness that "the last thing in the world that we want you to do is to tell a lie."

He then proceeded to ask some questions. Each time Miller stepped out of the room, consulted his attorney, and, returning, declined to answer on grounds that to do so might incriminate him. Finally he returned to say:

"Sir, my attorney suggested that I again advise you that I am prepared to answer any and all of your questions. You need only grant me immunity."

In answer to a question, Miller said he was willing to sit down in a conference room and, informally, give government counsel a preview of what his testimony would be if granted immunity. Woerheide told the jury that he would hold such a conference and report back to the jury at a later date. Miller was excused.

The conference was arranged for a few days later. Several of the Washington team took part, and Miller was accompanied by counsel. But Special Agents Stufflebeam and Witkowski, the men who had done the field work, were ejected by Woerheide.

It was a short conference. Woerheide asked several questions based on statements made by Marje. One, for example, concerned her meeting with Powell and various legislators at Washington Park. She said Miller also attended. When asked by Woerheide, he denied being there.

"I know nothing about it," he said.

"You're not being cooperative," said Woerheide, and a few minutes later he terminated the meeting. It was apparent to Miller that "cooperation" meant confirming Marje's tales of a Miller-Kerner conspiracy, and the government would accept nothing less. Not at that stage of the case, anyway.

Another curious fact didn't become apparent until much later. When Marje's former attorney, Judge Schaller, called Miller on April 21, 1971, to warn him he might be indicted, the judge didn't add that he was doing everything he could to achieve that goal. On the day before, when he talked to the IRS agents, he gave them a nine-page affidavit and many of his files. The affidavit dovetailed completely with the one given earlier in the year by Marje, and cast Miller in the role of mastermind. Of course, Schaller wasn't present when many of the events took place, but he indicated in various ways that he knew what happened.

It now is obvious that Schaller's warning to Miller was designed to accomplish what it did achieve — force Miller to take the Fifth Amendment and preclude any possibility he might tell the Grand Jury the truth. It caused Miller and his attorney to decide to take no chances — a mistake that was to prove very costly to the businessman.

On June 9, 1971, Judge Schaller appeared before the same Grand Jury and illustrated his skill at inference. He was there, of course, with the consent of his client. As he told the jurors:

"Many months ago when the various federal agents came to me and asked if I would cooperate and, if necessary, be a federal witness, I said I would, provided, of course, if my client released me. Mrs. Everett. Which she did."

Woerheide made no mention of constitutional rights and, by his failure, gave the judge what is known as "left-handed immunity." The entire examination was designed to blame Miller for everything Mrs. Everett had done. Schaller, an experienced attorney, told no lies, but suggested several incorrect inferences and conclusions.

Asked if Marje Everett and Miller "in your presence" discussed the formation of CTE, Schaller replied, "It's possible, yes."

The question was repeated in slightly different form, and Schaller said, "They could have been — I couldn't say about Miller at that point."

Was it Miller's idea to set up CTE?

"It could have been; I can't say that about Miller. It might have been Zoline's."

What was the relationship in 1960 between Miller and Mrs. Everett?

"There is no question in my mind that Miller was her total confidant," said Schaller, ignoring the fact that he had not met either Miller or Marje in 1960.

They reached the subject of harness racing and the formation of WPTA. Schaller said he helped form it. Asked if Miller was confident he could get dates for trotting, Schaller came out with an error:

"Yes, it couldn't have been formed without that. He was chairman of the board."

Miller was chairman of the Illinois Racing Board, so in one sense Schaller was correct. The implication, however, was that Miller was chairman of the board that gave racing dates to *harness* tracks, and that was a separate body. Presumably the grand jurors didn't understand the distinction, but certainly Schaller did.

When Schaller continued to qualify Miller's role, he apparently felt it necessary to explain — and, in doing so, cast another innuendo:

"Frankly, Miller was not — Miller did not say anything in front of me. Mrs. Everett told me that she discussed that with him."

"I see."

"He very carefully stayed out of that picture with me," said the judge.

Guilt by omission, so to speak.

On the other hand, Mrs. Everett gave him a list of politicians and the amount of shares each was to have, but, somehow, there was nothing wrong with that.

Applications for racing dates were made up at the track, Schaller said, and he checked them.

Q. And that was done at the track by Mrs. Everett and her advisers, which would include, of course, Mr. Miller, is that it?

A. To that question I can't actually say. I am sure Mr. Miller saw those applications before they were passed to the commission officials. As I say, Mr. Miller was very careful of Mr. Schaller.

Again the low blow.

Asked if there was any discussion as to the laws of Illinois and racing regulations about the disclosure of the names of nominees and identities of beneficial owners — all of which Schaller had helped conceal — the judge replied:

"My only concern, very frankly, was Mrs. Everett. She was my client. They [the politicians] were strangers to me."

If it occurred to any of the jurors that Schaller was still concerned only about his former client, Mrs. Everett, no one so indicated. Indeed, if any juror ever asked a question of any kind, the record doesn't reflect it.

Schaller, perhaps unwittingly, cast some doubt on the Miller mastermind theory when he revealed that Marje's decision in 1966 to repurchase stock in Washington Park Trotting Association was due in part, at least, to "the upcoming merger with Gulf & Western, which I didn't know of then." It took him a year to figure it out, he added.

When some of the dissident stockholders were ready to revolt, Schaller continued, it was Miller who settled things. They were all "prima donnas," he added, "and Mrs. Everett, of course, led the list, frankly."

Schaller also disclosed that Miller, far from trying to keep Ted Isaacs happy at all times, said "No" when Isaacs demanded 10,000 shares of WPTA. Schaller wrote himself a memo: "WSM says no to Isaacs."

"I recall very specifically why I wrote that memorandum," he said. "I knew who Isaacs was and I knew his relationship to Kerner and Mrs. Everett's relationship to Kerner, and I was very concerned that as long as I was in the middle that I had a record of what happened."

Woerheide asked Schaller about Isaacs' relationship to Kerner, but asked nothing about Mrs. Everett's relationship. Like Faith McInturf, Schaller had met the governor at the racetrack in Mrs. Everett's celebrity box.

Schaller said he didn't want to sell the 11,000 shares of WPTA stock he had bought for $1 a share for $5, but did so when Marje told him to. "Judge Lynch was on the bench and I was the sole attorney on the account, and you simply don't irritate a $50,000 a year client, gentlemen, so I sold."

At about this point in the Grand Jury hearing, a man entered the room and sat down. The foreman interrupted the proceedings to inquire, "Would this gentleman please identify himself?"

"This," said one of Woerheide's aides, "is the United States Attorney."

The episode illustrates how completely the investigation was being run by Mitchell's team from Washington. The local jurors didn't even recognize William J. Bauer, the U.S. Attorney for their district.

After a lunch break, the subject became Chicago Harness.

Q. Did it make money?

A. I think Chicago Harness made money from the beginning.

Q. Was Mrs. Everett gratified?
A. Oh, yes.
Q. She told you so?
A. They were paying a 2 per cent rental to her, each of the harness companies.
Q. How about Miller, what comment did he make to you about the success of CHR?
A. Basically all Miller said to me from time to time was that he was delighted because the revenues of the State of Illinois were being increased.

Another strikeout.

Schaller said Marje gave him 5,000 shares of CHR stock. "I performed many personal and confidential services for her and she made me a gift." His partner, Judge Lynch, was permitted to buy 40,000 shares at forty cents a share, and Lynch let Schaller have half of it. And, yes, that stock was in addition to the $50,000 a year retainer paid the firm by Mrs. Everett.

When trouble developed between some of the stockholders and Mrs. Everett, Schaller said Miller was asked to settle it and did so.

The questioning continued, moving all too smoothly over the scene in Miller's office when Isaacs paid for the fifty shares of CTE stock which Marje had signed and which Schaller brought to the office in person. Instead of asking for those details, Woerheide contented himself with this question:

"On this occasion you saw the stock certificates?"

"They were there," said Schaller with equal vagueness.

No point in overwhelming the jurors with little details, don't you know? Or such, at least, appeared to be the belief of the man from the Justice Department.

The hearing recessed on this note, but only after Schaller delivered himself of a complaint. He had been working for months, he said, with special agents, reconstructing records and searching files. When asked to testify to the Grand Jury, he had agreed, he said, because he assumed it would be secret. Yet, suddenly, there was a "whole headline" in the Sun-Times.

"Ladies and gentlemen," said the judge, "I think you are conducting a secret proceeding and I think you ought to look into the fact of where all these leaks are coming from that are headlines of the paper. I tried to cooperate and help my government and I find myself in the headlines before I am even here."

"We are very much concerned about this ourselves," said Woerheide, blandly ignoring the fact that leaks to the press were an important part of the prosecution's game plan. The leaks continued as the case moved toward its climax.

Already the tempo was picking up. After hearing Schaller on June 9, the Grand Jury listened to another judge the following day — Otto Kerner.

The distinguished-appearing jurist was warned that he was under investigation, and was told of his rights. Bravely he responded, "Mr. Woerheide, my purpose in being here is to be a witness, and to be as completely cooperative as I possibly can be."

He wasn't completely reckless, however, having brought counsel with him "because I learned a long time ago, like a shoemaker whose children go barefoot, a lawyer who is his own client is a fool."

Kerner remembered meeting Ted Isaacs in 1940 when both were active in the National Guard. He met Miller, he said, during his campaign for governor in 1960, but apparently Miller's role in providing collateral for a campaign loan, and twenty per cent of his campaign contributions, had been forgotten. Kerner never handled any funds personally, he said piously, "so I can't answer questions of that sort." His relationship with Miller had always been "a formal official one, not a social one and not a personal one."

Again and again he emphasized the same point — that he saw Miller very infrequently and always on official business. Apparently he was aware that Miller had been cast as the mastermind, and wanted to disassociate himself from such an allegedly unsavory personage.

When he took office, he said, he was told the Racing Commission wasn't held in high regard by the Jockey Club of the United States. Naturally, he sought to improve it, but in making appointments "I did not rely on Mr. Miller at all."

He met Marjorie Everett, he said, "through her father whom my father knew" when she was a young girl. His first memory of Joe Knight was of "this rather tall and handsome looking man with a white suit and a great big white Palm Beach hat" on a hot day in Springfield in 1932. Joe was a student at the University of Illinois and became active in politics, Kerner said.

A discussion of the development of the racing industry followed. Kerner took credit for the increased state revenue it brought about, but denied responsibility for any individual actions such as the introduction of harness racing at Washington Park.

"The governor," he said, "is not a member of the Racing Commission. It is a complete and separate entity, and, may I say, once you appoint them and they are confirmed they are completely independent and tell you where to go."

The largely fruitless questioning continued until the lunch break, and then resumed. Kerner, asked if he discussed his problems as governor with others, replied stiffly, "Mr. Woerheide, I think in order that you may know me, I keep my problems within myself. I don't find sharing them with anybody relieves me or solves the problem necessarily."

After more sparring, the special attorney finally got around to the CTE stock deal which, of course, was the central issue in the entire investigation. Kerner told it somewhat differently. He had been asked by Joe Knight, he said, if he wanted some stock in a racing association. Fifty shares were available, and he could have it all. Kerner replied, he said, that he didn't want it all. Knight didn't give him any details and he didn't ask for any because "I had confidence in Mr. Knight."

He told Knight, he continued, to "speak to Ted Isaacs and see whether he wishes half of it." Isaacs, he explained, had left a lucrative law practice to become director of revenue. "Whatever the arrangement is between the two of you is acceptable to me." (This was a contradiction of Knight's testimony.)

Here Woerheide made another effort to drag in Miller, but Kerner denied discussing the deal with Miller or referring Isaacs to Miller.

"I want you to know my only conversations with Mr. Miller were of a formal nature in reference to the operation of the Racing Commission," Kerner insisted.

Kerner claimed he didn't know what company was involved or who was actually selling the stock. He left all the details to Knight and Isaacs, and it was *not until the shares had been bought* "and a borrowing had been made" that he learned the facts.* He believed, however, that the deal was completed in 1962. Isaacs told him, he said, "that he had arranged to pick up the stock, and had signed a note, and that we

---

* Again, confirmation that Miller was not the first to present the stock offer in 1962 and that Marje's request that he "feel out" the governor was not sincere.

would be paying interest, as I recall, to Mrs. Everett. I never saw a note, I want you to understand. I never had any of these documents."

He considered himself obligated to Isaacs, not to Mrs. Everett, because he never signed her note.

The next step came "some time later." Isaacs told him that according to Knight "the CTE shares were necessary, I believe, to Mrs. Everett for some sort of loan, and would I have any objection to its being transferred to another company with shares of equal value?"

He was willing. Meanwhile, Isaacs told him on July 19, 1966, that some interest was due and he made out a check to cash for $4,479, and gave it to Isaacs.

Now Woerheide brought up the subject of Chicago Harness Racing stock — the stock Kerner had disguised as "Chicago Co." on his tax returns, and had denied to the special agents that it was racing stock.

Kerner said once again the matter was suggested by Knight, and, yes, it was Chicago Harness stock. He asked for no details since he trusted Knight, but he told him to split it with Ted. Knight did not tell him, he added in answer to a question, that Miller was the "beneficial owner" of the stock.

A few days later Isaacs asked for a check for $5,600 to pay for Kerner's share of the CHR stock. Once again he told him to make it out to cash. A short time later he got half of it back, a dividend check for $2,800. Two checks for that amount each were sent to Isaacs by Marje's attorney, George Schaller, on February 23, 1967. Schaller was nominee, although Kerner denied knowing it at the time.

Suddenly there was tension in the room:

Q. You received the dividend in February, 1967?
A. That is what the letter says, yes.
Q. And the dividend you received was fifty percent of the purchase price?
A. Yes.
Q. So you were aware at that time that you had made a bargain purchase when you purchased it?. . . .
A. Wait a minute.
Q. For $5,600.
A. Wait a minute, Mr. Woerheide.
Q. Paying a dividend of fifty percent of the principal, is that correct?
A. I happen to be a lawyer and I know precisely

what you are getting at. No, I did not know I made a
bargain purchase. I did not know that.
Q. You never discovered. . .
A. I would say that I made a good investment.

The wrangle continued over the legal implications of "bargain
purchase," a term of great importance to the government's theory that
in return for such bargains the governor did favors for Marje and
Miller. Kerner insisted that at the time the racing stock was purchased
he had the judgment of Joseph L. Golman, a certified public accountant, that the price paid was reasonable.

Woerheide moved on at last, asking why Kerner suddenly decided
to sell such a good stock. It was all Isaacs' idea, said the judge, and he
didn't question it. At first he thought he was paid $28,000 for his shares
in CHR, but, when prompted, acknowledged he received only $7,000.
Asked why the difference, he said simply, "We owed some money."

It was, he added, owed to Marje Everett. On second thought, "I
think we owed money to Joe Knight. I think he paid Mrs. Everett, and
we paid Knight. . . . Much of the information that I have is really
second-hand. Any statement I make may be in error. I don't know. I do
know that we owed money to people and that we paid it off. That I can
assure you. And the results of all these transactions are carried on my
returns, to the penny."

After Miller resigned from the Racing Board and acquired control
of Balmoral in 1967, Kerner and Isaacs sold their stock for a total of
$300,000 in 1968. Woerheide wanted to know why they sold?

"Because Mr. Isaacs indicated there seemed to be some sort of
abrasion going on between some of the owners," said Kerner. Isaacs
handled the deal, and, again, he knew very little about it. "All I know is
I received a credit memo from the bank for the sum of $150,000,
$15,000 of which was put in a savings account, and $135,000 was put
into a checking account."

Kerner acknowledged that the exchange of CTE stock for Balmoral
stock was not reported on his 1968 tax return and, "technically," it
should have been. His excuse: "There was no tax due" because the tax
had been paid in 1967. His failure to report the item had nothing to do
with the fact he was being considered for appointment to the federal
bench in 1968, he insisted, in response to a pointed question.

The final question concerned legislators owning racing stock. Was he aware that Miller had anything to do "with these people" being able to obtain stock?

"No, no," said Judge Kerner.

But the judge had more to say on other subjects. He told the jurors he had tried to cooperate with the government for a year and a half.

"Dick Tracy is running around," he continued, "and my mail here in my chambers and at home has been monitored. . . . I can't understand what this is about except for irritation. It is not the type of investigation that I participated in, shall I say, when I was United States Attorney. Anything you want of me you shall have. . . . When persons commit a crime they should be punished for it. If not, I would expect the Grand Jury to protect these individuals as well, and I am sure Mr. Woerheide and counsel would agree with me.

"Thank you very much."

"Thank you very much," said the foreman.

The Grand Jury was finished with Judge Kerner, but Judge Kerner wasn't finished with the Grand Jury. On August 5, 1971, he returned at his own request to make sure the jurors understood his answers the first time. He made a long statement, reviewing his previous testimony and perhaps putting it into better perspective but adding little that was new. When he finished, Special Attorney Woerheide also had some unfinished business to discuss. He asked about the interview Special Agents Stufflebeam and Campbell conducted in his chambers on July 15, 1970.

> Q. Do you recall that they asked you about an entry [on his tax returns] designated "Chicago Co."?
>
> A. Yes, they did ask me about that. And at the time I couldn't recall precisely what it was. I said, "Give me an opportunity to verify my records at home." . . . I said at the time, as I recall, "That might be an insurance company that was recently formed, but I am not certain. Let me check it out and I will give you all the details."
>
> Q. Do you recall the agents asking you specifically if Chicago Company referred to Chicago Harness Racing stock?
>
> A. At some time they did ask that question.
>
> Q. Do you remember informing them that it was not racing company stock?

A. No. I did not say it was not, I did not say that. I said I was not certain what it was but I would verify it.

Q. Do you remember informing them that Balmoral and CT were the only racetrack stock you ever owned?

A. I doubt very much that I would have made that statement, Mr. Woerheide.

Q. You were perfectly aware of the fact at that time that you had bought Chicago Harness Racing stock?

A. Oh, yes, surely.

So on the question of perjury, it was to be Judge Kerner's word against two special agents. On December 14, 1971, Stufflebeam was brought in to give the lie to Kerner. He gave his version of the interviews, and was quickly excused. The record shows that Samuel K. Skinner, chief of the Special Investigation Unit, Chicago, Illinois, then said, "Let the record show that I will be discussing with and reading the proposed indictment to the Grand Jury."

How difficult it is even for "informed
sources" to be informed.

ROBERT F. KENNEDY, 1960

8

The Indictment

Indictments in Project CRIMP were just a matter of time, but before
they could be returned it was necessary to complete the record by
bringing Ted Isaacs and then Mrs. Everett before the Grand Jury.

Isaacs appeared on the morning of June 15, 1971. In addition to the
grand jurors there were assembled to hear him the United States
Attorney, William J. Bauer; his chief aide, Richard A. Makarski; and
four special attorneys from the Department of Justice.

As usual, Woerheide acted as grand inquisitor, and began by
carefully warning Isaacs of his constitutional rights. No "left-handed
immunity" was wanted with this witness. After establishing that Isaacs'
law firm was retained in 1960 to handle the Ben Lindheimer estate,
Woerheide started up a familiar trail:

Q. Well, was it William S. Miller who introduced you to Mrs.
Everett?

A. I don't remember that it was. It could have been. I don't recall.

It took a dozen questions to get Isaacs to say he met Miller during
the political campaigns of Adlai Stevenson and no particular close
relationship developed between the two men. Small wonder, since
that meeting in Daley's office in 1960 to plan Kerner's campaign
finances was their first.

The Kerner relationship, which began with the National Guard and
continued during World War II, did become different, Isaacs acknowledged.

Q. When was that and how did it develop?

A. I can't say when. It's one of those things that just occurs.

Isaacs said he had no racetrack stock when he began working for the
Lindheimer estate, but learned a lot about the business while settling

125

the estate. He met with Mrs. Everett quite frequently as problems arose, and in 1962 "Mrs. Everett invited me to participate in CTE and at a point later on I did make arrangements to purchase stock in CTE."

Skeptically, Woerheide demanded details. Isaacs replied, "Mrs. Everett began talking enthusiastically about CTE during the period that the estate was open. She was then discussing the plans that she had to fulfill what she called her father's dream, something he had never been able to complete before he died. . . ."

Instantly, Woerheide tried to bring Miller into the discussion of the Lindheimer dream, but Isaacs couldn't confirm it. Nor would he say that Miller used him as a conduit to the governor. "Why should he come to me?" he asked.

Woerheide kept plugging. Twice he asked if Marje told him Miller would help get racing dates for harness meets, and twice Isaacs denied it. Nor was he present when she offered Isaacs CTE stock. Then this exchange:

Q. Do you recall Mr. Miller being present?
A. I just don't recall. I don't know.
Q. Well, do you recall that he was not present?
A. I don't recall that he was not present.

It was in a conversation with Mrs. Everett, he said, that a figure of fifty shares was agreed upon. He was very impressed with her "ability and aggressive nature" and happy "to be invited to purchase."

Q. You were impressed by her. Was she impressed by you?
A. I can't say that.
Q. What did she say, sir?
A. What do you mean?
Q. Well, as to why she was making the shares available to you?
A. She thought this would be a good business and, in effect, she encouraged me to get into it.

The grilling continued until Woerheide was asking if Isaacs had enough money to buy $50,000 worth of CTE stock. When he said his assets were sufficient, the special attorney asked, "Were you already a millionaire by that time or were you worth, say, $500,000?"

Angrily, Isaacs replied: "That's not a decent thing to ask anybody."

"I think it is a proper question," said Woerheide.

"No, it isn't."

He was a man of "modest means," said Isaacs, "and always have been."

Woerheide let it pass, and turned to Kerner. It was not Marje's idea to cut Kerner in on the stock, said Isaacs. When she first mentioned his buying stock, he told the governor that he would like to share the opportunity with him. Then he told Marje, and she agreed.*

Did Marje know Kerner? Yes, they often attended the same political meetings.

Q. Did you know that Bill Miller brought them together?

A. No, sir, I didn't know that.

Kerner gave him carte blanche to handle the stock deal as he saw fit, Isaacs said. Joe Knight was brought in, and George Schaller, and there was wheeling and dealing until 1966, and then a stock exchange later. It was all vague, somewhat confusing, and added little to the facts on record. Isaacs did add some details about Balmoral. It has 1,249 acres of land, some good buildings, and there were plans to set up a real estate development and an animal hospital there in addition to the track. This sort of thing appealed to him, he said.

The Grand Jury recessed at that point, and it was two days later before Isaacs returned to complete his story. The questioning was largely unproductive as Woerheide searched for evidence of the Grand Conspiracy and found nothing of value. As Isaacs told it, he, the governor, and Miller simply did their jobs and as problems arose they tried to solve them. Even the decision to combine harness and thoroughbred boards into one entity headed by Miller was Kerner's idea, he said, and was designed to save money by ending duplication of effort.

At one point Isaacs expressed reluctance to say why Kerner dropped Thomas Bradley from the new board. Woerheide lectured him sternly about Grand Jury secrecy, noting that even the reporter was sworn to secrecy.

"I have to be a little bit squeamish when I read headlines every day about what is going to happen to me before the Grand Jury," Isaacs countered.

They went on to the purchase of CHR stock by Knight, and the resale of part of it to Kerner and Isaacs. Again Isaacs refused to implicate Miller as being responsible. Woerheide wanted to know why Knight was willing to sell the stock at cost.

"Other than the fact that Mr. Knight and I were good friends and I

---

* Further evidence that Miller was not the first to convey the stock offer to Kerner.

liked him a lot," Isaacs replied, "he had the reputation of being a great fellow, always doing things for people. He was a bachelor who spent most of his time running around helping other people out. I don't know whether he is or not, but he had the reputation of being a very wealthy man. I have no idea that he is or was. And my friendship for him was really the only bond we had."

As to Kerner — well, "Mr. Knight would have done anything in the world for the governor. He really loved him."

The inconclusive interview ended shortly after that. Isaacs said nothing that confirmed the government's conspiracy theory, but, of course, he had given a possible preview of what his defense might be when brought to trial. As it developed, Isaacs did not testify in his own defense so his Grand Jury testimony remains the only version to which he swore under the possible penalty of perjury. It is perhaps significant that no perjury count was returned against him despite his contradictions of Mrs. Everett's statements.

Four Grand Juries had been meeting, each getting a bit from this witness and a bit from that. Now it was time to wrap it all up by hearing from the star — the deposed Queen of Racing in Illinois.

One month after Isaacs' first appearance, Marje Everett was in the Grand Jury room. It was the morning of July 15, 1971, and they wanted her to spell out the name L-i-n-d-h-e-i-m-e-r. She did. Then she was asked about Miller.

During the last years of her father's life, she said, she was "drawn a little closer to Mr. Miller who was very interested in racing and whom I got to know and respected and liked as a friend, a person I believed in and believed that his interests were similar to my father's, which was trying to elevate racing and make it successful for the state."

No problem here in putting the Racing Board chairman into the driver's seat.

After her father's death, "Mr. Miller was the friend I needed and with whom I counseled almost on a daily basis."

The formation of CTE "was the result of working with Mr. Miller, and, as you know, another gentleman who was a lawyer."

Woerheide was hitting his stride. Question after question began: "And as a result of these discussions with Mr. Miller, did you. . ."

And the answer usually was, "Yes, sir."

She credited Miller with introducing her to bank officials, but, curiously, said nothing about his cosigning her note. The decision to go into harness racing was a result of discussions with Miller, who assured her he thought he could get harness-racing dates. The meeting with Paul Powell in Springfield was described, but nothing was said of the presence of William Johnston of Sportsman's Park.

Q. Was there any discussion about Mr. Powell and certain of his associates participating in the ownership of this racing entity that would be set up?

A. Yes, sir, Mr. Miller discussed that in my presence.

Woerheide tried to move too swiftly at this point. Marje ignored his question to say, "I think, Mr. Woerheide, that you might want to mention that there was a later meeting which Mr. Miller and Mr. Powell arranged. And as a result of this particular meeting there was a meeting arranged at Washington Park Race Track during the spring meeting there. And Mr. Miller had arranged for Mr. Powell to come and certain associates of Mr. Powell. They had lunch at the track and it was agreed that there was going to be a block of stock set aside for Mr. Powell to distribute as he saw fit. And from that date to this day virtually I never participated in any future meetings."

The formation of WPTA was reviewed in detail and the names of the businessmen who held stock both for themselves and for the politicians were put on record. Marje admitted that she was aware of the use of nominees but "Mr. Miller *really masterminded* the manner in which this should be done and handled." (Emphasis added.)

Moving on, Marje said that Miller introduced her to Isaacs and suggested his firm be retained to handle the estate.

"Mr. Miller was working very closely with Mr. Isaacs on racing," Marje continued, "and had developed quite a close friendship with him. And I think in racing matters that he felt should be brought to the attention of the governor, Mr. Isaacs, I was led to believe, was frequently the liaison or courier. I was led to believe that Mr. Miller did not have any close contact with the governor."

No mention here, of course, that in 1960 and 1964 she gave money through Miller to Kerner's campaign.

As to the stock deal, this curious exchange occurred:

Q. In connection with these discussions did he make any proposal to you as to what you should do?

A. I indicated to Mr. Miller that I would make available to him, at his suggestion, what he thought I should do. I would, you know, *carry out any suggestion that he made.* [Emphasis added.]

The November 8, 1962, memorandum was discussed. It was made, Marje said, *at Miller's suggestion.* She was then shown a letter dated November 12, 1962, addressed to Ted Isaacs and signed Marjorie L. Everett. She agreed the signature appeared to be hers and added that she believed "that letter was dictated over the telephone by Mr. George Schaller to our secretary, Miss Carroll."

Asked whether it was dictated in 1962 or 1966, she replied: "I would have to think it was 1962."

Another document described as "a note written in Chicago, Illinois, on November 12, 1962, and signed by Theodore Isaacs," was shown. Marje said she had never seen it prior to the beginning of the investigation.

It was all very confusing so Woerheide moved swiftly to other matters after promising to come back "to this matter" later. The formation of Chicago Harness was discussed and, again, Miller was credited with being the *mastermind.* He invited such "outstanding businessmen and fine representative people" as "Mr. Crowdus Baker who was then with Sears, and Elmer Layden, the former football player of the Four Horsemen," as well as "Mr. Wacker who was of the Wacker Drive family, and Mr. Atlass who was with WIND [radio] and Westinghouse."

Q. Did Mr. Miller say anything about taking certain shares for himself or for people connected with him?

A. Yes, Mr. Miller and I discussed this and he had a block of 50,000 shares of Chicago Harness Racing set aside for his distribution.

Woerheide wasn't satisfied. After establishing that Atlass agreed to serve as nominee, he summed up: "So it was agreed between Mr. Atlass and yourself and Mr. Miller that Mr. Atlass would act as nominee for Mr. Miller for the 50,000 share block?"

Marje wouldn't go along. "He was to be, I had thought, a nominee for that block of stock. I did not know that that was Mr. Miller's — it was a block to be distributed by Mr. Miller. . . . Mr. Miller always indicated to me that under no condition would he or his family or Miss McInturf have stock in any of our companies or any other racing operation."

Woerheide had no comment on this heresy, nor is there any ready explanation why Mrs. Everett insisted on setting the record straight. The point wasn't vital to the conspiracy theory, but Woerheide had made much use of it in suggesting that Miller was unscrupulous and greedy.

Came 1966, and the completion of the stock deal. Marje said Miller called and told her to have prepared two certificates for twenty-five shares each of CTE stock. It was to be issued in her name and endorsed by her in blank.

"We called the bank," she continued, "who held the stock, and they were kind enough to return the certificate for the 2,000. I told them that when I received payment for the fifty shares that I would give them payment, which was $50,000, that the money would be turned over to them as against the collateral that they were releasing. They were then given a certificate for 1,950, which was the balance of the two certificates, and twenty-five each were delivered to Mr. Miller as per his instructions."

She added that "I had George Schaller handling all these matters, anything to do with this area."

They turned to Balmoral. Marje admitted that she had controlling interest in the company, but wanted to be rid of it. Miller, she said, told her he would like to quit the Racing Board and buy Balmoral.

"Frankly, it had some attractiveness to me," she continued, "because I was tired of truthfully battling the political — there was an element of politicians and a difficult element of sordidness in the west-side racetrack, Sportsman's, and I thought, here's a man who knows racing and he might take a lot of the unpleasantness that goes with trying to operate. And I could still have my pie. We could still try to develop the finest racing facilities without having to constantly compromise with your principles and worry about things that you really would like not to worry about."

This extraordinary statement was also accepted without question. Woerheide was satisfied to let Marje allege that Miller directed the creation of a new corporation by Webb Everett and the acquisition of outstanding stock. Miller "arbitrarily set a price of $30 a share that he would pay for it."

"Mr. Miller," she added, "if he ever turned and if he ever got his temper up, he was a very devastating individual."

Miller proceeded to buy control of Chicago Harness for "between $550,000 and $580,000." He got Balmoral when "he came in one day and handed us a check for $1,450,000."

A few more questions and the session wound up. The foreman thanked Marje "for journeying so far to testify before us."

Special Agents Stufflebeam and Witkowski began preparing final reports as quickly as they secured a transcript of Marje's Grand Jury testimony. The first was signed on July 2, 1971. On page 141 they wrote:

Based on the evidence as set forth in this report we recommend, therefore, the following:

1. OTTO KERNER and THEODORE ISAACS be prosecuted for wilfully attempting to evade and defeat a substantial part of their income tax for the calendar year 1966 in violation of Section 7201 of the Internal Revenue Code.

2. OTTO KERNER and THEODORE ISAACS be prosecuted for wilfully subscribing to false income tax returns for the years 1966 and 1967 in violation of Section 7206 (1) of the Internal Revenue Code.

3. WILLIAM S. MILLER be prosecuted for wilfully subscribing to a false income tax return for the year 1966 in violation of Section 7206 (1) of the Internal Revenue Code.

4. OTTO KERNER be prosecuted for wilfully making a material false, fictitious and fraudulent statement to special agents of the Intelligence Division, Internal Revenue Service, during the course of their investigation in violation of Title 18, 1001, USC.

5. OTTO KERNER, THEODORE ISAACS, WILLIAM S. MILLER and JOSEPH KNIGHT be prosecuted for conspiring to unlawfully, wilfully and knowingly use a facility in interstate commerce, to wit, the United States mail, by receiving and taking delivery by mail and sending through the mail numerous documents, with intent to promote and carry on activity, namely bribery, in violation of the laws of the State of Illinois, and causing to be filed false income tax returns by both ISAACS and KERNER for each of the years 1966 and 1967 in violation of Title 18, Section 371 and Title 18, Section 1952, USC.

6. OTTO KERNER and THEODORE ISAACS be prosecuted for wilfully and knowingly making

false statements before a Federal Grand Jury while under oath in violation of Title 18, Section 1623 USC.
7. Upon completion of the criminal proceedings, a fraud penalty be asserted on the deficiencies as set forth in this report.

The second final report recommended the prosecution of Miss McInturf, Miller's confidential secretary, and Joseph Golman, Isaacs' accountant.

The agents recommended Miss McInturf be prosecuted "for conspiring to unlawfully, wilfully and knowingly use a facility in interstate commerce, to wit, the United States mail, with intent to promote and carry on an unlawful activity, namely bribery, and causing to be filed false income tax returns by both Isaacs and Kerner."

Golman was recommended for prosecution for conspiring with Isaacs to "afford a bribe payment to Kerner and Isaacs in a form which could be reflected on their respective income tax returns calling for capital gains treatment," and for aiding in preparing false income tax returns on behalf of Isaacs.

Following this report on September 7, 1971, the agents put together a third one on October 15, 1971, dealing with Miller and Chicago Harness. It recommended prosecution of Miller and CHR "based on evidence that Miller, chairman of the Illinois Racing Board at the time, used the power of his official position to acquire controlling interest of CHR, and through CHR, controlling interest of BJC, at a per share price dictated by him, without regard to the actual value of the shares being purchased."

This, said the agents, was "extortion."

The report maintained that Miller reneged on an agreement with Webb Everett, and announced he had decided not to quit the Racing Board. He wanted to use Everett as a nominee to conceal his interest. Everett refused, the report said, and having done so "had no alternative but to sell to Miller at Miller's price." Likewise, he forced Marje Everett to sell Balmoral Jockey Club stock at the price he named, the report said.

Not mentioned was the fact that Marje had sent the special agents to attorney Henry Williams in Miami to get confirmation of the extortion story. Williams did not confirm it. Bewildered, the investigators called Marje who told them to try again next day. They tried again, as ordered, and failed. Williams, the Miami attorney who had been consulted by Webb Everett and Miller, knew nothing of any extortion. Nevertheless, Stufflebeam and Witkowski accepted the Everett version and recommended Miller be prosecuted.

In November, 1971, the last report was signed by the investigating agents. It concerned some of the legislators who had received stock in WPTA. Once again Miller, the alleged mastermind, was included in the list to be prosecuted. The report began:

> This report relates to an alleged conspiracy be-
> tween WILLIAM S. MILLER, CLYDE CHOATE,
> JOHN LEWIS, GEORGE DUNNE, JOHN MEYER,
> A. L. CRONIN, PAUL ZIEGLER, PAUL POWELL,
> WILLIAM POLLACK, ARTHUR BIDWILL,
> ROBERT McCLOSKEY, WILLIAM MURPHY,
> EVERETT PETERS, and CLYDE LEE to violate Sec-
> tion 1952, Title 18, USC, in violation of Section 371,
> Title 18, USC.

An alleged conspiracy, yes, but only Miller, Choate, Cronin, Dunne, Lewis, Meyer, and Ziegler were actually recommended for prosecution. Powell was dead, of course, but why was Republican Bidwill who, next to Powell, received more stock than anyone else — why was he omitted?

Years later, when asked that question, Stufflebeam replied, "We couldn't prosecute everyone; we had to have some witnesses."

The recommended charge was conspiracy to use the mails to carry on bribery. Miller was again cast as the mastermind who arranged for the legislators to receive forty-nine per cent of the stock in WPTA in return for the legislature's cooperation in establishing harness racing at Washington Park. The only testimony cited in support of Miller's alleged role was that of Mr. and Mrs. Everett.

It is interesting that had the special agents' recommendations been carried out, Miller would have been indicted in three separate cases: with Kerner, Isaacs, and Knight; with CHR; and with the legislators. Fortunately for the man from Crawfordsville, the final decision on who to indict was made by the Justice Department. The boys in Justice were more interested in Kerner than in crucifying Miller.

While experts in Washington debated technical aspects of the complex case, certain personnel changes were made. It was obvious to all with a political bent that the man in charge of prosecuting Judge Kerner would, if successful, have a bright career in Illinois politics. That meant then that Woerheide and others of the special team from Washington should be supplanted by local heroes. U. S. Attorney Bauer was the logical choice, but Bauer was considered too old and insufficiently aggressive. Beneath him, however, was "Big Jim" Thompson, first assistant U. S. Attorney and a man of talent and experience. Only thirty-five, he was a bachelor, a graduate of Northwestern University School of Law, and a collector of antiques who enjoyed playing with a snowmobile on his private retreat in Wisconsin. Six feet, six inches tall, he was softspoken and ambitious to be not only governor of Illinois but president of the United States. If any man would make the most of opportunity, so Attorney General Mitchell decided, it would be Thompson.

So far so good. Woerheide became angry when told he couldn't prosecute and went off to Europe in a huff. Illness kept him there for months. Meanwhile, Bauer was appointed a federal district court judge and Thompson promoted to his place.

Still no decision on the indictment came from Washington, however, where some politicians argued it was too close to election year to take a chance with a public hero such as Otto Kerner. Project CRIMP had taken too long to make its case.

Hesitation there might have been in Washington, but there was none in Chicago. A copy of the proposed indictment was leaked to Ron Koziol, investigative reporter of the *Chicago Tribune*, and on Sunday, November 21, 1971, it appeared under double banner headlines.

Koziol, of course, had to agree to play games before he was given his scoop. To take the heat off of local sources he flew to Washington, registered at a hotel, went over to the Internal Revenue Service building on Pennsylvania Avenue, entered through the front door and passed to the street again through the back door. Then he came home. His story carried a Washington dateline.

When IRS inspectors descended on the *Tribune*, Koziol's colleagues tipped them confidentially to check the records of a certain airline on a certain day, and to take a look at the guests registered at a certain Washington hotel on the day in question. The probe proved without a doubt that the reporter was in Washington just before the story broke, but that is all it proved. Today, Koziol still protects his sources, as a good reporter should, but some of the sources think it is too good a story to keep secret.

Koziol's scoop was comprehensive — he had full details of the pending indictment, and by publishing them he made it impossible for Justice to hesitate any longer. Indeed, Sam Skinner, now chief of the special investigation division under Thompson, was forced to scramble to complete a "prosecution memorandum" recommending the indictment of Kerner, Isaacs, Miller, Knight, and Miss McInturf. So great was the speed he spelled Isaacs as *Issacs* and McInturf as *McIntuff*. There wasn't time to retype the thirty-page document, so Skinner added a correction and an apology on the cover page.

In his memorandum, Skinner listed several "major facts" he expected to be contested. The first of these was whether Miller was the key individual in the CTE stock offer. Skinner noted that only Marje said he was, but he was confident the trial jury would believe her on the grounds the stories presented by the defendants "are so inconsistent that they defeat any one of the defendants' contentions." He noted, however, that if Miller and McInturf testified for the government, their testimony could "seriously impeach" Isaacs' and Kerner's versions.

Still unsettled, said Skinner, was whether the CTE stock deal was made in 1962 or 1966. He noted that Isaacs' attorney now admitted the promissory note was drawn in 1966 and backdated to 1962. So was Marje's letter to Isaacs. Yet Marje had claimed the sale on her 1966 tax return and the IRS had disallowed it on the grounds it was a 1962 sale. All very confusing, said Skinner, but in his opinion it really didn't matter. It was bribery whether in 1962 or 1966.

Did Isaacs commit perjury when he told the Grand Jury he dealt with Marje and not Miller? Skinner recommended the question be dropped since it was "another one-on-one perjury case." Moreover, it created "an Isaacs v. Everett posture which should in my opinion be avoided."

He also warned that "efforts should be made to keep the Everett v. Kerner testimony contradictions to an absolute minimum to prevent the case from drifting into an Everett v. Kerner posture which would not be healthy."

At the end of his discussion, Skinner recommended that Kerner,

Miller, Isaacs, Knight, and McInturf be prosecuted, and that the indictment naming them should be returned on November 30, 1971. That deadline wasn't met. There was still debate in Washington. Finally Mitchell conferred with President Nixon and won his approval. The final battle had been between Justice and the Internal Revenue Service. The latter agency, realizing how much of the case rested on the unsupported word of Marje Everett, wanted to file civil cases. Justice, under Mitchell, wanted criminal indictments, and it got them. The May Grand Jury, which waited patiently during the months of wrangling for the government to tell it what to do, was reconvened on December 14 to hear Stufflebeam rebut Kerner's version of his interview with the special agents. Then the sixty-five page, nineteen-count indictment was read and explained. The Grand Jury put its stamp of approval on the document the following day.

Announcement of the indictment was made December 15, 1971, by Mitchell in Washington and Thompson in Chicago. Before making it public, the U. S. Attorney personally conveyed the news to Judge Kerner in his chambers.

Count One accused all the defendants — Kerner, Isaacs, Knight, Miller, and McInturf — of conspiracy to travel in interstate commerce and with use of the mails with intent to distribute the proceeds of bribery.

Counts Two through Five accused all defendants of specific use of interstate facilities in furtherance of bribery. Counts Six through Thirteen charged all defendants with specific acts of mail fraud.

In addition, Kerner was charged with one count of perjury before a Grand Jury, one count of making false statements to Internal Revenue agents, one count of tax evasion, and one count of making false statements in a tax return. Isaacs was additionally charged with one count of tax evasion and one count of making false statements in a tax return.

The indictment was so complex that Chicago newspapers lacked time, space, and perhaps expertise, to explain it fully. Thompson, now in the spotlight, did his best. The indictment of Kerner, he said, was only the second time in history that a federal appeals judge had been indicted while sitting on the bench.

"Without the complete and full cooperation" of Marje Everett, Thompson said, the investigation would have been impossible. "The people of this community owe her a vote of thanks," he added. Later, when the government was forced to provide a bill of particulars, Mrs.

Everett was listed as "an unindicted co-conspirator."

From his office at Balmoral Park, Miller noted that "up to this very moment I never as much as received a single penny of profit or dividends or salary from racetrack stock or racetrack operations. I firmly believe my innocence will be established beyond any question of doubt. I have no fear."

Mrs. Helena Kerner, wife of the judge, commented that the indictment was politically motivated. Isaacs, Knight, and McInturf declined comment. Former Republican Governor William G. Stratton expressed sympathy for Kerner. Stratton, who had been indicted and acquitted on income tax charges, noted that "a defendant in a case like this certainly is in a difficult position." Neither Mayor Daley nor Governor Ogilvie had any comment.

Kerner did not resign his seat on the bench following his indictment but did ask to be suspended pending the disposition of the case. And acting chief of the U. S. District Court for the Northern District of Illinois, Judge Richard B. Austin, said he would ask U. S. Supreme Court Chief Justice Warren Burger to assign an outside judge to hear the case.

In Los Angeles, meanwhile, Neil Papiano, Mrs. Everett's attorney, was grateful for the kind words volunteered by Thompson about his client.

"She has said from the beginning that she has committed no wrongful acts, and it pleases all of us to find that the Grand Jury concurs," he stated.

How he arrived at the conclusion is difficult to fathom, but the Grand Jury indictment was timely from Mrs. Everett's viewpoint. On the day before, she had filed suit to be seated on the Hollywood Park board of directors. Despite the stock she had won from Levin, she had been denied a seat and thus a chance to exercise the control the stock gave her. The other directors cited her part in the Illinois scandal as reason for keeping her off.

"In view of the action today in Illinois," Papiano said, "we are demanding her immediate seating on the Hollywood Park board of directors. It is obvious that the Hollywood Park management not only owes Mrs. Everett her seat on the board, but also owes her a public apology."

The board didn't agree, and the legal battle continued. On January

11, 1972, she was in Los Angeles to give a deposition in the matter. Questioning her was attorney Frank Rothman, representing Hollywood Park. After about five minutes, Rothman began a new question:

"Mrs. Everett, while an owner of stock in a racetrack in Illinois, did you bribe . . ."

Papiano interrupted. "Come on!" he said.

Rothman continued:

". . . or offer to bribe any public official?"

"We are adjourning the deposition at this point," said Papiano. "I will seek a protective order."

Rothman replied: "May the record reflect that after having been asked the last question, Mrs. Everett has left her seat, picked up her coat and is in the process of leaving the deposition room."

"Pursuant to my instructions," snapped Papiano.

It looked as if Marje had backed into a corner. If she said yes, she might lose her chance to take over Hollywood Park. If she said no, she would imperil the case against Miller, Kerner, and the rest.

Appearances were deceptive, however. Marje knew the power she gained when that indictment was returned. The Nixon administration needed her desperately if Kerner was to be convicted, and his conviction was now essential if Republicans were to win in Illinois in 1972. Already she had put on the pressure. Four days before the deposition, U. S. Attorney Thompson and his chief aide, Skinner, flew to California and met with Evelle Younger, the attorney general of the state, and with members of the California Horse Racing Board. The decision was made to halt the probe then and there.

After Marje's walkout from the deposition session, Attorney General Younger warned the California racing board that if it attempted to make Mrs. Everett answer the question in a public hearing, he would seek a court order to prevent her from testifying.

Marje's Phoenix attorneys had good connections with Republican powers in both Arizona and California, and had contacted Governor Ronald Reagan in behalf of their client. Reagan, of course, had ambitions to succeed Nixon in the White House, and was alert to the political aspects of the situation. Much of Papiano's indignation at the question asked by Rothman stemmed from the fact that he thought the matter all wrapped up. It was, in fact, all settled, but a "decent interval" subsequent to Thompson's flying trip had been wanted. On

January 24, the California racing board granted Mrs. Everett a temporary license. She promptly dropped her suit and the question of a
public hearing became moot.

That didn't stop Marje from granting an interview in Los Angeles a
few days later and blaming Sidney Korshak for her troubles. Over
cornflakes at the Beverly Wilshire Hotel, she said Korshak — the
labor-relations expert hired by her father — had been at work behind
the scenes to keep her out of Hollywood Park. Why? Attorney Papiano
suggested that perhaps the management of the track didn't want Marje
"fooling around with their records and perhaps exposing links and
tie-ins they would just as soon stay hidden."

Marje agreed, and in passing blamed Korshak for causing the death
of her adoptive father by permitting a strike of mutuel clerks to develop
at Washington Park on June 5, 1960, the night Ben Lindheimer died.
Upon getting control, Marje fired Korshak. Several years later after
selling to Gulf & Western and being fired by Philip Levin, Marje could
do nothing when Korshak was rehired as labor consultant by Levin.
Whether or not he was engaged in a "Stop Marje" movement in
California was never proved, for Marje had gained the upper hand with
the men who mattered.

Hollywood Park soon capitulated completely and abruptly Marje
was galloping along on a fast track under sunny skies. In Chicago,
Thompson breathed a sigh of relief; his star witness would testify.
Later, Kerner's attorney would call the aid given Marje by Thompson'
an act of "bribery," but little good it did him to say so.

Special Agent Stufflebeam, a close friend of Thompson, did not
share the prosecutor's optimism. He felt that too much depended on
Marje's unsupported word. Another witness was needed, he told his
colleagues. While he personally preferred Miller, he was willing, if
necessary, to give immunity to Isaacs. "I'd as soon give immunity to
Pontius Pilate," someone replied.

Stufflebeam continued to think about Miller as a witness, and was
pleased when the defendant retained the attorney William A. Barnett.
His previous lawyers had advised Miller not to talk to special agents
and to take the Fifth Amendment before the Grand Jury. Perhaps an
opportunity might come along, Stufflebeam reasoned, to make Miller a
friendly witness.

On January 20, 1971, the defendants were arraigned before Acting

Chief Judge Richard B. Austin. They arrived early. Isaacs and Kerner sat side by side on the front bench. When an emaciated Knight ambled in, Isaacs got up to take his scarf and overcoat. Knight sat down next to Kerner, leaving Isaacs on his feet. Miss McInturf, her full-length mink coat safely in the closet, sat beside an impassive Miller. Reporters noticed that Miller's hair was white.

No less impressive than the defendants were their attorneys. Kerner was represented by Edward Bennett Williams. Boston lawyer F. Lee Bailey represented Miss McInturf. Thomas P. Sullivan, a Chicago attorney with the expensive firm of Jenner & Block, served Isaacs. George F. Callaghan was Knight's attorney. William Barnett, who had successfully defended former Illinois Governor William Stratton, represented Miller.

Everyone pleaded "not guilty" as expected, and the lawyers began to squabble when informed they would have to file all pretrial motions by January 31. The order came from Judge Robert L. Taylor of Knoxville, Tennessee, who had been assigned to the case by Chief Justice Burger. Judge Austin continued the matter until 2 P.M. The lawyers immediately headed for the courtroom of Judge James B. Parsons, the designated "emergency motions" judge for the month. Declaring that an emergency existed, Attorney Sullivan challenged not only the motion schedule but the assignment of the case to a Tennessee judge. He also maintained that the indictments were faulty in that they were returned before Acting Chief Judge Austin — who was over seventy years old and thus prohibited by law from serving as chief. Judge Parsons was obviously embarrassed, and promised to rule later. The lawyers then went back to Austin, who accused them of "sneaking" into another courtroom. He ruled they could go to Tennessee and make their protest in person to Judge Taylor. All in all an exciting day in Chicago's Federal Building, and perhaps an indication the actual trial would be delayed in starting. But despite the best efforts of defense attorneys, the legal confusion was eventually ended and Judge Taylor of Tennessee confirmed as the man who would preside when at last the trial began.

Meantime, while Marje was getting back into racing out in California, her former tenant was bowing out of racing in Illinois. On January 31, Miller announced his resignation as president of Balmoral Jockey Club and as executive director of Chicago Harness Racing. Repeating that he was innocent of all charges, he stated, "I, of my own volition, take my leave until my name has been cleared. I owe that to racing."

Miller did more than resign his jobs; he also sold his racing and breeding stock — some twenty horses — to William S. Farish III of Houston. Among the horses was *Bee Bee Bee*, out of *Paula* by *Better Bee*. When, a few months later on May 20, *Bee Bee Bee* raced through the slop to beat *Riva Ridge* and win the Preakness, Miller was about the only unsurprised man in Illinois. He pointed out that *Better Bee* had run through similar slop to set a track record at Arlington and beat the great *Round Table*. "The slop at the Preakness figured to be right up his alley, at least in my mind," he said.

Gerald Strine, writing in the *Washington Post*, noted: "The timing of the Kerner 'scandal' has cost Miller dearly. His name is under a cloud at a time when, otherwise, the midwestern banker-manufacturer would be enjoying his greatest moment in racing."

About that time, the Internal Revenue Service concluded that Miller hadn't paid enough. Or someone thought it might be fun to tighten the screws a bit. In April, 1972, a $2.4 million civil suit was filed against Miller. Its basis was allegations that Miller was guilty of fraud and tax evasion in his purchase of Balmoral and Chicago Harness from the Everetts. It was a live thing, growing every day as interest and penalties were added on top of interest and penalties. By the time it was settled in 1976, the total allegedly due had reached the $4.6 million mark.

Despite the money involved, Miller didn't take it seriously. It was, he believed, another effort by the government to make him testify, to make him corroborate Marje's tales. He remained willing to cooperate, he insisted, but only if he could tell the truth.

The criminal case didn't look so dangerous either after a meeting of the five defendants and their attorneys at the office of Albert Jenner. As soon as everyone was seated, Kerner took command with the announcement he had good news. During one of his Grand Jury appearances, he said, an unauthorized person had been present in the room — an Internal Revenue Service agent. This was stunning news. If true, the case against Kerner would be dismissed, and without Kerner there was no case against anyone else. Attorney Williams, who perhaps knew his client better than the rest, asked Kerner if he was sure of his facts.

"Of course I'm sure," replied the judge. He explained the agent had audited his taxes several years before, and he had seen him on almost a daily basis for a month or more. There could be no doubt — he knew the man.

The assembled lawyers agreed that such being the case, there was no need to waste time planning for a trial that wouldn't come off so the meeting adjourned in less than ten minutes.

In June a hearing was held on a defense motion to dismiss the indictment because of the presence of an unauthorized person in the Grand Jury room. Kerner described the intruder as having black hair. When the agent he named was brought in, he proved to have white hair. The motion was withdrawn.

Miller, meanwhile, had been quietly searching his files and assembling the facts. He wanted to be ready. One day in May, Miller, Miss McInturf, and Robert Boissenin, a skilled accountant employed by Miller, visited the Federal Building to examine some of the government's documents which under the legal discovery procedure had been made available to the defendants. He directed that each document he considered important be numbered and a record kept by Miss McInturf. Special Agent Stufflebeam was lounging around watching when Miller loudly pronounced a certain document a "phony." It was the promissory note which Isaacs had drafted in 1966 and backdated to 1962.

One of Kerner's attorneys grabbed Miller's arm and led him into the hall. "Don't talk like that in front of him," he said, pointing to Stufflebeam. Irritated by this unsolicited advice, Miller said nothing, but soon walked down the hall to a coke machine. Stufflebeam followed and out of the hearing of the others made his pitch.

"You belong on our side."

"I'll testify for the government if I'm allowed to tell the truth," repeated Miller.

They left it at that for the moment.

From that day until August 14, 1972, almost three months, there was no communication between Miller and his two codefendants, Isaacs and Kerner. Isaacs retained a new lawyer, youthful but aggressive Warren Wolfson, and Kerner began working with his trial attorney, Paul Connolly, a partner of Edward Bennett Williams. Miller had good sources, however, and word reached him that the strategy being discussed by attorneys for Kerner and Marje contemplated blaming Miller for everything.

A few days after sharing a coke with Stufflebeam, Miller was persuaded by a mutual friend that the special agent could be trusted. Taking a deep breath, he agreed to meet with the younger man. Upon receiving the message, Stufflebeam hunted down his good friend, U.S. Attorney Thompson, and obtained his consent. Next day he drove down to Crete and there at the racetrack built by Matt Winn he and Miller reviewed the case all afternoon while killing a bottle of Grant's Scotch. Two more meetings followed. It was soon apparent to Stufflebeam that Miller had been blamed by Marje for a lot of things he had nothing to do with. What's more he had vital documentation to prove his version of the facts correct.

The possibility that Miller would be on the other side, cross-examining Marje through his attorney, was enough to drive a man to drink. Stufflebeam soon reported his reactions to Thompson, and it was agreed a deal should be worked out. Attorneys took over, and a document on behalf of Miller and Miss McInturf was drafted. In essence it provided the two would testify truthfully, both in the trial and before a Grand Jury. In return, the charges against them would be dropped regardless of the outcome of the trial.

The agreement was signed on August 15, 1972. Later, Kerner's attorney was to call it one of "the most cynical deals I have ever heard of in the history of American jurisprudence."

With the signing of the agreement, U. S. marshals were sent to Miller's office at Balmoral Park to take possession of a large, vault-like cabinet in which Miller and Miss McInturf had stored some of the evidence they had assembled during their search of the records. Miller was moved into the Drake Hotel to a suite shared with Stufflebeam and paid for by the Justice Department. A two-day debriefing began.

Thompson still had his reservations. At one point he became annoyed when Miller insisted on his personal innocence.

"Oh, come on, Bill," he growled. "You know we've got you dead to rights on that income tax evasion thing."

"What income tax evasion thing?" demanded Miller.

"The cash you took from Marje which was supposed to be a contribution to Kerner's campaign," snapped the prosecutor.

Miller wheeled, picked up the telephone and called his office. A few minutes later Miss McInturf knocked on the door, entered, and gave him an envelope. Miller handed it to Thompson.

Inside the envelope was the receipt for the $45,000 Mrs. Everett had donated to the Kerner campaign in 1960. It was signed by Isaacs who had received the cash from Miller.

"Well, I'll be damned!" said Thompson.

After that, relations improved. Soon Thompson and Stufflebeam were coming down to Crete every Sunday. A routine developed: brunch at the Holiday Inn, and then an afternoon of Scotch and talk. The climax came when at last Thompson admitted:

"Bill, you should never have been indicted."

As if to illustrate how much time and effort had been wasted by Woerheide's determination to make Miller the mastermind, Thompson called his new witness before the Grand Jury on December 13, 1972. Kerner wasn't mentioned; the questioning concerned the formation of Washington Park Trotting Association and the forty-nine per cent interest in it of various legislators.

> Q. And did Mrs. Everett desire to increase her revenue at Washington Park at that time so she could obtain funds necessary for the rehabilitation of both Washington Park and Arlington Park?
> A. Yes, and to pay her bank loans.
> Q. Did you suggest to Mrs. Everett that in order for her to successfully enter the field of harness racing, it would be wise to obtain the approval of Paul Powell?
> A. Yes.
> Q. At that time, who was Paul Powell?
> A. At that time, in 1961, Paul Powell was speaker of the House of Representatives in the State of Illinois.
> Q. Do you now know that in 1960 and early 1961, Powell was a stockholder in every harness racing company in Illinois?
> A. Yes.

They went on to the "test question" Woerheide had asked Miller in conference:

> Q. Now, calling your attention to the year 1961, was there a meeting at Arlington Park Race Track where the subject of participation in the stock distribution of WPTA was discussed by Mrs. Everett and members of the Illinois legislature?

A. Mrs. Everett informed me that such a meeting occurred.

Q. Were you present at that meeting?

A. I was not present at the meeting, but I was present at the racetrack.

At the end of the short session, Miller was excused subject to recall for additional questioning. He was not recalled — the probe of legislators was postponed to permit Thompson to concentrate on his primary assignment, "getting Otto's ass." And then it was dropped, along with a lot of other things.

The world is full of people who can't talk straight.

FRED SIRICA, as quoted by
his son, JOHN SIRICA

9
The Witness

The Watergate scandal had been contained and John Dean congratulated; Richard M. Nixon had been re-elected in a landslide; and the season for good will to men having passed, Judge Robert L. Taylor, Chief Justice Burger's handpicked choice from the Tennessee hills, would brook no more delay.

Twice the case had been postponed, first until after the November elections — why gamble? — and then until after the holidays; all pretrial motions had been disposed of; and the cases of McInturf, Miller, and Knight had been severed, the latter because Knight's impending death could no longer be ignored.

So it was that on January 3, 1973, the case number, 71CR 1086, *The United States of America versus Theodore J. Isaacs, et al.*, was read aloud in the ceremonial courtroom on the 25th floor of the Everett M. Dirksen Federal Building. Two hundred prospective jurors, one-fourth of the number available, filled the benches. It would take all week to seat thirty-one potentials, but only a few minutes on January 10 for both sides, using their rights of peremptory challenge, to agree on a jury of twelve and an alternate panel of six.

The jury consisted of six men and six women, nine of whom were white. Two of the women were housewives, the others worked as secretaries or file clerks. The men, with the exception of an ex-pilot who worked as an agent for American Airlines, were blue-collar: a brickmason, a sheetmetal worker, a forklift operator, a typesetter, and a machinist. Only the ex-pilot had any college training, but the forklift operator, a black, had two sons attending college. One of the two black women, a widow, was the mother of two Chicago cops. The brickmason ultimately became foreman. He was a member of the Sons of Norway.

147

A newspaper professed to see a wide gulf between Kerner and the jurors:

"Kerner is impeccable, still handsome at sixty-four — the distinguished appellate court judge, a man educated at Cambridge and Northwestern Law School. He is Lake Shore Drive.

"The jurors are bedroom suburban, city bungalow and walkup apartment."

Instant aristocracy, in other words, for this grandson of immigrants. Did the jurors look up to such a man as living proof of the American Dream, or did they think of him as a Bohemian who had forgotten his roots? Conceivably they simply accepted him as a man accused, and concentrated on comprehending the facts, leaving it to the press to speculate about the mighty brought low, the patrician humiliated.

Edward Bennett Williams was not present on behalf of Kerner. The assignment had gone to his partner, Paul Connolly, a veteran with silver hair and a handsome face that could flush with indignation as occasion required. During the series of pretrial hearings he had been a bitter foe of Marje Everett, even suggesting that Thompson's intervention in her behalf in California amounted to bribery to secure her testimony. Nevertheless, the rumor around the courtroom was of a change in strategy — Miller, not Marje, would get all the blame.

Warren Wolfson, a short, younger man who early in his career worked as a reporter for WHAS-TV in Louisville, represented Isaacs. He had a good reputation in Chicago legal circles as an aggressive, intelligent attorney, but it appeared he would have little opportunity to display his talents since Isaacs' fate almost surely was tied to Kerner and, under the circumstances, the less the jurors saw and heard of "the bungling bagman" the better.

"Big Jim" — by now he had become "Giant Jim" Thompson — towered above everyone. Surrounding him were a gaggle of assistants and three special agents of the IRS, including, of course, that handsome swinger, Peter Stufflebeam.

Judge Taylor sat almost hidden behind the bench, his bald head a pale moon above the rim of the wood. When occasionally he hunched forward, his black, hornrimmed glasses covered his face like a mask. The judge was seventy-two, and looked it. He was also hard of hearing. Even so he was not overawed by the historic occasion, and he remained feisty throughout the weeks of trial.

Thompson opened, and talked for ninety-one minutes, filling sixty-four pages of trial transcript. "In the end," he said, "this is a simple case. At the heart of the matter it is a case of bribery and fraud and lies to evade that bribery and fraud."

Connolly talked even longer, his opening filling eighty-nine pages. And as he held his audience, those who had heard the rumor of a shift in tactics listened closely for a hint. It came when the attorney began discussing the various counts in the indictment.

"What the government must prove in the first count is that the persons named — Isaacs, Kerner, Knight, McInturf, Miller — agreed to bribe Kerner, agreed with one other person, because although she is not indicted, she is named as a co-conspirator. You won't see her named as such as you read that indictment. You will see her described as 'the principal stockholder of Chicago Thoroughbred Enterprises,' or 'the principal stockholder of CTE,' never by name. The lady they are talking about is Marjorie L. Everett.

"They say that she intended to bribe Otto Kerner and these other people helped her. Well, ladies and gentlemen, as I stand here and say to you this morning, Marjorie Everett will not so testify. *She will not.*

"So, they say these people entered into an agreement to bribe Otto Kerner.

"Now, what is bribery? Mr. Thompson says it is sophisticated and subtle. I say baloney. If it was a bribe, you would see it, and it isn't. He says that the bribe was that they made arrangements to get $300,000 worth of stock in 1966 to Otto Kerner, when he had to pay only $50,000. So the difference between $50,000 and $300,000 is a bribe. The evidence will not support that.

"The evidence will support that this stock was made available in 1962 when it was worth just what was eventually paid for it, $1,000 a share. That Marje Everett looked upon it as an option, a commitment, an irrevocable promise. Kerner looked upon it as if he in fact had purchased it. Either way, there was a binding contractual obligation made in 1962, which both sides recognized, that the stock would be available at $1,000 a share."

Moving on, Connolly came finally to William S. Miller:

"As you heard Mr. Thompson this morning, and as you read this indictment, you will believe that the sinister Machiavelli of this entire case is this man named William S. Miller, who manipulated his governor, breached his trust, involved his governor in a terrible conspiracy, and corrupted all of Illinois racing. That is what the indictment says in so many words, and from his opening statement this morning you will conclude as much.

"I am going now to inform you about one of the most cynical deals I have ever heard of in the history of American jurisprudence. This man [Thompson] has given immunity to William S. Miller. . . .

"In short, this means that Mr. Miller and Miss McInturf are to be called as witnesses by the government in this case. While they are on the stand, their testimony, if it satisfies Mr. Thompson as to its truthfulness — and he is to be the judge of that, and not you and not the judge — if he is satisfied with their testimony, the indictments against them are dismissed. They walk out of here; just walk out. Since that very moment, Mr. Miller has refused to talk to me, has refused to talk to *me*. I don't know what he is going to testify to. However, he had a file cabinet, and in that cabinet he kept a pretty good history of Illinois racing, and the court has given me the opportunity to look at that file cabinet, and I can tell you from the documents in that file cabinet, many of which will be introduced as evidence, what happened. . . ."

Connolly wound down by declaring the charges against Kerner "are the product of a very busy imagination of a very vigorous and ambitious prosecutor. They do not hold water. They do not establish bribery. They do not establish a fraud on the people of the state of Illinois. The attempt to torture the facts into a criminal charge is manufactured, unjustified, unreasonable, and not in good faith."

With that, the court adjourned for lunch.

Isaacs' attorney, Warren Wolfson, kept a low profile when he addressed the jurors after they had eaten, but he did admit the famous promissory note was written in 1966 and backdated to 1962 "on the advice of his tax adviser."

"Ladies and gentlemen," he said, "again, nothing improper about that; done all the time in the business world. It was dated 1962 because that's when the agreement of the parties took place."

And, like Connolly, he took a dig at Miller:

"Mr. Connolly, I believe, has given you a pretty good idea of what it was all about when Everett, Miller, Schaller, and some others, got together.

"These aren't the kind of people that perhaps you are used to in your everyday dealings, so I hope you will listen carefully. When you listen to Miller, see if he isn't the kind of person who will say things to suit his own purposes, do things to suit his own gain, not only in this courtroom but, as you saw from the contract with the government Mr. Connolly read, he is ready to do or say whatever he has to do that suits his purpose. I hope you will use that test as you listen to his testimony."

Already it was clear to observers that Miller's reputation was on trial regardless of his agreement with the government. The defense would attack him brutally. As a witness, he had no one to defend him — no one save Thompson, and how far could the U. S. Attorney go without hurting his case? Of course, Mrs. Everett was in the same position — or was she? Either Miller or Marje had to be portrayed as the villain, the *mastermind*, if that dubious distinction was not to be placed on Kerner-Isaacs. Which was the most logical choice: the woman who had talked in the first place and gained "left-handed immunity" by so doing, or the man who had to be indicted before becoming a government witness? The opening statements on both sides indicated the nod had gone to Miller. This deduction was confirmed as Assistant U. S. Attorney Skinner called the first witness — Marjorie Everett.

For more than a year Skinner had been working with Marje. He had made many visits to her Scottsdale home to review her testimony. Only a few nights before, she had been given a dress rehearsal in the courtroom. She had sat in the witness chair to be cross-examined by strange attorneys and be told of various things she might do to project a less masculine-executive image. Marje seemed to enjoy the play-acting.

Now the double doors at the back of the room opened and down the center aisle came Marje. People turned to look at her — as one observer put it — "like wedding guests watching a bride." She was tall for a woman, yet chunky, somehow, with a cropped thatch of brown-gray hair and a lined face. Seating herself carefully, she drank from a paper cup of water, seemingly trying to wash down her nervousness. Yet when asked her name, she replied in a little-girl, almost inaudible, voice, and Skinner asked her to speak louder.

"Yes, sir, excuse me," said meek, mild-mannered Marje.

A reporter wrote next day that Marje "looked like a little girl who had been called down to the principal's office, or a poker player staring at a royal flush."

In answer to questions she said she was married, and married to

Webb A. Everett. That stirred the memory of a female reporter who recalled "the quote she gave long ago to an interviewer about her one real love — the racetrack: 'When we were growing up I didn't have as many dates as my sister so I'd sit around the house on evenings talking sports with Dad or listening to him and his friends talk about them — and racing.'"

The preliminary questions concerned the racetracks Marje took charge of in 1960. Quickly she set the stage. Arlington Park, she said, "had thoroughbred racing dates which they received on a year to year basis."

Miller met her plane when she returned to Chicago the day after her father died. Joe Knight was introduced to her "at the undertaking parlor when my father passed away."

The employment of attorney Joseph Zoline and the formation of CTE were described. When asked, Marje painted a bleak picture of her personal finances:

"I had to take everything I owned in the world and put it up as collateral against the loan that the bank made me. Additionally, sir, that loan, everything I had borrowed and everything I owned, what I owned, also, sir, was put up against not only my personal loan but also against the company's loan."

Marje was proving she knew how to be polite, deferential. Almost every response she made contained at least two "sirs," and sometimes three or four.

And now Otto Kerner was mentioned. "Yes, sir," she knew him. She first met him, "I believe, sir, at Rosehill Cemetery when my father passed away."

(One curious observer later checked the trial transcript to discover that Marje referred to her father no less than ninety-seven times in the course of her testimony.)

The question of political contributions was brought up. Marje remembered discussing it with Miller.

Q. Was anyone else present at this conversation?

A. I don't believe so.

The vital importance of Miller as a government witness was thus early apparent. Again and again, Marje was to make crucial statements, and then admit that Miller was the only witness to them.

Judge Taylor took occasion at this point to tell the jury that it must first establish to its satisfaction that a conspiracy did exist and that each

defendant was a part of it. Only then could the jury consider the acts
and declarations of co-conspirators as evidence. "Now, if you don't find
these factors, then what Miller allegedly said to this lady in the absence
of Mr. Isaacs and Judge Kerner would be known as hearsay testimony
and it would not be competent for any purpose."

A conspiracy indictment casts a wide net. In a furious exchange at
the side bar, Thompson emphasized: "This indictment doesn't charge
the offense of bribery; this indictment charges a conspiracy to bribe,
and a conspiracy to commit mail fraud."

Marje was finally permitted to tell what Miller allegedly said to her
about contributions, but she had to be reminded to speak "a little bit
louder." She, to no one's surprise, said the idea to give Kerner money
came from Miller who, she said, told her that if Kerner was elected
there was "a strong possibility" he would be made chairman of the
racing commission. All she asked in return, she said, was that Miller
not solicit other racetrack interests because certain ones "were owned
by hoodlums" and she didn't want Kerner to be under obligation to
them.

Just under obligation to her, presumably!

So she gave Miller $45,000 to give to Kerner's campaign.

Continuing, she said she was introduced to Isaacs by Miller and
that Miller later recommended Isaacs' law firm be retained to work on
her father's estate. No, there were no witnesses to these conversations
nor could she recall exactly where they took place. Yes, it was her
brother, the executor of the estate, who met with Isaacs and retained
him.

Skinner soon departed from his main line to explore the powers of
the Illinois Racing Board. Marje did nothing to underestimate them.
After listing, sir, all the various powers, she summed up, sir, by saying,
"It had what I would call life and death powers over all the racing
associations and all licensees."

Mrs. Everett discussed the decision to go into harness racing, the
changes and improvements at Washington Park costing $5.5 million to
implement that decision, and the fact that the gamble was dependent
on the whim of the Illinois Harness Racing Board. Had the harness-
racing tenants lost their racing dates, she explained "the improvements
that had been put in would, pardon the expression, go down the drain."

It was fairly routine stuff; the interesting action took place at the
bench out of the hearing of the jury. At one point, Connolly objected to

a line of testimony, but then relented after a fashion:

"Your Honor, we are going to be here a long time, but they can do it because I will tell you I will blast them right out of the water. . . . It will take me a half day to get rid of that, but I will get rid of it and pour blood all over their desk."

After that outburst Marje lost her voice and had to be reminded by the court to speak up.

"Surely," she said. "I am sorry, sir."

They arrived at the Kerner-Isaacs stock deal. Marje was permitted to testify about her alleged conversations with Miller — more one-on-one sessions. Miller, she said, suggested "it would be valuable and helpful" to make some stock available to the two officials. She had to be prompted, however, to add the oft-repeated lines that Miller thought it important to have a friend in the administration. She then was asked to read the note she had sent to Miller on November 8, 1962. In the second paragraph she *inserted* a verbal comma and *changed* a couple of words:

The handwritten memo stated:

> We did not issue the above as you had suggested that I hold this stock until we received further instructions from you.

As Marje read it:

"We did not issue the above as you had suggested, *but* I hold this stock until we *receive* further instructions from you." (Emphasis added.)

The result was to change the entire meaning. In the original, Miller suggested she *hold* the stock; in Marje's version it was Miller who suggested she *issue* it.

Why she would ignore one suggestion and then hold the stock to await other suggestions from Miller, she didn't explain. Nor was she asked to do so. Both sides were content in this instance to allow the bribe offer to originate with Miller.

With perfect timing, Skinner asked Marje why she agreed to make the stock available. In reply, she made something of a speech in which she repeated that Miller had "life and death power" over the racing industry, that she was deeply in debt, that it was imperative she continue to have harness-racing revenue or else she could go bankrupt overnight, and, finally, that she did not feel she "could gamble" by crossing Miller.

With those words ringing in the ears of the jurors, and the press, Skinner noted that it was "just about 4:45, Your Honor."

(It is yet again evidence of the one-sided treatment afforded Marje to note that nowhere in his questioning of Marje about the misquoted memo, did Skinner inquire into the actual reason for the 1962 stock offer: Marje's fears stemming from the misuse of Balmoral's restricted funds. If, in fact, the prosecutors ever discussed that important episode, they did not do it on the record.)

Judge Taylor took note of Skinner's hint about the time and adjourned court until 9:30 A.M. Before leaving, however, he informed the witness not to talk to any attorney other than her own.

"Yes, sir, Your Honor," said Marje cheerfully.

"I wish the lady would talk to me," said Connolly.

No one laughed.

The direct examination continued on the morning of January 10, 1973. Mrs. Everett, attired in a blue and white dress with a floral pattern, had to be reminded at the beginning to speak louder. The first questions disposed of Kerner's contention that it was Joe Knight who arranged the stock deal. Marje emphatically denied she had ever asked Knight to convey an offer. The knowledge that Knight was dying and couldn't testify one way or the other hung unspoken over the courtroom.

Skinner took up the formation of Chicago Harness Racing. Marje admitted she assisted in creating that tenant, and to talking to — whom else? — Miller about it. Asked when the conversation took place, she lunged like an anxious filly at the starting gate and was halfway down the track to the point where, sir, "Mr. Miller suggested that a block of stock of . . ."

Isaacs' attorney, Warren Wolfson, interrupted to point out the only question asked was, "When was that conversation?"

"Excuse me, sir," said Marje.

No one was present, of course, when Miller allegedly suggested a block of 50,000 shares of CHR stock be set aside "for distribution to persons whom he thought might be helpful." She assured him she had no holdings in the new company but would "assist in seeing that the

50,000 shares of stock were set aside."

No one asked how she could assist if she didn't own any stock. Turning to the 1964 campaign, she told of contributing $25,000 in five checks of $5,000 each — one for her two companies and three for her tenants — plus $15,000 in cash to the Kerner camp. Presumably the tenants' share came out of the S Account, although that private slush fund was not mentioned. Miller was mentioned, of course. The contributions "were transmitted, sir, to Mr. Miller, who had given me the instructions."

Some private conversations with Isaacs concerning racing matters were next discussed, and at last they came again to the 1966 meeting when Isaacs, with a little help from Knight and Miss McInturf, paid for the fifty shares of CTE stock. She told of getting the 2,000-share certificate from the bank, and replacing it with a 1,950-share certificate and two twenty-five-share certificates. *The latter, she said, she sent to her attorney, Judge Lynch, who, presumably, gave it to his partner, Judge Schaller, to deliver to Isaacs.* She remembered receiving two checks from Isaacs in payment.

Skinner drew an admission from his star witness that CTE's 1966 application for racing dates was inaccurate in that it didn't reflect her true holdings or list the parties holding stock through the use of nominees. He also brought up the 1966 promissory note which Wolfson, in his opening remarks, had admitted was backdated to 1962. Marje agreed her signature was on a letter accepting the note, and the letter was dated November 12, 1962. Obviously if the promissory note was backdated, Marje's signed letter acknowledging receipt of it in 1962 was also a fake. Yet she wasn't asked to explain the contradiction.

The government was satisfied to get her informed "opinion" that a share of CTE stock in 1966 would have been worth "in excess of $6,000." Obviously, then, if the stock deal had been a 1966 transaction, at $1,000 a share Kerner and Isaacs had indeed obtained bargains.

"The government passes the witness," said Skinner.

Long after the trial was over, Special Agent Stufflebeam admitted that Marje's version of events had been carefully tailored to conform with Miller's recollection and exhibits of important points. "If you have a witness who is wrong, and you know it, you show her and work to correct it," he explained. "What's wrong with that?"

From the viewpoint of someone who has been smeared by such lies, plenty is wrong, but for an ambitious politician who is already on record as Thompson was that the erring witness has performed a public service, such a reshaping is obviously necessary. Marje, having been fitted with a halo, could do no wrong.

Apparently Paul Connolly agreed. In keeping with his new theory, he was kinder to her than even Skinner had been. Indeed, Isaacs' attorney, Warren Wolfson, said the day and a half of cross-examination conducted by Connolly amounted to "making love" in the courtroom. Even the press commented: one writer reported that although Connolly had promised to discredit her, he "appeared to be enjoying her company."

Suspiciously, Connolly began by making an elaborate attempt to prove that he had never seen or spoken to the witness prior to that moment. Marje agreed repeatedly, but, somehow, she knew his name despite the lack of introductions. To his self-serving questions, she replied:

"That's right, Mr. Connolly."

Perhaps her attorney, Neil Papiano, had identified the defense attorney. Marje had been ordered to talk only to her own attorney, but no restrictions had been placed on whom her attorney discussed the case with. And Papiano was there, in the front row, anxiously listening to every word. There were a lot of words for Marje, enjoying her new freedom, tended to ramble and make speeches when asked any question. Connolly made no attempt to stop her, to demand she be more responsive. Sometimes her answers made no sense. Asked if she ever discussed the Kerner-Isaacs transaction with Stufflebeam, she replied:

"I don't recall, sir. When I did show the government my records at some time during the over-all period, I did not discuss handling it, to my knowledge, or to my recollection, I should say."

Asked how many sessions she had held with government lawyers since November 15, she stated:

"All right, sir. From November 15th, because of Thanksgiving, I don't think I met with them thereafter. I think I met with them — I know I met with them in November, but I don't think we met because of the holiday. I think in December, sir, that I met with them either two or three occasions. That is the best of my recollection, sir."

Asked how CTE wound up with stock in Balmoral, Marje began: "It was sort of strange, and part of this, sir, for a year or two I was out because of surgery, but it was part of the formative years. Lincoln Fields Race Track — excuse me, I may have to be a little lengthy — Lincoln Fields. . . "

And on she rambled for some four hundred words as she explained how her father got control of Balmoral without wanting it. As she said, "It was sort of strange." Unhappily, Connolly didn't ask about her surgery so that mystery remained.

Connolly moved on to what he called her father's attempt to up-grade racing by attracting "blue ribbon" type people. Marje took the bit in her teeth and babbled away for several minutes, dropping such names as Lawrence Armour, meat packer; Daniel Rice, grain broker; Modie Spiegel, mail order; Ralph Atlass, Westinghouse; Henry Strauss, Inland Steel; Mr. Cuneo, Cuneo Press; Fred Hooper, Derby winner; Travis Kerr, Oklahoma oil.

Why was it important to have such people?

"I think, sir, that while frequently the public don't know these persons personally, if they are identified with any industry, they are recognized as fine, high type of people in the community, and it gives the industry an identification of respectability and acceptance, sir."

What the blue-collar jury thought of all this, not even Connolly could know.

Leisurely he moved along, allowing Marje to make speech after speech on the various aspects of racing. She acknowledged that "Arlington actually was owned by hoodlums initially," and she discussed society figures "like Mr. Whitney and Mr. Baruch and Mr. Knight" who were members of the track's Post and Paddock Club. When she expounded at length on the seating capacity of the various tracks, the judge at last interrupted.

"The jury wants a recess, Mr. Connolly," he said.

Returning, Connolly led the witness into a long and confusing — even she admitted it was confusing — discussion of racing dates. All of which was perhaps a prologue to an admission that during the Kerner years the dates remained "relatively the same." He then wanted to know if the dates changed when Ogilvie became governor. Marje said they did, "dramatically." What she didn't say was that the changes greatly *favored* CTE under the Republicans.

The speeches continued with the witness permitted to ramble on for minutes at a time about escalators at the tracks, emergency telephones in every barn, bus service from enlarged parking areas, dining rooms, closed circuit television, and beds and electric heat in living accommodations for the hired help along the backstretch. Her father wanted to "provide for the little man and the less fortunate." All of which was supposed to show that Arlington was designed to produce more revenue for the state than could any other track in Illinois. Not mentioned, of course, was the fire in 1970 at Washington Park in which a stablehand as well as every thoroughbred in one stable burned to death. The investigation revealed that not a single fire extinguisher was operable and the fire wagon didn't work. So much for the less fortunate.

Still, harness racing at night was promoted with the working man in mind, Marje testified, and "the majority of the people are the working persons." So she got some more fine people such as Charles Wacker of Wacker Drive and Harold Anderson of Publisher's Syndicate to buy stock and, incidentally, serve as nominees for Illinois politicians. Control was in a voting trust so that control "was lodged not in any particular stockholder." Not mentioned was the fact that the trustees consisted of her husband, her attorney, and the distinguished Mr. Wacker.

Connolly, at length, asked why Chicago Harness Racing was created, and got this reply:

"Well, we had had, as I said, a very successful meeting, and so far as most segments, except that the time originally the initial shareholders, and as we landlords did not — we deferred the rent the first year so that the new shareholders did not have to pay the rent, which they wouldn't have had, actually, but it had been very successful. It had handled far more than had been handled in the area, and we now had a facility that we called all-weather. It was the only racetrack in the area at that time that could handle winter racing dates, dates like the weather we have today, because it was enclosed. I think we even advertised that it's as comfortable as being in your own home. There was no other facility in the area, sir, that could provide that, and we were desirous, obviously, of putting a lot of money in, of trying to utilize it to the maximum, and to derive as much rental as we could, sir. That's what conceived the idea. . . ."

Neither the judge nor Thompson protested such excursions, and the jurors sat helplessly. Otto Kerner kept his handsome face impassive. If he wondered how such a cross-examination was going to help him, he made no sign.

They came at last to the formation of the Illinois Race Track Police. Marje stated that Chairman Miller simply ordered the racetrack operators to finance it. She ignored the existence of an executive order by Governor Kerner on August 26, 1963, directing Miller to form a police bureau and stating: "All expense will be shared on a pro rata basis by all the racing associations."

Connolly brought up the subject of racing legislation. Mrs. Everett admitted that certain bills were helpful. Blandly, the defense attorney asked a key question:

"Did you pay any money in the form of bribes, or make any gratuities available to induce any vote on that bill?"

"*That,*" sidestepped Marje, "*was a matter that the attorneys handled for our company, sir.*"

A long, involved discussion of technical matters followed as Marje provided the jurors with a broad education on the subject of taxation, "breakage," and the like. Things livened up a bit, however, when Connolly asked her opinion of Kerner's administration insofar as racing was concerned. Skinner objected, and Judge Taylor upheld it. "You are going too far, Mr. Connolly," he said.

"Your Honor," said Connolly, "don't get mad."

"I am not a bit mad," roared the little judge, pounding the bench with his gavel, "not a bit mad. I'm asking you to stay on point. That's the only thing I'm doing. I'm not mad."

"All you have to do is say that," said Connolly.

"I have said it now," replied the judge. "Go on to something else."

The exchange, at least, woke up the jury.

Connolly obediently turned briefly to campaign contributions, eliciting from Marje the admission she was but following in her father's steps when she gave Kerner $80,000 over five years. She also made substantial contributions to others, she said, but Connolly promised not to ask her to name them. Instead, he turned to Miller and began to develop the theory that Miller was the evil mastermind. Miller talked her out of accepting partners, persuaded her to "go it alone," relying on him, of course, all the way. He helped her get loans. Indeed, Connolly showed her a letter from a bank showing that Miller endorsed her note. She had forgotten it, she said.

Miller was also credited with persuading her to hire Zoline to manage her affairs and form CTE. Zoline had "ability," she acknowledged, and she gave him stock, but eventually she had to buy him out.

"A bitter loss," she called it, but she didn't explain why the misuse of Balmoral funds made it necessary.

Again the complicated events that led to Miller buying Balmoral were rehashed. Connolly moved along steadily, pausing only to get the government's witness a cup of water. His solicitude continued when, after a little more than an hour, he suggested the witness needed a recess. Marje admitted that both her father and she wanted to be rid of Balmoral if the right group came along. Late in the afternoon, Connolly established to his satisfaction that there were 108,000 shares of Balmoral stock outstanding, and to get control of the company one would have to have "54,000-plus" shares. Marje agreed that CTE didn't own 54,000 shares, and that anyone getting control would have to have her 10,000 shares in addition to whatever CTE possessed.

Adjournment interrupted the detailed discussion, but Connolly picked up next day where he had stopped. And soon his goal came into view — the 10,000 shares of Balmoral stock at $30 a share for which Kerner-Isaacs swapped their fifty shares of CTE stock to obtain, and then sold to Miller.

It was devious, it was complex, but, if Connolly was right, then perhaps it proved that the original stock offer to Kerner-Isaacs was but a preliminary step in Miller's alleged master plan to gain control of Balmoral. For, according to Marje, those 10,000 shares did represent control and enabled Miller to push out Webb Everett and George Schaller.

Unfortunately for the theory, Connolly had his facts wrong. And he proved it so himself by introducing a February 11, 1967, letter to Marje from Rudolph Palluck of the First National Bank of Chicago. Among other things, Palluck wrote that "Illinois Racing Enterprises will control approximately 65 to 70 per cent of Balmoral, as it will own in excess of 60,000 shares, and there will be approximately 90,000 shares issued and outstanding."

Only the day before, Connolly had proposed his theory on the basis of 108,000 shares outstanding. What he failed to say was that the 18,000-share difference represented treasury stock which, according to Illinois law, had *no voting power* and could not be used to control a company. Therefore, it was 45,000-plus that was needed for control, not "54,000-plus," as he stated, and the 10,000 shares that went from Marje to Kerner-Isaacs to Miller were superfluous.

And so was Connolly's theory.

There is irony in the fact, however, that none of the principals in the alleged search for truth that the trial was assumed to be had any interest in clarifying the situation. As far as the government was concerned, the question of who masterminded the Kerner-Isaacs stock deal was immaterial. If Connolly wanted to blame Miller, so what? Certainly, Marje was happy to go along, assuming she knew what Connolly was trying to do. Miller, of course, wasn't even in the courtroom and had to depend on the newspapers for his knowledge of developments. The press, of course, was concentrating on what Connolly was saying, not on the things he neglected to say.

Apparently the only man in the room who was upset by the turn of events was Neil Papiano, Marje's lawyer from Los Angeles. From his seat in the front row, he had been discreetly flashing signals to his client from time to time. Now he became so agitated that Special Agent Witkowski moved his chair to the other side of the table and sat with his back to Marje staring at the lawyer. Papiano, aware of his gaze, became visibly angry. Later, during a recess, he talked to Stufflebeam about it in the hall. He was trying to help, he said, because Marje had not been given a permanent license in California and a bad image at the trial "could cost her a lot of money."

Connolly, meanwhile, was moving on toward the inevitable — the split between Marje and Miller. Marje obviously enjoyed telling the sad tale, and she went into great detail about the various events that changed her image of her father's friend in her eyes. He began writing "the most insulting letters and the harshest letters that I can ever recall receiving, lengthy, insulting, and abusive." He threatened suits, but, instead, "he just didn't pay the money, Mr. Connolly, in some cases substantially, several hundred thousand dollars." This referred to her many improper charges and of course to the S Account.

Connolly got her to admit that there came a time when she stopped speaking to Miller. As she put it, "I don't have any respect for the man. I don't trust the man. I think I have grounds for those evaluations."

Connolly then asked the big question: "And you think, do you not, and you have thought for several years, that Mr. Miller schemed and conspired to cheat you out of Chicago Harness Racing and Balmoral?"

Skinner objected. The attorneys went up to talk to the judge. Said Skinner:

"Judge, he has established and gotten the testimony from the witness and we have refrained from objecting to the form of the questions, to putting words in the witness' mouth almost entirely. *This is now his entire theory*, and he is now asking her in summarizing what he thinks her testimony is, and taking away from the jury and putting his own words in and asking for a yes or no." (Emphasis added.)

The judge sustained the objection, but ruled Connolly could ask her "if she thought that." Connolly did, and Marje replied: "Yes, sir."

Connolly, having made his point, shifted subjects. Turning to the famous memo of November 8, 1962, he read the letter, inserting the invisible comma but leaving the word *received* alone. As recorded by the court reporter, the sentence became:

> We did not issue the above as you had suggested, that I hold this stock until I received further instructions from you.

Connolly wanted to make sure he understood.

"Do I understand that *your commitment was to hold this stock*, and you would let Mr. Miller handle it in the way he wanted to do it?" he asked. (Emphasis added.)

"That is correct, sir," said Marje.

They came to a discussion of Mrs. Everett's 1966 tax return, and Connolly requested a conference at the bench. He told the judge that the government had given him a copy and "ordinarily I would introduce it but Mr. Papiano, Mrs. Everett's personal attorney, has said that there are matters in here that don't pertain to the case. He would appreciate it if I not do that. I have no reason to invade her privacy."

Skinner had no objections to questions about specific items on the return, so the privacy of Marje was maintained. The episode is significant largely in that it confirms Connolly had been talking to Marje's attorney even if, according to Connolly, he had not been talking to her.

It developed that the fifty shares of stock Marje allegedly had been holding for Kerner-Isaacs at $1,000 a share was valued by her for tax purposes at the price she had paid off her ex-attorney, Zoline: $3,200 a share. Consequently she had claimed a $110,000 capital loss on her 1966 tax return. The government — according to Skinner's prosecution memo of 1971 — had denied the claim, but in 1973 Marje testified the matter had not yet been resolved.

Connolly continued to skip about. In passing he got Marje to say she was not represented by counsel when she signed her affidavit in Scottsdale or later when she appeared before the Grand Jury, although Stufflebeam had consulted her lawyer in Phoenix months before.

Q. Did they tell you you needed one?

A. I didn't feel I had anything to hide, sir. I just came and told, as I have tried to here, testify to the best of my ability, sir, as to the facts.

The implication was clear — Marje had been given "left-handed immunity" in return for her cooperation. Connolly did not push the point, however, but turned to some inconsistencies in her previous statements and Grand Jury testimony. Marje admitted she had been confused about the facts in several instances, but had since refreshed her memory. And so, still sparring with padded gloves, they came down to the final question:

"Mrs. Everett, in your transactions with respect to the fifty shares of stock of CTE, did you intend to bribe Otto Kerner?"

In his opening statement, Connolly had assured the jury she would not say she intended to bribe Kerner. He was right; she didn't. Deviating from her affidavit and her Grand Jury testimony, Mrs. Everett answered:

"When I made this stock available to Mr. Miller — I have tried to testify to the court the tremendous pressure, the point of no return, the problem I had and the impossibility I felt in turning down Mr. Miller as chairman."

This was an answer? Apparently Connolly understood it to be one. He asked: "So you gave it because of the pressure Mr. Miller imposed upon you?"

Marje nodded. "When he told me that he wanted to deliver this stock to Theodore Isaacs and Otto Kerner — and he had the type of power, and as I have tried to testify to the best of my emotions and feelings — I felt I had been extorted."

"Thank you," said Paul Connolly.

The character assassination of Miller complete, without further ado, court recessed until after lunch. The afternoon papers had their headlines.

Warren Wolfson, Isaacs' attorney, took the center stage when the afternoon session began. Apparently he had been aware of the Witkowski-Papiano byplay earlier, so immediately he asked Marje if her attorney had coached her about how to handle herself on the stand. Marje was bewildered at the sudden change of pace and asked for clarification. Skinner objected. Judge Taylor said he had never heard "that kind of question before so I cannot intelligently rule."

"Well," said Wolfson, "I've never heard this kind of witness."

With that he was off, barking sharp, incisive questions at the witness who replied with rambling, evasive answers. Wolfson pictured her as a strong executive in full command of her business, not as a frail woman being bossed by Miller and by her attorneys. When she said that Miller "actually took me down to Springfield" to meet Paul Powell, he inquired:

"When you say he 'took you,' Mrs. Everett, you do not mean he took you forcibly, do you?"

"No," she replied, "I went with Mr. Miller, if that's the way. . . ."

"You went because you wanted to go, did you not, Mrs. Everett?"

"I went because I thought it advisable to go," she replied sullenly.

It took a lot of repetition but finally Wolfson made the witness admit that the government never warned her she might be in danger by testifying.

Turning to her statement that she felt Miller had extorted her as far back as 1960, Wolfson asked if she had ever reported the alleged extortion to a law-enforcement agency.

"Obviously not, sir," said Marje.

"You did not feel that you had done anything improper, did you, Mrs. Everett?"

"I didn't think I had done anything improper, no."

Suddenly, in response to a new line of questioning, Marje admitted that she liked Ted Isaacs. In fact, "he used to come over and watch football games with his family. I have never been in his home, but we were certainly good friends." Nevertheless, she didn't recall ever discussing the stock deal with him.

They came to the commitment, and under sharp questioning Mrs. Everett's inability to recall when the deal was made became embarrassing. She tried to bluff her way out:

"There has been reason for me to believe that I was mistaken in my original statement at that time, and why should I continue to make a misstatement if I feel it is a misstatement?"

Then she added, "I did not lie intentionally."

It was Connolly who came to Marje's rescue time after time, making objection after objection to Wolfson's questions. It was as if Marje had by some alchemy become *his* witness instead of the government's. And it finally got him into trouble.

"Your Honor, may I come to the bench?"

"Well, if you think it is necessary," said the judge.

"Well, I do," replied Connolly. "I wouldn't say it if I didn't."

At the bench, Judge Taylor waxed wroth: "I don't want to hear any more comments like that. You have been going over from time to time, 'Judge, are you mad,' and things like that. Now, that has no place in this record, and I am not mad, and you shouldn't talk back to the court like that. . . ."

"I don't think it was improper, Your Honor," said Connolly.

"Well, I do," retorted the judge.

Connolly then made an amazing admission. "The witness," he said, "has a tendency to ramble in her answers. She does not direct her attention to the question. She has a tendency to talk too much."

Even Thompson was startled. "For a day and a half that was [the kind of] answer he wanted. Now he doesn't want it and he objects."

The upshot of this crisis was a request by Judge Taylor that Marje "do your best to answer the question without going into peripheral matters." Then he added hastily, "This isn't a criticism by the court of you."

"I apologize for rambling, sir," said Marje bravely.

They took a recess to cool off — and to straighten out defense signals. Connolly and Kerner went first to Isaacs in the hall, and then the three of them cornered Wolfson. Nearby, watching, was Papiano, Marje's attorney. Connolly wasted no time: "Hey, look," he said, "don't be so rough on Marje. I worked with her for two days. You're ruining everything."

Wolfson resisted, but when his own client joined in, he decided he had no choice. Years later, on looking back, he commented that "I acceded, and I'll regret it to my dying day."

Wolfson, in the course of the trial, became convinced that Connolly had indeed made a deal with Papiano, and the squeeze play in the hall was only one of the reasons. He "made love" to Marje on the stand, Wolfson said, and "he had information that he could only have obtained from Papiano."

In the younger lawyer's opinion, "Connolly misconstrued the case and fell in love with his own theory." The theory, of course, was that Miller had a complicated scheme to get control of Balmoral. "If you spend your time making love during cross-examination the way Connolly did," added Wolfson, "it supports the government's case."

The jurors' verdict would seem to confirm that analysis.

They returned to the courtroom and Wolfson let Marje get off the ropes and backpedal. Late in the afternoon, Connolly interrupted his examination.

"Let me get some water," Connolly volunteered. "I think the lady is going to choke over here."

He rushed about solicitously, demonstrating by his concern that he was still Marje's friend and perhaps indicating to the jury that she had not hurt his client's case. Judge Taylor, who had said nothing during earlier displays of waterboyishness by Connolly, finally took exception:

"These marshals are going to furnish the water for the witnesses in the future, gentlemen," he announced. "It looks better."

The sport of kings—Arlington Park, 1975 *(Chicago Tribune photo)*.

Darkness falls on Washington Park *(Chicago Tribune photo)*.

Balmoral Park before . . .

. . . and after.

Mrs. Vera Lindheimer, 1958.
(Chicago Tribune photo)

Ben Lindheimer, 1953.
(Chicago Tribune photo)

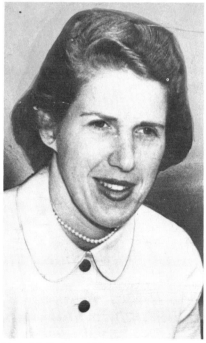

Sidney Korshak, Ben Lindheimer's "labor
consultant." *(Chicago Tribune photo)*

Marje Lindheimer, 1953.
(Chicago Tribune photo)

The Racing Board meets: from left, Ernest S. Marsh, William S. Miller, Donald McKellar, and Schaefer O'Neill (representing Cahokia Downs).

Power moves from left to right as Illinois Racing Board Chairman Paul Serdar prepares to step down and William S. Miller becomes boss at a November 16, 1960 session. *(Chicago Tribune photo).*

William S. Miller beams on his wife, Catherine, at the 1961 running of the Washington Park Futurity. *(Chicago Tribune photo)*

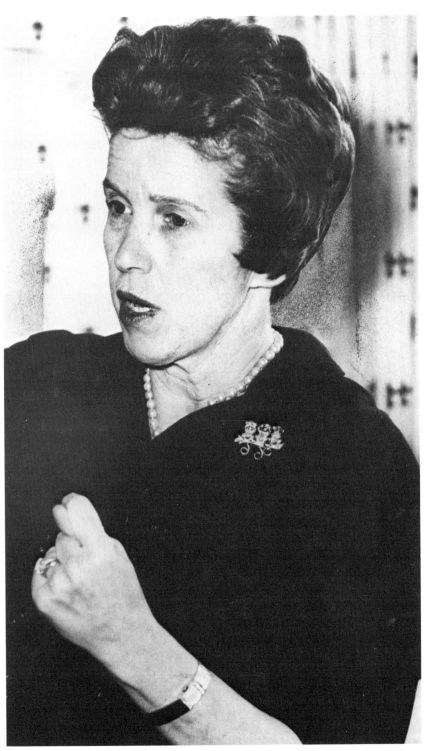

Mrs. Marje Everett—ready to fight in 1965. *(Chicago Tribune photo)*

The Big Deal, 1969: Gulf and Western buys out Marje Everett. From left, Webb Everett, David Judelson, (President of G&W), Marje, Philip J. Levin, and Edgar Janotta. *(Chicago Tribune photo)*.

Anton "the Boss" Cermak, builder of the Chicago Machine and father-in-law of Otto Kerner, Jr. *(Chicago Tribune photo)*

Jake Arvey—successor to Cermak. *(Chicago Tribune photo)*

Mayor Edward J. Kelly—successor to Boss Cermak. *(Chicago Tribune photo)*

Happy 44th Birthday to an Ally of Boss Cermak. From left, State Attorney L.H. Geiman, Baliff Charles Timlin, Clerk Matt Vogel, and Circuit Judge Otto Kerner, Sr. It is February 22, 1928, and Kerner is on his way with a little help from his friends. *(Chicago Tribune photo)*

Henry Horner on the eve of his 1932 election as Governor of Illinois. His subsequent veto of a bill legalizing handbooks brought down the wrath of the Mob and the Machine. *(Chicago Tribune photo)*

The Last Hurrah of William "Big Bill" Thompson as he attempts a comeback in 1939. The old magic had faded, corruption had become organized. *(Chicago Tribune photo)*

This headline was right. Mayor Martin Kennelly savors another victory of the Machine Cermak built as he rides to City Hall in 1951. *(Chicago Tribune photo)*

THE BOSS—Richard J. Daley. *(Chicago Tribune photo)*

All the way with Adlai in 1952: Governor Stevenson sets a precedent by eying the White House from Springfield. *(Chicago Tribune photo)*

The rewards of clout are obvious as William J. Lynch, former law partner of Mayor Daley and counsel to Marje Everett, takes the oath as a federal judge on April 4, 1966. At left is Chief Judge William Campbell. *(Chicago Tribune photo)*

Paul Powell, Politician Personified *(Chicago Tribune photo)*.

Governor and Mrs. Otto Kerner, Jr., leave Chicago for the 1961 Inauguration of President-elect Kennedy. After Camelot came Project CRIMP. *(Chicago Tribune photo)*

Report on Project CRIMP: At Key Biscayne session in 1970, Attorney General John Mitchell briefs his colleagues. From left: President Nixon, Donald Rumsfeld, Mitchell, John Ehrlichman, Charles Colson, Bryce Harlow, Robert Haldeman, Robert Finch with back to camera. *(Official White House photo)*

Otto Kerner, Jr., arrives at prison in a Mercedes.

Home from prison comes Otto Kerner, Jr., flanked by his son, Tony, and daughter, Helena. It is March 7, 1975 and he has fourteen months to live. *(Chicago Tribune photo)*

Theodore Isaacs arrives at prison in handcuffs.

The VICTORS: James "Big Jim" Thompson, left, and his assistant, Samuel Skinner, hold press conference after winning guilty verdict in the Kerner-Isaacs case. Both would go on to higher office. *(Chicago Tribune photo)*

James "Big Jim" Thompson campaigning for Governor in 1976. *(Chicago Tribune photo).*

My pocket was picked in the Vatican, but I certainly didn't believe that His Holiness had anything to do with it.

WILLIAM S. MILLER, 1973
U.S. v. Isaacs, et al.

10

The Mastermind

Friday, January 12, 1973, promised to be Dullsville, reporters told themselves. After Marje's charges of extortion, only the testimony of the man now branded as the Villain-in-Chief, William S. Miller, would restore a sense of drama. Witnesses for the day were routine, there primarily to introduce records.

Who wanted to write about Richard Roggeveen anyway? More to the point, who wanted to read about him? Roggeveen, one of five witnesses heard during the morning session, identified himself as treasurer of the corporation that succeeded Chicago Thoroughbred Enterprises, part of the new team installed by Levin of Gulf & Western. Obviously he had little personal knowledge of Mrs. Everett's business affairs, but he was custodian of records covering her long reign. Those reporters who daydreamed about sensations to come as he testified missed some intriguing information and an opportunity to get a really big story.

Of course, it was all very confusing.

Under direct examination, Roggeveen testified that CTE stock certificate Number 106 for 2,000 shares was issued on October 8, 1962, replacing Certificates 4, 7, and 8. In turn Certificate 106 was replaced by Certificates 158 for 1,950 shares, 159 and 160 for twenty-five shares each. The change was made on February 8, 1966.

All of which was apparently connected with the Isaacs-Kerner stock deal, and was routine enough. The witness also produced what he called the books of the company, financial records, and they were introduced. Whereupon the government was through with the wit-

168

ness. Kerner's attorneys worried, however, and requested a conference at the bench to find out what the books contained. Assistant U. S. Attorney Kadison explained that the books apparently contradicted the stock certificates. Instead of totaling 2,000 shares, the records indicate the total of those certificates was only fifteen shares, he explained.

"There are some entries that indicate that there is another common-stock book," said Kadison.

Two sets of CTE books? Astonishing. Yet the government had not intended to make the point to the jury — it was but playing safe by introducing as evidence only the books that contained the damning data.

Skinner emphasized the point. A common-stock book was missing, and if the defense wanted to explore the subject it could do so. Judge Taylor interjected: "He [Skinner] doesn't think you will hear of it in argument." Wolfson asked, "The case doesn't turn on that?" "No," said Thompson.

Nevertheless, Thomas Patton, one of Connolly's assistants, explored the subject for the jury. He got the witness to admit that Certificates 4, 7, and 8 totaled only fifteen shares, but were somehow transformed into Certificate 106 for 2,000 shares. Roggeveen couldn't explain how the miracle was performed.

There was also an intriguing notation on the back of Certificate 1. Issued to Marje Everett on February 1, 1961, and worth 4,900 shares, the certificate was stamped:

"The shares of stock represented by this certificate are subject to a certain agreement dated January 2, 1962, between Chicago Thoroughbred Enterprises, Inc., et al."

Was this then the source of the stock sold to Kerner and Isaacs? Roggeveen didn't know what the statement meant, and, of course, Marje had not been asked. So the mystery remained. On redirect the witness was asked if he knew whether or not there was another stock book. He replied he did not know, and, hastily, both sides dropped the can of worms. Mrs. Everett's secrets remained unplumbed. Did she have two sets of books? Who in this strange trial really gave a damn? Besides, it was time for the lunch break.

There was a stirring of interest after the noon recess when Circuit Judge George J. Schaller was called to testify. His importance, however, lay not so much in the fact that he formerly represented Mrs. Everett as in the fact that he had formerly been a law partner of Mayor

Daley. Together with another partner, now Federal Judge William J. Lynch, he possessed that magic quality known to Chicago citizens as *clout*. One reason it was so wondrous, of course, was the reluctance of those in positions of power to take public notice of it. If you had it there was no need to advertise.

Schaller was polite, deferential in fact, on the witness stand. Gone was the ambiguity, the innuendo directed at Miller, that had characterized his Grand Jury testimony. In open court with reporters present, he selected the role of impartial judge in preference to that of Marje's attorney. That he represented her personally as well as her corporations for ten years prior to his appointment to the bench, he quickly acknowledged.

On October 3, 1966, Schaller said, he was asked by Joe Knight to serve as nominee for the owners of 28,000 shares of Chicago Harness Racing stock. He immediately called Mrs. Everett to find out what she wanted done. "She said: 'I wish you would do so,' and I did." In February, 1967, Knight told him CHR was going to declare a dividend and he wanted it to go to "the true owners." "He named Isaacs and Judge Kerner." Again, Schaller consulted with his client, Mrs. Everett, and got her approval.

Later, on instructions from Knight, Schaller sold the CHR stock for $2 a share. Abruptly, his testimony faltered. The letter of instructions from Knight had been prepared — prepared by Schaller — *after* the sale had taken place. Asked why, Schaller was saved from explaining by a Connolly objection. At the bench Connolly said he understood Schaller once said he kept certain papers "because he knew people were going to get in trouble." The prosecutors were accommodating. Assistant U. S. Attorney McGowan stated for the record, "I think I will just strike that last question, Your Honor, and avoid any controversy."

"All right, sir," said Judge Taylor.

Schaller said he sold the stock as ordered, deposited the money in his personal checking account, and wrote two checks to Knight for the amount. The checks were sent, however, to Isaacs and later endorsed by Knight. That Schaller in his capacity of Mrs. Everett's attorney personally contributed to the concealment of the Kerner-Isaacs stock ownership apparently didn't surprise or shock anyone. Nor was any effort made to credit the maneuver to Miller.

They turned next to the meeting in Miller's office when the CTE stock was paid for by Isaacs with money borrowed from Knight who, in turn, had borrowed from Miss McInturf. His instructions to attend the August 10, 1966, meeting came from Mrs. Everett, Schaller said, and no one else. He carried with him the two stock certificates, delivered to him the night before by Sidney Karras, comptroller of CTE. He turned over the certificates to Isaacs upon receiving Isaacs' checks for $50,000 in principal and $8,958 in interest. The checks he sent to Mrs. Everett.

Schaller testified he then signed the promissory note dated November 12, 1962, as "paid in full." This, of course, was the note that everyone admitted had been written in 1966 and backdated. Accompanying it was a letter dated November 12, 1962. Schaller was asked if he recognized it.

"I believe this is the language I dictated," he replied.

Asked when he dictated it, Schaller wasn't sure. Wolfson and Connolly objected to the next question: "Would it or would it not have been after August 10, 1966?"

Judge Taylor then made this astounding ruling: "Judge," he said, addressing Schaller, "do you know about it? You are the judge as to whether you can properly and legally answer the question. If you can, I will let you answer it. If you say you can't, then it will not have an answer."

Schaller replied, "The contents of this letter was dictated by me some time after the meeting of August, '66."

And it was done, he said, after a conversation with Mrs. Everett, who asked him to dictate it to her secretary, Mary Carroll. So much for that backdated bit of evidence.

Moving on rather rapidly, the government attorney asked about a memo from Mrs. Everett to Schaller. A paragraph was read into the record:

> The Balmoral surplus is to be used to buy up all available stock in Washington Park Trotting Association, Inc. and Chicago Harness Racing, Inc., so as to secure ultimate control of both companies. GJS is acting as agent for the company for this purpose, and has $150,000 at his disposal.

Schaller, the GJS of the memo, proceeded to use Balmoral funds to buy control of the harness companies. Mrs. Everett's authority for such action was, according to the attorney, that "she was executive director. She ran all the racing companies."

That she ran the racing companies there is no doubt, but the record shows she was *not* executive director or an officer of any kind of Balmoral. Yet Schaller's error wasn't challenged in the courtroom — to do so would have been to cast doubt on Star Witness Everett, and neither side wanted to do that. While buying up stock from the businessmen who had fronted, perhaps unknowingly, for various legislators, Schaller also sold stock he and his partner, Lynch, owned. Each received $2 a share for 30,000 shares.

Dullsville, indeed. Under certain circumstances, it might have been solid stuff, but Judge Schaller was on the side of Marje Everett, of the federal prosecutors, and, of the Daley Machine. Had Nixon and Daley made a deal? A deal that would sacrifice Kerner but save the mayor's friends? No matter — the implications of *clout* were best not discussed in the courtroom or in the press.

When Judge Taylor decided that because of Friday afternoon traffic problems it was necessary to quit early, there was a general sense of relief. Next week Miller would testify, and he would be fair game for everyone.

Schaller wasn't excused, however, and on Monday he returned to admit he had acted as nominee for politicians ranging from Arthur Bidwill to Paul Powell. Under respectful but sharp cross-examination by Isaacs' attorney, Warren Wolfson, he also made a startling admission:

"I would say, Mr. Wolfson, that I very likely on five or more occasions have given statements inconsistent with my present testimony which is based on the documents I now have. At that time, I don't know if any documents were in front of me." (They were in Miller's files at the time.)

Thus Judge Schaller joined with his former client, Mrs. Everett, in admitting that statements which earlier had brought the indictment of five people were often in error. Several of those erroneous statements put responsibility for actions taken on Miller. In becoming a federal witness, Miller, at least, had been successful in setting the record straight on some key points. Ironically, however, Connolly remained as loyal as ever to the theory of Miller the Mastermind. Only Wolfson, neglected by the press and patronized by Kerner and Thompson, continued to dig for the facts. At one point he asked Judge Schaller, "So it is possible even to be positive and be wrong at the same time?"

"Absolutely," said the judge.

No one even sniggered.

(If Judge Schaller got off lightly, his former law partner, Federal Circuit Judge Lynch, was treated even more gingerly when three weeks later he appeared as a *defense* witness. Connolly asked him only three questions, each an attempt to transfer responsibility for the Kerner-Isaacs stock deal from Mrs. Everett to Miller. The judge couldn't remember the alleged conversations. On cross-examination, U. S. Attorney Thompson was equally kind. He allowed Lynch to deny that Miller "in effect" ran Marje's corporation or that Marje was ever "in fear" of Miller. In fact, he said, the Miller-Everett relationship as he observed it was "very confidential, cordial, friendly."

Thompson didn't ask Lynch about Marje's statement that the bribing of legislators "was a matter that the attorneys handled for our company, sir." Nor was the subject of *clout* discussed. As with Schaller, the treatment accorded Judge Lynch was deferential in the extreme.)

Meanwhile, the bored reporters waited for Miller and listened for yet another day to big-name businessmen who had been involved for better or worse with Mrs. Everett's racing enterprises. Ralph Atlass described his career as a nominee at the request of Marje. "I agreed to be so used," he said, "even though she never mentioned any names and did not even tell me how much stock she wanted me to hold as nominee." He was president of Washington Park Jockey Club, he said, but WPJC was just a name for a racing meet and the title was strictly honorary. Surely, WPJC's applications for racing dates bore his signature, but he did not examine them in detail.

Harold H. Anderson had even less to say. He didn't think there was anything wrong in holding stock as a nominee for others, and, in fact, he could see practical reasons for the practice. Made it easier to sell or transfer stock for one thing. He was "quite friendly" with Mrs. Everett. "She would ask me to do various things in connection with the racing industry," and he was happy to oblige.

Albert Bell, former secretary of CHR, and Modie J. Spiegel were not so accommodating, and their testimony supported each other's version of events. It was Mrs. Everett, they said, who asked Spiegel to be president of Chicago Harness Racing, and who created the voting trust. Later it was Mrs. Everett who demanded the trust be dissolved.

When Spiegel didn't agree, he received a visit from Attorney Lynch. Things became "a bit unpleasant," and Lynch made some veiled threats that harm might come to Spiegel's mail-order business.

How could Spiegel's business be harmed?

"Well," said Bell, "the city had a lot of power over a corporation in this community."

The subject was not pursued.

Spiegel and Bell finally sold their stock, but only after obtaining an inflated price for it. Similarly did socialite Charles Wacker sell out at a huge profit. There was, after all, some advantage in being wealthy, possessing a famous name, and being willing to raise hell if necessary.

At last! The crowds were back, the reporters eager. Word passed that "Giant Jim" Thompson would personally examine the witness, proof if needed of the importance of Miller's testimony. The two men exchanged smiles as Miller, erect and vigorous despite the gray in his dark hair, made the long walk down the aisle to the witness chair. One observer wrote, "He looks like Colonel Sanders with no goatee."

The ex-ice-cream-freezer manufacturer settled comfortably, aware perhaps that days would pass before he and the chair finally parted company. The former high school and college debater adopted a deliberate style, thinking before speaking, choosing carefully the word that best expressed his meaning. To some in the audience this concern smacked of arrogance, of an overwhelming vanity ill-suited to a man who had "flipped" to escape prosecution. Miller was unaware of this reaction. As he saw it he had from the beginning offered to tell the truth, no more, no less. Eventually the government had accepted his offer and privately, at least, admitted he should never have been indicted. The trial, he believed sincerely, would clear the air and, by so doing, restore his own tarnished reputation. So thought William S. Miller, but William S. Miller was naive.

Thompson began slowly, creating some mild amusement when the witness listed "cow pokes" among the articles his J. E. Porter Company manufactured.

"What is a cow poke?"

"A cow poke is an instrument that one places around a cow's neck and has a piercing instrument in a small pole that pricks the cow when it attempts to eat. In other words, the object of the instrument is to restrain the cow from eating too much."

"Can you use that on human beings?" asked Judge Taylor, the man from the hills of Tennessee.

Moving on, Thompson asked Miller his net worth in 1965 when he sold his company. "It was less than four million and perhaps slightly more than three," said the native of Indiana.

Turning to politics, Miller told about his breakfast meeting with Mayor Daley and candidate Kerner at which time he agreed to under-write Kerner's preliminary campaign expenses. The arrangement was worked out in detail with Isaacs, Kerner's manager, he added.

Having helped Kerner financially, Miller then proceeded to back Marje's efforts to buy control of Washington and Arlington Parks from her mother and brother. He took her, he said, to the City National Bank and Trust Company where he introduced her to the senior vice president, a man "by interesting coincidence" named William Miller.

They broke for lunch at that point and when they resumed the courtroom was graced by the presence of the huge fireproof filing cabinet in which Miller and Miss McInturf had stored all documents relevant to the case. Connally had demanded it be produced so it stood there, looking somehow sinister and forbidding.

Thompson ignored it and pushed ahead with the development of the Miller-Everett relationship. Miller explained that Marje was tak-ing too much of his time so he recommended she retain Zoline to manage her affairs. It was Zoline who ultimately arranged the loan with the First National Bank of Chicago that enabled Marje to get control of her father's companies. Meantime, Miller said, he had cosigned a note for Marje at City National Bank.

The next testimony concerned Marje's decision to donate $45,000 to Kerner's 1960 campaign. Later, after Kerner's victory, Miller was asked by Isaacs to recommend two new members of the Illinois Racing Board. He said Ernest Marsh was one he suggested, and Crowdus Baker, president of Sears, was another. Baker, he continued, declined the post after being told by his superior, Charles Kellstadt, chairman of the board of the huge firm, "that he would prefer that Mr. Baker refrain from being associated in an official capacity in racing for fear that the stockholders might think he was spending too much of Sears' time on racing matters." Subsequently, Miller explained, Donald McKellar was named to the board. Miller's own appointment as chairman was delayed, he said, when Serdar refused to resign, but pressure was applied and the problem soon solved.

The introduction of Marje to the harness-racing industry was related by Miller as the questioning continued. When asked, he explained that to finance her debt Mrs. Everett needed additional sources of revenue. Even bowling was considered, he said. Apparently becoming suddenly aware that his assistance to Ben Lindheimer's adopted daughter might be questioned, Miller interjected this explanation: "I should like to emphasize I am not acting in the role of a patriarch. I am acting in the role of trying to help the daughter of a man who was a friend of mine."

The meeting in Springfield with Paul Powell in the hotel suite once occupied by Orville Hodge was described, but when Miller was asked to relate the subject matter of the conversations at that meeting, Connolly objected. A long session out of the jurors' hearing was held at the bench. Judge Taylor commented about the witness:

"He is the most detailed man I have heard in a long, long time . . . he is lecturing to us. A person who has ever been around legislative halls has heard these lectures a thousand times, with their big cigars and all that kind of business."

Apparently Taylor identified Miller with lobbyists he had learned to dislike in Tennessee, and the bias implicit in his remark was obvious to all. It would surface again and again during Miller's long ordeal on the witness stand. Somehow, the subject of Connolly's original objection got lost, and Thompson proceeded without drawing from the witness an account of Marje's talk with Powell about legislators getting stock of WPTA. Miller, out of hearing of the side bar conversations, didn't know it but the effort to smear him while protecting Marje was under way.

They came to the chain of events leading up to Miller's meeting with Kerner on November 9, 1962, in which he reported on Mrs. Everett's problems and her expressed intent to provide stock for the governor and Isaacs. Asked why he relayed "Mrs. Everett's offer of stock," Miller replied:

"I relayed that message, which she on two occasions mentioned to me, because she was in need of the favor of both Governor Kerner and Mr. Isaacs. She was eager to ingratiate herself on a continuing basis with Governor Kerner and Theodore Isaacs, and she certainly wanted to avoid any adverse influence in connection with the racing dates that were being considered at that moment by both the Harness Commission and the. . . "

Connolly interrupted to ask for a conference at the bench. There he moved for a mistrial on the ground that Miller had been permitted "to rationalize and give his private interpretation of why he communicated this."

After much pro and con, the motion was denied. "In my opinion," said the judge, "that is competent evidence."

Connolly still argued, his point being that Miller's intent in relaying the message was immaterial. Skinner replied that Miller "is a briber just as much as Mrs. Everett, and is charged in the indictment."

No one mentioned that under Skinner's logic the reverse must be true: that if Miller was a briber, so was Mrs. Everett, and she *was not charged* in the indictment.

Court recessed with Connolly still unhappy, and when it resumed next day it began with a long conference in the judge's chambers. Connolly presented a copy of instructions he wanted read to the jury, instructions which, according to Thompson, would destroy the government's case. "You might as well grant a motion for a directed verdict," he told the judge. It was necessary for the jurors to infer what happened at that meeting in Springfield, Thompson insisted. Otherwise you could never have a bribery conviction "unless the briber sat on one side of the table and said, 'I am handing you this $5,000, governor, with the intent to influence your acts with respect to A, B, C and D,' and the governor said, 'Thank you, I am accepting that $5,000 with the intent to have my action influenced on A, B, C and D.' "

Continuing, the U. S. Attorney noted:

"What you have to remember is this situation, the delicacy of it. This is the governor of the State of Illinois. He is not going to sit in his office and talk right out, even in front of his closest friend and the chairman, about why he is taking this stock. Miller is a person of sensibilities, with long experience in state government and on the racing board, and he is chairman of the board. He is not going to sit there and tell the governor of the State of Illinois, 'Governor, here is a bribe from Marje.' They are sitting there and talking in code, but it is apparent what they are talking about, or Miller would not have started off with a recitation of her problems, her problems that she had told him the day before she was worried about."

Interestingly enough, Connolly made no use of a fact admitted by Thompson in the course of his argument: that Marje had *already offered* the stock to Isaacs before Miller went to Springfield. It would follow then that Thompson's theory about their conversation on November 9, 1962, was in error. *The bribe had already been accepted before Miller learned of it.* A few minutes later when Connolly complained that the government was now picturing Miller as the "briber," Thompson made his feelings very clear:

"We think you will agree," he told the judge, "at the end of the case, when we submit our instructions on the mail fraud, the conspiracy and the bribery, that it doesn't make any difference whether Mrs. Everett or Mr. Miller proposed the bribe to the governor, or both of them, as it appears to me now developing, acting in concert with each other.

"It doesn't make any difference," he continued, "whether Mrs. Everett was compelled to do so by Miller, if the jury wants to believe her on that point, or whether Miller agreed to help her original intention. *All we have to prove is that a bribe was offered and they accepted it,* knowing the intent with which it was offered." (Emphasis added.)

In other words: the goal of the government was to get Kerner, and Thompson was completely unconcerned about which of his two witnesses would be forever branded a giver of bribes. To win Marje's cooperation, he had helped her get a racing license in California; to attempt to win Miller's aid he had first caused him to be indicted and hit with a multimillion dollar tax bill. Now, having obtained the essential testimony, he was completely indifferent about the matter of truth, of what really happened. If Connolly wanted to blame all the plotting on Miller, well, apparently that was all right with Big Jim. As far as he was concerned, it made absolutely no difference to Kerner's guilt or innocence. That it made a lot of difference to Miller wasn't important. In the legal jungle it was everyone for himself or herself, and the conviction of Otto Kerner would mean much to Jim Thompson and his ambitions to be president.

Judge Taylor accepted Thompson's argument, and the trial moved back to the courtroom where Miller — ignorant, of course, of Thompson's willingness to throw him to the wolves — sat waiting. They began discussing various racing bills passed by the legislature and some Miller in his capacity of chairman had opposed. Long wrangles resulted. Miller made it clear all bills favorable to the racing industry were approved by all racing associations and by no stretch of the imagination favored Marje over anyone else.

The examination continued with Miller relating Isaacs' impatience with Marje's slowness in producing the CTE stock promised, with Joe Knight's unhappiness at being the only politician of note not owning racing stock, and his efforts to satisfy both men. He described the difficulties Mrs. Everett encountered with such business friends as Wacker and Spiegel, and told how those problems were resolved. When Connolly objected to what he called editorializing, Miller proved he could speak to the point.

"I told Mr. Knight we were in a hell of a fix," he said.

His resignation from the Racing Board and subsequent acquisition of Balmoral and Chicago Harness Racing were related. Connolly made only routine objections to what he called leading questions, but it was obvious he was biding his time. At the noon recess he won from the judge an instruction to Thompson not to talk to or have lunch with the witness. The effort to isolate Miller was beginning.

After only a few questions in the afternoon, Thompson was through and Connolly took over. He found Miller on guard.

"I haven't seen you for several months, have I?" asked the defense attorney.

"Well," said the former defendant, "you act gleeful about it, but that is true."

"I don't act gleeful, sir," said Connolly, and the long-anticipated battle was joined.

Connolly produced what he called Document 546 and asked Miller if he recognized that it contained a series of questions "posed to you" on July 28, 1972, before the agreement making Miller a government witness was signed.

The elderly witness examined it carefully and replied, "Mr. Connolly, I presume you want me to be very careful about my scrutiny of this document, and it consists of about fifty questions. Do you want me to acquaint myself with — forty-seven to be exact. Do you assure me that this is the correct document?"

"Well . . ." said Connolly.

"I'll take your word for it," said Miller. "Otherwise I think I'd better read it all."

The defense attorney suddenly became evasive. "Let's back up a bit, Mr. Miller," he said, and switched abruptly to the large filing cabinet that for two days had stood silently in the courtroom. He got Miller to identify it as one that had been in his possession until the previous August when federal marshals took custody of it and the documents it contained. Did the cabinet contain that aforementioned series of questions?

As a matter of fact it did not, but Miller, playing it cautiously, replied only, "I have no recollection of that."

"Well," said Connolly, "go down and look and see if you can find one."

Thompson intervened and requested a conference at the bench. There, out of the hearing of the jury and of Miller, he protested Connolly's tactic. The defense had been given access to the cabinet and had copies of its contents. Connolly replied, "This man [Miller] is beginning to fence with me. . . . There is no reason for him to deny they are the questions."

"He didn't deny they were the questions," replied Thompson. "He said he wanted a chance to look at them before he answered and you went right on to something else without giving him a chance to do it."

"All right," said Connolly. "That is your interpretation."

Judge Taylor asked if the government could stipulate that the list of questions was the correct one. Skinner said he did not know that it was the correct list. Connolly said he was willing to say that "to the best of my recollection," he got the list from the file cabinet. Again Skinner insisted he did not recall the list ever being in the cabinet.

He was permitted to look at the list, and finally said, "Mr. Connolly can go ahead and assume that those are the questions, just the questions."

The decision expedited matters, but there was still one thing wrong with it — as was later established, the list offered by Connolly *wasn't correct.*

Nevertheless, the defense attorney began reading the questions to Miller, one by one. After each question he inquired if Miller replied as follows, and he read the alleged reply.

Miller looked in vain to Thompson and Skinner for aid, but the two men ignored him. In the brief second he had to think he concluded that only one answer was safe, and he repeated it over and over:

"I can't remember."

His caution was justified, as a comparison of the *original* list of questions and answers with Connolly's version makes very plain. A few examples follow:

Question: When did you first discuss with Marje Everett making stock available to Kerner and Isaacs?

Connolly's version: "November 1, 1962."

Miller's actual answer: "She initiated the subject with me of racing association stock on or about November 5, 6, or 7, 1962."

Question: Why was this stock made available?

Connolly's version: "And did you answer in substance, 'Assume she wanted to ingratiate herself.' "

Miller's actual answer: "She doubtless believed it would give her special advantage with them. Her father followed a pattern of this kind but seemed to be more selective or at least more specific in his calculations and contemplations. For example, when he gave Arvey an option to buy stock, Arvey was national committeeman and chairman of the Democratic Party of Cook County and close to Governor-elect Stevenson. But Marje Everett offered stock to a wide variety of individuals: Mortimer, the highway engineer; Janotta, the man she thought was close to Ogilvie; Henry Williams; Mrs. Weisl; the jockey, Eddie Arcaro; Jimmy Jones, the trainer; Republican legislators as well as Democratic legislators in spite of her 'in' with Kerner. What answer, therefore, could one give to the question: 'Why was this stock made available?' "

Question: After November of 1962, how many times did you discuss with Isaacs and Kerner the fact that Marje Everett would make available CTE and WPTA shares to them upon request?

Connolly's version: "Not with Otto Kerner. Three or four times with Theodore J. Isaacs, probably in 1964."

Miller's actual answer: "Several months after November, 1962 — I can't recall the exact date — I gave Isaacs Marje's memo of November 8, 1962. I never discussed this subject with Kerner. It is my surmise that I discussed with Isaacs three or four times in 1963 and/or 1964 this subject."

Question: When did Marje give you the two twenty-five-share certificates of CTE?

Connolly's version: "She gave them to William J. Lynch."

Miller's actual answer: "She never did."

Question: Did you discuss the tax consequences of CTE and CHR purchases with Kerner, Isaacs, Schaller, Marje Everett, Lynch, and Joseph Knight?

Connolly's version: "Discuss with Marje Everett."

Miller's actual answer: "No."

Question: When did you first discuss with Marje Everett the obtaining of stock in BJC and CHR?

Connolly's version: "Late 1966."

Miller's actual answer: "Marje Everett probably discussed with me the possibility of obtaining stock in BJC and CHR in 1965."

And so it went. Sometimes Connolly's version contained the gist of Miller's answer, but at the expense of additional information. And sometimes Connolly's version was simply *incorrect*.

Miller knew that the answers, and some of the questions, were not on the original list, but he feared a denial might wreck the case. Better, he decided, to plead loss of memory than risk falling into a trap. Again and again he looked to his former drinking partners for aid. Stufflebeam seemed stricken, moving his hands wide in a gesture of hopelessness. Thompson stared impassively at the table. Later he was to call those few minutes "my darkest hour in the entire case. I thought he was going to be destroyed as a witness." Yet, at first, he made no move to protest. Miller was uniquely alone in that crowded room.

Finally Thompson objected, but at the bench he only wanted the judge to tell the jury the procedure was for the purpose of testing the responsibility of the witness. The judge obliged, and the strange farce continued.

(Ironically, one of the questions was of great importance in proving that Miller did not lie in order to win a promise of immunity. It asked if he discussed the stock deal "at any time between 1960 and 1968," and he replied: "No." Later he was to be accused of inventing that meeting in Springfield with Kerner in order to win immunity, but at the critical moment when the issue of immunity was at stake, he did not remember it and gave a negative reply.)

Ultimately the list was exhausted, and Connolly turned to other things. As if to dramatize his cheap victory, however, he told Miller, "You understand, I am a lawyer. I don't have any personal hostility toward you. Don't you understand that?"

"I have nothing but affection for you," replied Miller, "so proceed."

The tension eased.

Connolly then proceeded to quote from a document Miller had prepared in reply, point by point, to the indictment. The document, Miller admitted, was a self-serving statement, but many of his comments made while he faced trial were valid still. While seeming to attack the government's case, the document when put into perspective did little more than clarify Miller's contention that he was not — as Marje had charged — the master plotter. When this became apparent Thompson finally awoke to Connolly's tactics.

"No," he interrupted, "that is not what it says. Can we have that whole paragraph, please?"

"Sure, let me read the whole thing," replied the defense attorney.

"I want what you are reading to him, not your version," replied Thompson.

On that note court adjourned for the day. When it resumed Thompson's brief flurry was forgotten. He sat silently as for hours Connolly asked general questions about the state of racing in Illinois during Miller's tenure as chairman, and such things as the witness' prestige on the national level. Miller, happy enough to advertise his achievements, answered the questions in some detail. Nevertheless he was a bit puzzled. What was Connolly up to? The answer came at another side bar conference, but Miller didn't hear it. Judge Taylor suddenly blurted:

"I doubt if you can do anything about it — Mr. Thompson could — but this man is just continuing to go into these long excursions and talking about himself. I don't feel like I should interfere, but if you men, you lawyers, can tell him to refrain from that, I think it would help . . . he brags on himself tremendously."

"He has a monumental ego," said Connolly, the man who had asked those very questions about Miller's achievements.

"I have never seen a man like that, but he seems to be a kind man," the judge continued.

"Not to us," interjected assistant defense attorney Patton.

"He seems to be just overwhelmed with himself," Taylor added.

"I, of course, don't mind it too much," said Connolly. "I'm in a little different position than Mr. Thompson. I think this reflects on his credibility a little bit."

"I know what you're doing," said the judge.

And now Thompson joined the knifing: "In fact, I can't put up with him any more," he muttered.

Contrast that statement, and the attitude it expressed, with the treatment earlier afforded Marje Everett who had rambled and evaded without protest from either side or the judge. Miller's lack of friends, his isolation, was now complete. The court and the officers of the court knew it. The press sensed it. Miller, however, did not know it.

"You are an excellent lawyer," said Taylor to Connolly, "and you are playing up to his egotism. I can see that just as well as anyone, and I don't blame you for it. I don't blame you for it."

"I think I have done almost enough of it," said Connolly. "The people of the United States like the people of Illinois are stuck with this man."

"The government is always stuck with all their witnesses," said Thompson.

"All right, gentlemen," said Judge Taylor.

And the game went on. A bit later in another side bar conference, Connolly said he was attempting to show that Miller had "a personal animus toward Marje Everett which is motivating his testimony at this trial." He acknowledged, however, that it was "the same animus that motivated Mrs. Everett. We find ourselves in a conflict between two powerful egocentric individuals." In an effort to develop proof of the alleged animus he then asked Miller if he "got pretty steamed up" while reading newspaper accounts of Marje's testimony.

"I never get steamed up, Mr. Connolly."

"You always have a great feeling of equanimity for your fellow man, is that right?" sneered the attorney.

"A great deal of solicitude, and I probably prayed more than I cursed, if that is any satisfaction to you," retorted the witness.

"You viewed Mrs. Everett's testimony such as you read in the paper with equanimity, did you?"

"I viewed it with considerable compassion."

"Was there a bit of contempt involved also?"

"Yes."

"Thank you. We can recess now, Your Honor."

After lunch, Connolly began a serious effort to prove his famous theory — that all the intrigue and corruption were planned by Miller to give him control of Balmoral. The exchange grew heated as the two men fenced with naked blades. Miller brought the duel to a temporary halt by remarking, "I read in the paper that you were solicitous about somebody having some water. I would like a glass of water."

"Let's refrain from too much of this frivolity. A little of it is all right to break the tension, but let's not turn this into a . . ." Judge Taylor sputtered helplessly.

"Do you want to take an afternoon recess?" interrupted Connolly.

"Yes, let's take our afternoon recess," said the judge.

There were amused smiles in the courtroom. Miller sauntered over to the press box and remarked that only Al Capone had been more harassed. At the defense table sat Judge Kerner, ramrod straight, and almost forgotten.

Things didn't go much better for Connolly after the recess. Once more he returned to the transactions involving Balmoral and — with Miller contesting his "theory" at every point — began building to a climax. As he did, he moved physically backward down the aisle and asked, "Mr. Miller, follow me now. Would you look at me, please, sir?"

Miller looked. When the dignified lawyer reached the double doors at the back of the room, he fired his climactic question:

"You arranged for Joe Knight to induce Ted Isaacs to transfer fifty shares of CTE for ten thousand shares of Balmoral, a company you intended to acquire — is that not so?"

As cool as ever, Miller seemed to be waiting for the shout to reach him from afar. And when it did, he replied, "I don't know why you have to be so dramatic about it."

There were snickers from the audience. One writer said Connolly looked "foolish, back there, so far from where he should be." As he walked forward, Miller continued his reply:

"I did not intend to acquire the company."

The purpose, he added, was to get Kerner and Isaacs out of the racing business. When Connolly, trying to regain his dignity, asked how that was going to get him out, Miller — his good humor restored — noted, "Oh, I seem to think that it worked out very well. His stock was taken in as treasury stock in a relatively short period of time."

Connolly tried again:

"Well, Mr. Miller, won't you agree that one of the incidental, fallout benefits of that noble purpose of yours was to give you control of Balmoral?"

"No," said Miller, "I won't even give you the slightest comfort in that erroneous conclusion."

With that, Connolly had enough. He turned to the judge and suggested an early adjournment.

"I know it's early," he said, "but I'm tired and I think the witness is, too."

"Your traffic is bad today, is it?" asked Taylor.

"Yes," said Connolly.

"All right, we will adjourn until Monday morning at 9:30."

Monday, January 22, was devoted to "trivia" as Connolly admitted at the end of the day. Endlessly he questioned Miller about previous testimony concerning racing legislation, the meeting on November 9, 1962, with Kerner and Isaacs, and various documents taken from Miller's files. At the day's end Judge Taylor told Connolly and Thompson, "I don't think either one of you heard me when I said I am depending on the good judgment of each of you to do your best to keep this case in focus and not get lost."

"I am sorry I did," said Connolly.

Next day the jousting resumed. Connolly wanted to know how the meeting on August 10, 1966, when Isaacs paid for the CTE stock, happened to be arranged for Miller's Chicago office on Michigan Avenue.

"It is a pleasant place," said Miller, "a convenient place, a comfortable . . ."

"Well," interrupted the attorney, "so is Scottsdale, Arizona," a reference to the Everett home.

"Pardon me," said Miller. "All of you can apparently testify as to that. I have never been to Scottsdale, to the residence you speak of . . ."

Connolly continued for several hours, dealing with what he called odds and ends of testimony. Finally he announced, "I am done."

"Mr. Wolfson," said Judge Taylor, "do you want to ask this gentleman anything?"

The younger man, counsel for Ted Isaacs, replied with unconscious irony, "I have a few questions, Your Honor."

Tigerlike, Wolfson tore into Miller's purchases of Chicago Harness Racing stock, and in a minute did more damage than Connolly had achieved in days. He drew from the former chairman of the Racing Board the admission that he testified falsely about the stock in a 1971 appearance before the Republican-dominated Racing Board.

"I was untruthful," said Miller.

He had less success in making Miller admit that the 50,000 shares of CHR stock purchased in the name of Ralph Atlass for Joe Knight were, technically, his own. However, he got Miller to agree he did not tell the other Racing Board members about the transaction.

They paused for lunch, but those few minutes of testimony were to cost Miller dearly. The Racing Board used his admissions as a basis for denying him further racing dates, and suddenly Miller, the principal stockholder in three associations, was without authority to operate. In contrast, Marje Everett had been re-established in Hollywood Park thanks to the intervention of the Nixon administration and prosecutor Thompson.

When after lunch Wolfson completed his examination, Miller still had his sense of humor intact. Asked about his agreement to tell the truth in return for having the indictment against him dismissed, he confirmed that he would be the judge of whether he testified truthfully.

"Well," said Wolfson, "if your opinion differs from the prosecutor's opinion, who do you think is going to win that one?"

"Oh, I have sort of an innate feeling of confidence," said Miller.

"I'll bet you do," said Wolfson.

Wolfson also brought up the $2.4 million civil suit filed by the IRS against Miller, and on redirect examination Thompson sought to clarify the situation.

"Have I ever told you," he asked, "that the claim would be compromised by one penny because of your testimony here?"

"No, sir."

"Do you have an expectation that because of your testimony here, the government is going to let you take back one penny of that claim?"

"No, sir."

"Is that civil litigation going forward in the Tax Court?"

"Yes, sir."

Thompson then asked about Miller's "frame of mind" following his indictment. The witness replied, "I believed that the United States District Attorney was politically motivated. I believed that Mr. Stufflebeam and Mr. Witkowski were using their best efforts to accommodate the United States District Attorney's motivations. I was bewildered. I was mad. I felt the government, my government, was being used. I don't believe that I ever had such a low regard for the United States Department of Justice as I did when I wrote that statement."

He was then asked about his present attitude.

"Mr. Thompson," he replied, "I believe the United States government has done everything in its power to read and digest the documents that I have presented to the representatives of the government, and I believe that regardless of my unrelenting attitude of contradiction about certain of the contentions of that document, of that indictment, that the government has accepted my version in many, many instances. In consequence, my whole attitude has been nourished; my good feeling and my confidence have been restored."

"I don't have any other questions," said Thompson.

Connolly returned to try once more to prove his theory about Balmoral being the prize for which Miller had long intrigued. His questions brought a reply that surprised him: Miller said that he bought stock in Balmoral and Chicago Harness as a favor to Marje Everett.

"How was it a favor to her?" demanded Connolly incredulously.

"First of all," said Miller, "when her husband, Webb Everett . . . acquired Chicago Harness Racing, they were in violation of the law because they owned or controlled two harness racing institutions. So they had to dispose of one of them."

In addition, Miller continued, Mrs. Everett permitted her attorneys to use unauthorized funds to buy back the stock owned by members of the legislature.

"The money was used," he explained. "It had to be accounted for. Annual meetings were in the offing. There was $560,000 or $550,000 in that package. There was — I don't know how much more — six or seven hundred thousand in the other package. And so I, imprudently, unwisely, stupidly, came to the rescue."

"This act of nobility," sneered Connolly, "and gentlemanly conduct was not the product of a plan you had hatched over a year before?"

"No."

"I am finished," said Connolly for the second time.

But of course he wasn't finished. After a conference at the bar, Miller was ordered to return next morning, Wednesday, January 24. Again, the lawyer from Washington tried to replow the turned earth of Balmoral, and finally Judge Taylor lost patience.

"All right," he said. "That ends it. That ends it. Now go to something else, Mr. Connolly."

"Don't get mad, Your Honor," said Connolly.

Taylor's face turned red. "I am not mad. I am not a bit mad. Proceed."

But this time Connolly *was* finished. The judge ordered him to the bench.

"Mr. Connolly," he said, "I want you to quit stating in the presence of this jury, 'Don't be mad, Your Honor.' "

"You turned on me," said Connolly. "You turned on me, really. You may not have realized it, but you did."

"No, I haven't turned on anybody," said the judge, "but this is the fourth time you have stated for this record, 'Don't be mad, Your Honor.' Now that isn't the way to try a lawsuit."

"Your Honor," said Connolly, "you really were mad. You may not have realized it, but you were."

"I think I know my own feelings better than you do," said Taylor.

"Well, you certainly looked at me. I know you have heard enough of this witness and you want to get rid of him and I do too," said Connolly.

And after only a little more wrangling, the attempt to portray Miller as the sinister schemer of Illinois racing ended not with a bang but a whimper. The trial of Otto Kerner and Theodore Isaacs resumed.

If we are going to have freedom, we are going to have to let people act foolishly as well as wisely."

SAM J. ERVIN, 1970

11
The Defense

At last it was time to "make love" to Otto Kerner.

A week had passed since Miller was excused. The United States had run a score of minor witnesses before the jury in an effort to prove the various counts of perjury, false statements, and mail fraud, but there were few surprises in the testimony elicited and very little drama. At last Thompson was satisfied.

The defense made the usual motion for a directed verdict of acquittal. Connolly, with the jury absent, told Judge Taylor that there was nothing wrong in public officals engaging in private business while in office. President Eisenhower got a farm at Gettysburg, President Johnson got a television station in Texas, President Nixon got homes in California and Florida.

"If this is bribery," said Connolly, referring to Kerner's racetrack stock, "a lot of public officials are going to stand before the bar."

Judge Taylor denied the motion and ordered the defense to proceed.

Complications!

Connolly demanded that Isaacs take the stand first and testify. Wolfson declined to make "a final decision" as to whether Isaacs would testify at all. Judge Taylor said he could not tell Wolfson what to do.

Connolly blasted ahead, telling the judge — and the prosecution — what Isaacs would say as a witness: a denial of the November 9, 1962, discussion of stock in Kerner's office; the fact that Kerner did not agree to do anything in return for the stock; and Isaacs' assignment by Kerner to handle details of the stock purchase.

As Wolfson protested that Connolly was violating a confidence in

190

revealing Isaacs' defense, Judge Taylor denied a motion by Connolly
for severance of the defendants.

Only then did Connolly call his first two witnesses. They included
two bank officials and two attorneys. One of the lawyers was, as
mentioned earlier, Federal Judge Lynch. He was on the stand for less
than ten minutes, receiving the same kid-gloves treatment his former
partner, attorney, now judge, Schaller, had received. The situation
tickled the fancy of *Daily News* columnist Mike Royko, who noted that
the presence of three federal judges in the courtroom was unique: one
on the bench, one on the witness stand, and one at the defense table.
Unfortunately, said Royko, Lynch didn't remember much, which was
"too bad because if he ever got his memory clicking, he could probably
hold the city spellbound except for those who would pack their bags
and flee the country."

Essentially, however, Lynch and the other witnesses heard February 6, were but filling in until Connolly could set the stage for
Kerner's appearance. On Wednesday morning, various past members
of the Illinois Racing Board testified. One was Donald McKellar, a
former executive vice president of Field Enterprises and, also, a
former director of Arlington Park. He surprised everyone by stating
that during his tenure on the board, he learned "that Governor Kerner
did, indeed, hold shares in the corporation in 1963 or had options
therefor."

He obtained the information at a reception at the Savoy Hotel in
London. Mrs. Kerner, "who didn't seem to realize that I was a commissioner — she thought I was connected with Arlington Park" — asked
about the safety of their investment.

*Here was a chance to resolve the central question: Did the stock deal
take place in 1962 or 1966? But no one was in a mood to seize the
opportunity. Nor did anyone ask why McKellar did not feel it necessary
to take official action, knowing as he had to know that Kerner's stock
was concealed under someone else's name. Hastily the witness was
excused.*

In the afternoon, a parade of character witnesses began. Connolly
started with Senior Federal District Court Judge Joseph Perry and
continued with that old kingmaker, Jake Arvey. College professors and
businessmen were also included. After eight had been heard, the
defense attorney announced that more would be available later. In the
meantime he would call Judge Kerner.

The courtroom filled to capacity. Wearing a black suit, white shirt, and blue patterned tie, the silver-haired judge took his seat in the witness chair. He held himself with military erectness, and spoke with that tinge of British accent he had picked up as a schoolboy in Cambridge. According to intimates, he was eager to testify, impatient with the long delay, confident he could sway the blue-collar jury.

In the front row were his adopted children, Helena and Anton. Few in the courtroom realized that they were the grandchildren of a 1926 first marriage by Boss Cermak's daughter, and were no blood relationship to the man they were proud to call father. In bad health was their mother, the woman who in London in 1963 had been worried about the safety of the family's "investment" in racetrack stock. Her fears had been justified, but neither the son nor the daughter would admit it. Passionately they believed in Judge Kerner's innocence.

Connolly, equally handsome in a sleek, polished way, began slowly to trace Kerner's career. The judge revealed that it was a prediction of German students he met in 1930 that caused him to become active in the Illinois National Guard. Those students at Munich warned him, he said, that war would break out in 1939. From private 7th class, he rose ultimately to major general.

Thanks to his father, he also became active early on in politics, taking part in his first campaign at age seven. His father, he noted, was ultimately appointed to the U. S. Court of Appeals, Seventh Circuit.

"And you succeeded him to that bench, did you not, sir?"

"Yes, and very proud to."

Connolly backtracked a bit to bring in the immediate postwar era when Kerner served first as U. S. Attorney and then as Cook County judge. The latter he described as "a very important political role because of the supervision of the Board of Election Commissioners." He resigned from that office to run for governor in 1960, and won by "about over a half million vote majority."

Asked about Nixon's charge of vote fraud in that election, Kerner said that "As a matter of fact, the electoral board, which consists of certain state officers, refused to sign my certificate of election. Mayor Daley appeared before that state electoral board and said that if they had any doubt about the authenticity of the election he would guarantee the Democratic Party would pay one-half of the cost of recanvassing every single vote in the State of Illinois if the Republican Party would assume the other half of the cost. Immediately after that, the electoral board signed our certificate of election."

Kerner's work as chairman of the Civil Disorders Committee, set up by President Johnson, was elaborated upon. In the middle of it, Connolly interrupted to ask if the witness wanted some water. "No," replied Kerner, "it is just sinus that kicks up every now and then."

Turning back to the court of appeals, Connolly asked how long such a federal judge served. It was an opportunity. Kerner gestured with his hand: "Life tenure, good behavior, and that's why this suit, this action, is so very important to me. It's my life."

A very dramatic moment, the press decided.

Abruptly, Connolly switched to Kerner's long friendship with Ted Isaacs. It began, said the judge, as "a casual, military relationship." When he became active in politics, Isaacs and another old friend, Joe Knight, helped in his campaigns. Elected governor with their aid, he brought them both into his cabinet. He decided to make Miller chairman of the Racing Board, he said, before he took office, but Mayor Daley's recommendations had nothing to do with it. He knew Miller's reputation in the racing field, and thought he was the best man for the job.

The financial condition of the state and the measures taken to correct them were the subject of a long discourse. Connolly asked short questions, each serving as the topic of a minispeech by the defendant. Thompson made no move to interrupt. New business came in, unemployment dropped, tax revenue increased. Programs and progress: "I just can't cover all of them, Mr. Connolly, without boring you."

Ultimately they came to the issues in the case at hand. Speaking of a bill to allow racetrack owners and operators to do legally what they had been doing for years, shift meets from one track to another, Connolly asked if Kerner signed it into law because of "any gratuity or offer made to you whatsoever?"

"Of course not," said Kerner.

As if to prove the point, Connolly introduced an unsigned copy of a letter to Kerner from Miller, the last paragraph of which stated:

"If you will continue to shift your troubles and worries about Illinois racing to me, I will do all in my power to handle things well and merit the great confidence that your procedure implies."

With that, Connolly said he wanted to adjourn for the day. Judge Taylor complied.

"It was great theater," wrote *Sun-Times* columnist Tom Fitzpatrick. "Everything went right. There was a house packed with a hushed and attentive audience. All it required was a bravura performance by a star to make the day memorable. Otto Kerner gave them that and more Thursday. He was spellbinding. Before court recessed for the day, Kerner had every member of the jury nodding agreement with him as he told them of the tremendous burdens of being governor of Illinois. . . ."

But what did performance have to do with facts?

Unorthodox or unorganized, Connolly interrupted himself the next day and with the resigned permission of Judge Taylor, halted the examination of Kerner to present additional character witnesses: more judges, a sportscaster known as "the Voice of the Chicago Cubs," Kerner's minister from Springfield, and another professor. That made thirteen in all, and annoyed Taylor, who said he had been told there would only be twelve. Connolly promised that he would end it with General William Westmoreland, who was scheduled to come in on the following Monday. Meanwhile, he only had Roy Wilkins, executive director of the National Association for the Advancement of Colored People, remaining.

Character reconfirmed, Connolly was ready to proceed with his client, General-Governor-Judge Kerner. But, alas, waiting in the wings was Marje Everett, now officially a *defense* witness. There was no choice — she and her California attorney, Neil Papiano, had "very pressing, unbreakable engagements on Monday," so it was hear her now or never. It wouldn't take long — about ten minutes.

"Mrs. Everett, welcome home."

"Thank you, sir. Good morning, judge."

It was quibbling. Marje denied she had a discussion with Isaacs about the stock deal prior to calling Miller about it on November 8, 1962. She also said she didn't express any concern about the libel suit she had filed against the *New York Post* in her conversation with Miller, and she went to New York to see Alice Weisl, an old friend, who was about to undergo surgery for cancer. Nor was she worried about her relationship with Zoline.

It was an effort to impeach Miller's testimony as to minor details, while, at the same time, acknowledging she had written the note about the stock deal. She was close to Miller at the time, she added, and simply wanted him to know where to find her if needed so she had written the second note telling him where she would be in New York.

Thompson's cross-examination of his former witness took longer than Connolly's direct. Marje sparred with him, putting all the blame as usual on Miller while agreeing she was willing at the time to do whatever Miller suggested — even bribing a governor. But her memory was bad — some things she just couldn't recall.

Curiously, she disclosed that not only did she trust Miller more than her personal attorneys, Lynch and Schaller, in 1962, but she trusted him more than she did her husband, who wasn't informed of the stock offer either. "Webb handled his business," she explained, "and I handled *ours*. No, he did not know it, sir."

For those who remembered the pretrial hearing when Connolly virtually accused Thompson of bribing Marje by helping her gain a California license, an intriguing footnote was added during this second appearance of Mrs. Everett.

Connolly, on redirect, asked Marje about Thompson's public statement on her behalf. She said she was afraid she might misquote him, so Thompson — in effect — became a witness and testified as to what he had said about Marje being a "public-spirited citizen." His statement was not made under oath, however, which was probably just as well since it wasn't accurate. Nevertheless, Marje thanked him in open court.

An amazing exhibition, but, as usual where Marje was concerned, there was no one to object. It remained for Warren Wolfson, the man who had put Marje on the ropes before, to spoil the scene. He asked:

"Mrs. Everett, are you aware that after the indictment was returned, and after all those laudatory remarks by Mr. Thompson, that he referred to you in official court papers as a co-conspirator?"

"Obviously, I do, sir," said Marje.

"Thank you," said Wolfson. "That is all."

Thompson then thanked the witness. The witness thanked Thompson. Judge Taylor excused the witness. The witness thanked the judge.

"We will take a short recess," said Taylor.

Kerner returned to the stand with a fine if dignified display of indignation as he denied making statements ascribed to him by Special Agent

Stufflebeam and his IRS colleagues. Attempting sarcasm, he said Stufflebeam asked him if he owned a yacht, and, turning toward the special agent, he allowed that "I really didn't quite tell the truth then, Mr. Stufflebeam. I'm sorry. I do have a secondhand aluminum row-boat."

His version of "Chicago Co." and his reference to Isadore Brown were sluffed off. He just didn't remember at the time, he said, but he tried to help and promised to find out and tell them later. He did find out, he said, and told his accountant, Mr. Hyman, to tell them that Chicago Co. meant Chicago Harness. The second conference, Kerner admitted, was at his request. "I called them in and told them I was very irritated with them. . . ."

"Do you want some water?" asked Connolly.

"No, I have some. Thank you."

In the afternoon, Connolly brought up the subject of Mrs. Everett. Kerner said he had known her for perhaps thirty years. "I met her through my father and her father" — those old political allies in the days of Henry Horner. "After I returned from the wars, occasionally when we would have out-of-town guests and they would like to go to Arlington to see it, Mrs. Kerner and I would take them out on rare occasions. At that time we would see Mrs. Everett."

He never discussed his ownership of stock in her racing enter-prises, he said. "I saw no reason to bring it up and she did not." Nor did he discuss appointments to the Racing Board with her or any proposed legislation.

Isaacs was another matter. Even after "he left office" (his indict-ment wasn't mentioned) he continued to act for the governor in a political sense. He was not, however, a "liaison man for racing."

Joe Knight was a personal friend, and worried about how Kerner would make a living when he got older. He promised to tell Kerner about any good investments he discovered. In the fall of '62, he reported there was "some stock available, some racing stock," at $1,000 a share. Kerner told him to "speak to Ted" about it and, later, asked Isaacs to take care of the details. Ted eventually reported "that we didn't need any money at that time, that Marje Everett was going to lend us the money until some later time."

The only person he mentioned the stock deal to was his wife because, since he had no records, he wanted her to know about it "in the event something should happen to me." The lack of records bothered him, he added, and in November, 1962, he asked Isaacs for "some explanation for my records as to what this transaction is." Apparently he didn't get anything because it was during the Christmas-New Year holiday of 1970-71 that he first saw the backdated documents prepared in 1966. When Connolly asked why he didn't "do something" about it until 1966, Kerner replied, "I had other things taking up my time, and it never crossed my mind to ask about it. I had trust and confidence in Mr. Isaacs. I presumed the stock might have been in his name, I didn't know, and I just didn't worry about it."

Meanwhile, on the day Isaacs asked for and got a check from Kerner for $4,479, to pay interest on the "loan" Mrs. Everett had extended to us "for the purchase of stock," Knight reappeared with an offer to sell some racing stock he owned at cost. Isaacs handled details, and Kerner wrote a check for $5,600. In August, Isaacs came back with a request for another check, this time for $5,000, to pay off Mrs. Everett for the stock. Knight was going to take over the remaining $40,000 the two men owed. Still later, in 1967, Isaacs said Marje needed the fifty shares of CTE stock, and did Kerner object to exchanging them for Balmoral stock of the same value? "I said, 'No, I have no objection. If it accommodates her and aids her in her problems, I have no objections whatsoever.' "

That, as far as Judge Kerner was concerned, covered the stock deal. When asked, he estimated he devoted "not more than three or four hours total" to the complex transaction. Nor did he in the period from 1962 to 1968 discuss racing stock with Miller. Asked specifically about the November 9, 1962, meeting in Springfield with Miller and Isaacs, he denied that the subject came up. Of course, by his own admission, he was already aware that CTE stock was available and had told Knight to arrange its purchase with Isaacs. Under the circumstances, the question of Miller's alleged discussion was immaterial to everyone but Marje and Connolly, who had theories to sell.

Connolly turned to racing legislation and immediately became embroiled in an argument with Thompson, who accused the defense attorney of "trying to sneak in the back door" with testimony already ruled inadmissible. Taylor sustained the objection. Kerner then reviewed various racing bills passed during his tenure in office — always with Miller's support — and one bill he vetoed. That one, he said, would have made it impossible to start a new racetrack in the state and thus would have created a monopoly for tracks and associations already doing business.

Asked why he held stock in racing associations during this period, Kerner replied that he considered it "an investment." Did he feel any conflict of interest in holding such stock? No, because "any time any racing bill came up where my personal interest might be affected, I ruled in favor of the state."

With that to be featured in tomorrow's headlines, Connolly suggested adjournment until Monday. Fitzpatrick was not so upbeat in his description of Kerner's second day of testimony. In fact he noted that "we live in a strange world. The more you observe it the less you become certain of anything." For a newspaper columnist, that was quite an admission.

A new week began, and just in case the jurors had forgotten what a sterling character defendant Kerner possessed, here was William Chiles Westmoreland, former general, former chief of staff of the army, former commander-in-chief in Vietnam, to remind them. The handsome general still had a military air about him despite his well-tailored civies, and he spoke with the authority of a man accustomed to respect. Kerner, he said, served as his executive officer when he commanded the 34th Field Artillery Battalion of the Ninth Infantry Division. They saw active duty in North Africa and Sicily.

"I saw him shoulder his responsibility in the most admirable way. He was brave under fire. He had an excellent rapport with the officers and men of the battalion." He was, in short, entitled to be "taken at his word." Under cross-examination, Westmoreland admitted he only saw his friend once while he was governor of Illinois. Moreover, he knew little about the case. "Frankly."

Columnist Mike Royko couldn't resist the temptation to have a little fun with the general:

> When a man like Westmoreland says somebody has "unquestioned honesty," a jury of ordinary people has to be impressed.
>
> Westmoreland, remember, is the kind of person who would not say something without really knowing what he is talking about.
>
> As evidence of that, just consider some of his best

known utterances from those years he ran the war in
Vietnam.

In 1966, for instance, he was asked by a Pentagon
official how many troops he needed to do the job. He
said, "175,000."

"With that figure," he said, "they [the enemy] will
give up the war."

April 24, 1967: "The military picture is favorable."

Nov. 15, 1967: "The situation is very, very en-
couraging."

June 9, 1968: "The enemy has been defeated at
every turn."

When a man who has said that tells you about
"unquestioned honesty," you know you are getting it
right from the horse's mouth, or at least from some part
of the horse.

But if Royko wasn't impressed, who could say the jurors weren't?
Placidly, Connolly plowed ahead, building up his client to make the
gulf wider and wider between Kerner and ordinary mortals. The
examination broke no new ground but served to expose the jury to the
personality of the defendant.

In some respects, at least, the ex-governor seemed quite devoid of
gratitude. He did not know, for example, that Marje contributed
$45,000 to his campaign in 1960 until years later "when the govern-
ment filed some papers." A committee took care of such matters. He
did recall, however, a visit in 1964 from Miller at which time the Racing
Board chairman turned over $15,000 from Marje, in an envelope.

"I didn't open it at the time. I opened it later and saw it was cash and
turned it over to my treasurer."

Jumping about, Connolly went over Kerner's Grand Jury testimony in which he denied ever having discussed with Harness Board
Chairman Thomas C. Bradley a proposal to take away the racing dates
of Maywood Park. Bradley had testified to the Grand Jury, and earlier
in the trial, that such conversations had indeed occurred. Again Kerner
denied it. He explained he had asked for Bradley's resignation early in
1965 because in the 1964 campaign Bradley "sat on his hands" despite
being a township committeeman. "I got fewer votes in that area in the
1964 campaign than I got in 1960, and I was displeased."

The unspoken implication of Kerner's comments was that Bradley's testimony stemmed from his unhappiness at being forced from office, but he was careful not to say so.

Abruptly, Connolly was finished.

"Judge Kerner," he said, "I think I have covered the details of this case. I want to ask you, sir, in conclusion, whether during your term of governor you accepted a bribe, literally, morally, or legally, from William S. Miller or Marjorie L. Everett or anyone else?"

"Absolutely not," said the judge, finality vibrating in his voice.

"Did you deprive the people of the State of Illinois of their right to honest, good government?"

"No, I did not."

"Did you intentionally tell a falsehood before a Grand Jury that was investigating this matter?"

"Never."

"Thank you," said the defense attorney.

And that was the defense. Essentially it consisted of Kerner's word against everyone else. Nothing more, nothing less.

Before "Big Jim" Thompson could begin "to get Kerner's ass," as he had confidently predicted, the record had to be corrected. It seemed that Connolly had put some words in Miller's mouth and then asked Marje about them. She had, naturally, denied Miller's alleged remarks. When Thompson objected that Miller never said it, Connolly had cited the page number on which the testimony appeared. Without checking, Thompson accepted it. Now Connolly admitted that "my digest of the testimony was wrong, Mr. Thompson, and I apologize."

The incident was a reminder to some of the manner in which both sides had earlier played football with Miller's reputation. That Thompson belatedly bothered to check the transcript was proof, perhaps, of his growing realization of the importance of Miller to his case.

With the record corrected, Thompson wasted no time in challenging Kerner. He began by referring to the ex-governor's ignorance of campaign contributions. When the witness repeated that he never knew the amounts contributed, he was asked, "For the purposes of fund raising, it doesn't make any difference to a candidate whether somebody gives $45,000, or ten dollars — is that right in your experience?"

"It didn't make any difference," said Kerner.

A giggle of amusement, of disbelief, rippled across the courtroom. Several jurors were seen to smile. Apparently some cynics questioned that even Mr. Clean could be so far above the battle. Thompson struck again.

"So then there was no way, when you thanked people for their gifts, to differentiate in degrees of warmth, let's say, between a $45,000 gift and a ten dollar gift, is that right?"

"That is correct as I told you before . . ."

Laughter interrupted him. Judge Taylor rapped his gavel.

"Let's not have any of these laughing-outs at these questions," he ordered. "This is a serious matter and we don't want any of that in the courtroom. It isn't proper."

Thompson pursued the matter, ultimately asking if it weren't true that Marje Everett contributed 10 per cent of Kerner's total campaign fund in 1960. Kerner agreed it was 10 per cent, but insisted he wasn't aware of the amount until the indictment mentioned it in 1971. When the loan Miller made was added to the $75,000 he raised, the total came to 29 per cent of the campaign fund.

Turning to Kerner's contention that the November 9, 1962, meeting in Springfield was only for the purpose of informing the governor of the 1963 racing dates, Thompson found Kerner anticipating the key question.

"I know what your next question is going to be, probably," said the witness.

"What is my next question going to be?"

"Because," said Kerner, "I have found out since, in reviewing the minutes, that he came and spoke to me about the dates before the commission met and approved the dates. Am I correct?"

"That is correct," said Thompson. The dates were awarded on November 20, he added, eleven days after the meeting with the governor.

Nevertheless, Kerner insisted he was told the dates on November 9, and he saw nothing extraordinary about it even though there was a conflict in applications for certain dates. Why, since the dates had not been decided, Miller bothered to come to Springfield to tell him, he didn't explain.

"I know what he did and said," added Kerner. "That is all I can testify to."

But it wasn't quite that simple.

After the break for lunch, Thompson established that Kerner had told the Grand Jury he was notified of racing dates only twenty-four or forty-eight hours before publication, not eleven days. Kerner had also denied that Isaacs ever attended such sessions, yet he admitted Isaacs was present for the 1962 discussion.

Somehow, it didn't add up.

And there were other matters in which his Grand Jury testimony was incorrect. Kerner explained he knew more about the transaction now than he did when he testified before the Grand Jury. When the Grand Jury testimony was read, he was forced to reply, "I don't recall that question or answer. If I did say it some time in the interview, I was incorrect when I made that statement."

Thompson turned to Joe Knight and the CTE stock deal. In a series of rapid questions and answers, Kerner emerged looking somewhat less than discreet.

"Is it your testimony, sir, that he did not tell you the name of the stock that was available?"

"No, he did not."

"Did you ask him?"

"No, I did not."

"Did he tell you where it was located, where the business was located?"

"No, he did not."

"Did you ask him?"

"No."

"So you didn't know whether it was an upstate racing association or a downstate racing association?"

"No, I did not."

"Did he tell you what the assets of this corporation were?"

"No, I didn't ask the question."

"Did he tell you who the other shareholders were?"

"No."

"You did not ask?"

"I did not ask."

"Did he tell you who the management was?"

"No."

"You did not ask?"

"Correct."

"Did he tell what racing dates that company had held in the past?"

"No."

"You did not ask?"

"I did not ask."

"But you on that occasion agreed to invest in the shares, did you not?"

"Yes."

"More than that, you told Joe Knight to talk to Ted Isaacs and see if he wanted some?"

"Yes."

Perhaps the best example of Kerner's reliance on his friends came when on May 22, 1967, he received a check for $7,000 from Knight. It represented, of course, Kerner's share of CHR stock after it had been sold to repay the money Knight had borrowed from Miss McInturf and loaned to Isaacs, but Kerner knew nothing of that at the time. When he received the check, he told Thompson, "I wasn't certain what it represented." Nevertheless, he deposited it and didn't bother to ask Knight what it represented. After all, he said repeatedly, he trusted Knight.

Further interrogation brought disclosure that Kerner had given 275 "legal packing cases of papers" to the State Historical Society without looking at them. Later he deducted the value of the gift — $70,000, according to appraiser Ralph Newman, who had testified earlier as a character witness for Kerner — from his 1968 income taxes.

Connolly objected to the line of questions: "It is a perfectly proper legal thing to do and this is prejudicial. Franklin Roosevelt, Harry Truman, John F. Kennedy, Lyndon Johnson, Dwight Eisenhower, have all built libraries and have done the same thing." His voice rose.

"Look, Mr. Connolly," said the Tennessee judge, "that is not the way for a lawyer . . ."

"I know it isn't," said Connolly, "but this man should know better than that."

"Don't talk like that during this trial," ordered Judge Taylor. "If you have an objection, make it."

"I'm trying to. I'm sorry I lost my temper."

Thompson, who seemed to be having trouble keeping a straight face, announced, "I think I have developed this all I care to."

"You certainly have," said Connolly.

Amazingly, the defendant saw fit to make bad matters worse.

"I might add," Kerner volunteered, "Mr. Thompson . . ."

The U. S. Attorney tried to stop him, but Kerner continued: ". . . that Mr. Newman is appraising Mr. Nixon's papers, or so he has told me."

"All right," said Thompson. "Add that to the jury if you will."

"I think we should, to be perfectly fair," said Kerner.

"Mr. Nixon has not deducted them from his income tax returns, has he?" asked Thompson.

"Not yet."

"He will when he leaves office," said Connolly.

"Do you know what he will do?" asked Thompson.

"Certainly," said the lawyer from Washington, D. C.

"Gentlemen," said Judge Taylor, "stay away from those things."

For the day they obeyed. Kerner, somehow, was no longer looking so god-like, and his attorney appeared downright foolish in the eyes of some observers. Perhaps Connolly was aware of it for, next morning in chambers, he brought up the subject once more.

"Your Honor," he began, "yesterday afternoon I went into a towering rage in this courtroom because of what I thought was one of the cheapest shots ever taken in a case that I have tried — the reference by the district attorney to the fact that this man on trial took a deduction in a subsequent tax return that is not an issue in this case, not even in the indictment, and made it appear in front of the jury that the man was a cheater in his tax . . ."

"No such thing," said Thompson.

"I am still mad about it," continued Connolly. "I think it is so prejudicial that I move for a mistrial."

"The motion," said Judge Taylor, "is overruled."

The judge and the defense attorney argued. "Yesterday," said the judge, "it rather shocked me, the way you behaved. But, in justice to you, you are under a strain, and, of course, I accepted your apology fully, and I do now."

Connolly's associates insisted that their colleague had properly objected at the beginning of that particular line of questions, and the judge commented, "That is the trouble with you boys."

Connolly didn't like that remark, but urged the judge to read the transcript. "I don't have to read it," said the judge. "I heard the testimony, and I am not going to sit here and read the record."

Then it was the government and the defense attorneys who squabbled. Skinner jabbed at his opponents, saying, "I have not yelled in the courtroom, and I have not objected when you have accused me of tapping phones, and I won't do it again. I won't do it in the courtroom ever." Thompson noted there "was no objection for a page and a half." But Connolly again promised to "blow you right out of your chair when you have finished."

The judge tried to soothe bruised egos. "You should be kind to each other and go on the idea that you want to live and you want your adversary to live instead of just coming in here with brickbats to hit the adversary over the head — that isn't proper. . . . It grieves the court to see counsel and to hear counsel abuse each other."

"I think it was a very dirty shot, Your Honor. I still do. Nothing is going to change my mind about that," said the red-faced Connolly.

Finally Thompson wrote out an instruction to the jury and Judge Taylor read it aloud when the day's proceedings at last began: "Members of the jury, yesterday you heard some evidence that in 1968 Judge Kerner deducted the value of the papers he donated to the Illinois State Historical Society. The court instructs you that persons may donate materials of this sort to libraries and deduct the value of the gift from income, and you are further instructed that you should not be prejudiced against Judge Kerner in this regard."

Thompson began to chip away once more at Kerner's Grand Jury testimony. The former governor came up with a new reason for not remembering certain conversations he had been asked about.

"I received so many conversations of various sorts, Mr. Thompson, where I turned my hearing device off."

"Your hearing device?"

"Yes. I am not hard of hearing, but, I say, physically, I really wouldn't listen, and this occurred very frequently." He added that he stopped listening when he wasn't interested in the subject being explained.

Kerner then proceeded to charge he had been "led down the primrose path" by Woerheide at his first Grand Jury appearance, and was consequently "misled." Asked specifically, the judge said he thought the misleading was deliberate. Whereupon, Thompson got him to admit that in his second appearance he told Woerheide and the Grand Jury: "I think I have been treated fairly in here. . . . I have confidence in you and I have confidence in this Grand Jury and you may have all the information from me that you desire at any time."

In explanation, Kerner said that "when the indictment was returned, I could see how certain of my understandings of questions and
my answers were deliberately twisted."

Again and yet again, Thompson found the defendant in error, even
on testimony given the previous day. Nevertheless, Kerner's poise
wasn't shaken and he could still muster strength to refer to one allega-
tion as "an outright, blatant lie."

On that note, Thompson ended his cross-examination.

On redirect, Connolly skipped quickly over a number of subjects
and paused to bring up the matter of private papers appraised by
Newman at $70,000. Kerner, still dropping names, volunteered that
"Mr. Omar Bradley, General Omar Bradley himself, told me that
Ralph was doing his papers."

"Now that," said Judge Taylor, "is hearsay testimony and incompe-
tent. . . ."

Still trying, Kerner began again: "I know a president who stated
that Ralph. . . " Thompson objected and the presiding judge told the
defendant jurist, "Judge, don't repeat that hearsay testimony. That
isn't competent."

"Well, I do know . . ." began Kerner, but Connolly interrupted
him, and finally established that Kerner had *seen* work Newman did for
Bradley, Carl Sandburg, Senators Dirksen and Douglas. With that the
man Thompson was later to describe "as our most beneficial witness"
was excused.

"The defendant Kerner rests," said Connolly.

The defendant Isaacs mounted no defense. Wolfson, still angry with his
fellow defense attorney and still feeling he had been misused by his
client when Isaacs joined with Connolly and Kerner to persuade him to
"go easy on Marje," contented himself with a short statement of facts to
which both sides agreed. Wolfson, in fact, was afraid to subject his
client to a cross-examination such as had badly wounded Kerner. With
his history of wheeling and dealing Isaacs was even more vulnerable,
but beyond that was the knowledge that Isaacs' fate rested with the
former governor. If by some miracle the jury bought Connolly's theory
of Miller's complex scheming and decided that poor Kerner was but a
pawn in the evil game, then it would almost have to acquit Isaacs as

well. Personally, Wolfson was not sanguine about it, but given the state of the record it seemed about all to hope for. So, after only a few minutes, the defendant Isaacs rested as well.

Assistant U. S. Attorney Skinner, the man who had written the official prosecution memo back in 1971, began the closing arguments at 10 A.M. February 14. He had valentines for Judge Taylor, "who has taken the winter off to come to Chicago"; for the federal marshals, "who have also made sacrifices"; for other members of the staff "who have worked many hours of overtime without compensation"; and, finally, for the jurors, who had not seen their families for seven weeks. With that duty done, he proceeded to throw rocks for most of the day at Kerner and Isaacs, and a few pebbles at their alleged co-conspirators, Miller and Marje.

As Skinner outlined the plot, it was a joint venture on the part of the latter two. No longer did Miller get the blame for all decisions. Marje was in there too, said Skinner, in effect, and the pair worked to build up a racing empire by any and all means. Of course, he acknowledged, Mrs. Everett said it was all Miller's idea, and Miller said it was Marje's idea, but that really didn't matter.

Continuing, Skinner traced the development of the conspiracy as he saw it, and began outlining the "proof" he asserted existed to support each count in the indictment. By lunch he still had far to go. Connolly used the break to tell Judge Taylor once again not to get mad. The dangerous remark came after Taylor denied a series of motions relative to alleged misstatements of fact by Skinner.

"I am not mad," roared the little judge. "I am not mad. I say the argument was proper."

And of course he had his way.

It began snowing in mid-afternoon so at Skinner's suggestion the usual recess was cut short and he hurried forward to finish earlier than planned. His job was to lay out the facts of the complex case, choosing, of course, those that best suited the government's purposes. Building to an emotional climax, he said of Kerner:

"His motive to lie is clear. The evidence shows that he and Theodore Isaacs are guilty of bribery. They are guilty of mail fraud. They are guilty of perjury. They are guilty of lying to agents. They are guilty of lying to the Grand Jury. They are guilty of lying to you and they are guilty of lying to the people of this courtroom who have been here."

He called for "a verdict of guilty on all counts," and all parties left the black tower that is the Everett Dirksen Federal Building and went out into the white snow.

Thursday, February 15 — and tension filled the courtroom. It was as if the bell was about to ring for a heavyweight championship fight. Scheduled was Paul Connolly, the big gun from Washington, D.C.; Paul Connolly of Williams, Connolly & Califano; Paul Connolly, the man with a theory.

Everyone was there: Kerner's adopted children, Connolly's wife and daughter, who had flown in for the occasion, special writers from area newspapers supplementing the regular reporters.

"I have never undertaken a more momentous task," began the lawyer, sounding almost privileged to have the job of defending "this man, who is an honor to his nation and his state."

Denouncing the government for applying "the conspiratorial theory of history" to Kerner, and comparing such application to the methods of Hitler and Joe McCarthy, the attorney proceeded to do two things: defend Kerner, and blame all of his troubles on another conspiracy by the man he called "Machiavelli" — William Miller.

All day he talked, pausing only for the noon recess. He reviewed the case in great detail and with considerable eloquence, but in the last analysis his torrent of words seemed designed to overwhelm by sheer volume rather than by weight of logic. Even so, there came a time when he seemed to put all his eggs in one basket.

"One of the most significant factual determinations that you must make in this case," he stated solemnly, "and I say to you with all the power and force at my command — if I am wrong about this, I think you are going to have to return a verdict against Otto Kerner — one of the most significant factual determinations that you will have to make is whether or not on November 9, 1962, William S. Miller discussed Marje Everett's stock offer with Governor Kerner, because you have a major conflict. Kerner says it did not happen. William Miller says it did happen."

Warren Wolfson suddenly felt sick at his stomach. He glanced at the prosecution's table. U. S. Attorney Thompson had turned to look at his assistant, Skinner. Both men were grinning in delight. "It was incredible," Wolfson said later. "He let the case rise or fall on that one point."

At the end he put the outcome on yet another basis. "Weigh the life of Otto Kerner when you are in that jury room," he said, "against the hard-charging, vigorous imagination of an ambitious prosecutor, and decide for yourself whether the interests of the United States of America are served by having Otto Kerner in your midst or not. . . .

"There is no compromise with freedom and acquittal."

"Members of the jury," said Judge Taylor, "the arguments will end tomorrow." The big day, the "happening," was over.

Wolfson, who had called no witnesses of his own but who had fought as best he could for the silent Isaacs, led off for his client at 10:05 A.M. Friday. He sought to impress the jurors with the importance of their decision, supplying, as it were, continuity with Connolly's closing comments:

"Your verdict will have a lasting impact on the men who sit at this table. If you are wrong, your word can mark them forever and bring terrible consequences to them and to their families."

Leading into his summary, he reminded the jurors that he had told them in his opening statement "that you would not be used to people like William Miller and Marjorie Everett. . . . First Marjorie Everett. Mr. Thompson said she is a public-spirited citizen, entitled to the gratitude of the public. And once that is said, they call her a co-conspirator. . . . That makes her a public-spirited co-conspirator. Then they go on to place Bill Miller on the stand, and he calls her a liar. If you listened closely to what the government has told you, so do they."

The attorney went on for some minutes, detailing the conflicts of testimony between Miller and Mrs. Everett. He had great fun in describing the transformation of Miller from a defendant to a government witness, although he found it incredible that Marje should appear as a government witness and then as a defense witness.

"What difference does it make, they say," Wolfson continued, "if you can't believe both Marje Everett and Bill Miller? The difference should be clear. You are being asked to convict people on their word and on their thoughts as they say they have expressed them."

He offered a third alternative: "Marje Everett and William Miller fulfilling some joint plan to be king and queen of racing, to cut up the world, at least the racing world, which is the only world they knew or cared about."

Occasionally, Wolfson got Marje's statements mixed up with Miller's, but it didn't seem to matter very much. Fair enough, for, according to Wolfson, the government attorneys were just as inconsistent.

When they wanted Marje Everett to pay more taxes, he explained, they said she sold the CTE stock in 1962. When they wanted to prosecute Isaacs and Kerner, they made it a 1966 transaction.

Mixing sarcasm and sincerity, Wolfson tore holes in the government's case, but he was effective chiefly in the less vital areas. His theory of the case came clear: Kerner and Isaacs had taken advantage of a stock deal, but had done so without giving anything in return. In other words, there was no vast conspiracy on the part of anyone — it had been merely business as usual in Illinois. In that context, neither man had done anything illegal — at least until the investigation began. And, Wolfson reminded the jurors, *his* client, Isaacs, had not been charged with perjury or making false statements.

The case, said the young attorney who soon would become a circuit judge, boiled down to what Humpty-Dumpty replied when Alice said he had given the wrong meaning to a word.

" 'When I use a word,' Humpty-Dumpty said, 'it means just what I choose it to mean — neither more nor less.'

" 'The question is,' said Alice, 'whether you can make words mean so many different things.'

" 'No,' said Humpty-Dumpty, 'the question is which is to be master.'

"You are the final master," Wolfson told the jurors. "You have the last word. You can take us out of Wonderland."

(Wolfson was in error. The quote was from Lewis Carroll's *Through the Looking Glass*, not *Alice's Adventures in Wonderland*.)

He was winding up.

"You have seen in this trial an exercise of awesome power, power to bring men to trial on innuendo, guesswork, to charge Bill Miller and then turn him into a friendly government witness, so he can go ahead with his plans to rule racing; to charge Faith McInturf, sign her up on the prosecution team, and then not put her on the stand; to praise Mrs. Everett with one hand and with the other call her a co-conspirator and then vouch for a witness who calls her a liar; to overlook the phony applications knowingly filed and passed on by William Miller and Marje Everett, but to ask you to hold two men responsible for those applications without a hint of evidence that they knew anything about them. . . .

"Could it be someone wanted to get to Otto Kerner so badly that the only way to do it was trample over Theodore Isaacs? He is here because he bought stock twice and he sold it twice and he made a profit. That and no more. Don't let Ted Isaacs become a sacrificial lamb. Don't let that happen."

It was an intelligent and eloquent closing, but it was largely ignored by the press and the audience, who were waiting to hear that other big gun, the prosecutor who hoped to be President, James "Big Jim" Thompson, reply to Connolly's blasts.

Thompson paid tribute to Wolfson for "one of the best defense arguments I have ever heard," and proceeded to some of the questions raised by that young attorney. Of Marje Everett he said:

"She provided that first basic information. Without that, there would be no case here today. . . . She is a co-conspirator because she did the acts and she joined in this agreement about which we have heard evidence for the last six weeks. She wanted to protect her racing enterprises."

He emphasized the point: "It is not because she should go unpunished for what she did, but because a determination was made long ago that without her there would be no case. Somebody had to testify. We took Marje Everett as we found her."

As to Miller: "It wasn't to his advantage to convict himself out of his own mouth so long as he was a defendant."

Speaking of Kerner and Isaacs, he commented: "The plain fact is the stock was offered and they took it. I suppose what it boils down to is Marjorie Everett and William Miller were *our* witnesses because they were *their* conspirators."

Thompson said he was willing to trade a "seventy-two-year-old man who is out of government" for "a man who, if the charges in this indictment are true, was a corrupt governor and who now sits as a judge, judging other people's property and lives and fortunes."

Soon Connolly, the irrepressible, was interrupting Thompson's statement with objections. Judge Taylor told him coldly, "You had your talk to the jury. Let him finish his argument."

Thompson turned to Connolly's gamble — the meeting November 9, 1962, in Kerner's office at Springfield. Noting the defense attorney had stated the day before that if the jury believed Miller's version it had to bring in a verdict against Kerner, the prosecutor proceeded to tell why Miller should be believed. It took several minutes. Once again

Wolfson experienced that sinking sensation in his stomach. Connolly's face became redder.

They paused for a recess, and the lawyers gathered at the bar. Wolfson made several objections and was commended for doing so "in a proper manner," but he was overruled. Judge Taylor then glared at Connolly.

"I direct Mr. Connolly not to interrupt this man again."

"I don't think you have the power, Your Honor," said Connolly.

"I don't want you to disobey what I told you."

"I will have to make a judgment when the time comes," said Connolly.

Thompson resumed, discussing in detail the perjury, false statements, and mail-fraud counts. He tore Kerner's testimony to pieces, and laughed at it. Finally he mentioned Connolly's charge that he was ambitious, and he quoted an unnamed federal judge as telling him, "Ambitious prosecutors don't indict federal judges."

The man who would run for governor of Illinois in 1976 admitted, however, that he did have ambitions. He listed them as a desire "to serve in the office [of prosecutor] with honor and distinction. . . . I want you to be proud of me."

He asked the jury at the end to do "what your consciences and your view of the evidence leads you to do, and return verdicts of guilty on the counts that you think warrant that finding."

Next morning, Saturday, February 17, 1973, the jury listened to Judge Taylor instruct on the law of the case for more than three hours. The doors to the courtroom were locked during the lecture. Thereupon, the jury took one final look at defendants Kerner and Isaacs and marched out to do their duty as they understood it.

The waiting, and the sweating, began.

Our long national nightmare is over.

GERALD R. FORD
August 9, 1974

12

The Verdict

In Washington, Senator Sam Ervin is preparing to hold hearings of his newly authorized "Watergate Committee." In less than a month John Dean will warn President Nixon:

"We have a cancer within, close to the presidency, that is growing. It is growing daily. It's compounding, growing geometrically now because it compounds itself."

The Imperial Presidency is beginning to totter, its base eroded by cynicism, corruption, and fear. Yet, ironically, Project CRIMP is about to achieve results in Chicago. More than three years have passed since that autumn day in 1969 when Marje Everett talked to George Mahin and John Walsh, and on Monday, February 19, 1973, a trial jury agrees on a verdict.

Sixteen hours have been spent in deliberation since the jury got the case on Saturday afternoon. Now, after ninety minutes on Monday, foreman William Michael knocks on the door of the Grand Jury room and tells the marshal stationed outside that the jury is ready to report.

"Relax," says the marshal. "It'll take an hour or so to get everybody here."

The first phone call goes downstairs to the fifteenth floor where in his office Thompson and his aides have been waiting in growing confidence. The time taken by the jury in such a complex case is too much for an acquittal, and not enough for a hung jury. Obviously, then, someone has been convicted of something.

It is the holiday of George Washington's birthday and in honor of the man who would not lie, the modernistic Federal Building is almost empty. Unsmiling, a bust of Everett Dirksen stares at the vast expanse of red carpet and the black columns that rise at regular intervals until the glass walls are reached. Not on duty in the information booth is the

213

girl who says of her job, "I burn up in summer and freeze my ass in winter."

Isaacs, thin, nervous, and wearing a sports jacket, is first to arrive. He paces the hall, chatting with reporters who rush in worriedly and then relax. Soon Wolfson appears, leads his client into the courtroom and seats him at the defense table.

Kerner walks in, accompanied proudly by Connolly, trailed by Connolly's young associates, Tom Patton and Jim Hubbard. Kerner is pale beneath his tan, and he is breathing rapidly although he has come from his chambers two floors above. For Kerner is still a sitting federal judge; suspended, yes, but still entitled to his privileges of salary, offices, elevator, and parking space.

Kerner sits down, carefully, consciously, as if posing for an official portrait, and begins talking to Isaacs. At 11:25 o'clock, Thompson leads in his retinue. Skinner cannot conceal his confidence, his joy: he greets reporters in a loud, cocky voice. It becomes quiet now as the tension grows.

At last the jurors come in, single file. Connolly, who has asked them to look Kerner in the eye, notes with horror that everyone is looking at the floor, all but Alfred Kunde whose gaze is steady and defiant. Everyone stands, nevertheless, even the reporters. Judge Taylor enters, and they stand again.

The ritual begins. The clerk takes an envelope from foreman Michael, fumbles with it, tears it open, reads aloud:

"We, the jury, find the defendant Theodore Isaacs guilty as charged in the indictment."

A muscle flickers in Isaacs' left cheek, but his face is expressionless. Did he expect a guilty verdict?

The second envelope is opened. The clerk reads:

"We, the jury, find the defendant Otto Kerner guilty as charged in the indictment."

Kerner's mouth sags open. Connolly reaches for his arm, but the proud man regains control as quickly as he lost it.

A sigh sweeps the courtroom. Skinner shakes Thompson's hand and other assistants pound him on the back. They are happy.

Judge Taylor polls the jury. There is no mistake, no disagreement. Reporters are running for the nearest telephones and the jurors leave the courtroom. Motions are made — strictly routine business. The defendants sit quietly until everything is done that must be done. Sentencing will come later. Kerner faces a maximum sentence of eighty-three years in jail; Isaacs could be sentenced to seventy-three.

Jurors return and are thanked by Judge Taylor. He also admonishes them to keep secret their deliberations. They go to the hotel near Arlington Park where they have been sequestered. Marshals will drive them home after they pack their suitcases. Juror Kunde tells the press, "I'm going home and kiss my wife."

Court is adjourned.

Late in the day, Kerner issues a statement which says in part, "I have been in many battles in my life, where life itself is at stake. This battle is even more important than life itself because it involves my reputation and honor, which are dearer than life itself, and I intend to continue this battle."

Isaacs declines comment. "I would have to sit down and write out my whole philosophy," he tells reporters.

Thompson, besieged by reporters, agrees to a press conference. For the first time he gives Miller equal praise with Marje. Miller, he says, "withstood a withering cross-examination. . . . The jury must have believed him." The U. S. Attorney denies that there were any political motivations in bringing Kerner to trial. It is all in a day's work, he implies.

Shortly thereafter Thompson receives a telephone call from presidential assistant John Ehrlichman who is high above, somewhere, in what was, and will be, *Air Force One*, now dubbed *The Spirit of Seventy-Six*.

In the name of the president of the United States, Ehrlichman offers congratulations for a job well done. The president was especially pleased with the remark about no political motivations, Ehrlichman adds. "Deniability," there's nothing like it.

From Los Angeles, Marje Everett comments, "I regret that others should have involved a man of Otto Kerner's reputation and standing in their maneuvers and caused him to pay such a high penalty.

"Naturally, I am gratified that the verdict of the jury upheld the truthfulness of my testimony and the circumstances under which I was forced to make stock in my racing enterprises available."

Mrs. Everett doesn't explain which testimony has been upheld —

her statements as a government witness or her answers as a defense witness.

Columnist Mike Royko, as often happened, comes closer than most to telling it like it was:

> Even now, there are many tears being shed, some of them by naive journalists, about the "tragedy" of Otto Kerner and his shattered career.
>
> And his friends are explaining that poor Otto just isn't very bright.
>
> In fairness, there is some evidence of that.
>
> He didn't show much brains in getting tied in with Isaacs, who has to be one of the all-time bungling bagmen.
>
> He didn't have as much brains as William Miller, the wealthy former racing board chairman. Miller was up to his eyeballs in the payoffs. But he was smart enough to squeal on Otto, so he is walking away rich and free.
>
> He didn't have as much brains as Marje Everett, the former racing queen. She handed out bribes, and she kept her mouth shut as long as the bribes helped make her rich. Only later did she get indignant and blow the whistle on Kerner. She is walking away rich and free.
>
> A lot of other politicians got theirs, too, and they are still running around loose.
>
> Only Otto and Isaacs are prison-bound at this point.

On the day after the verdict was returned, banner headlines in *Chicago Today* proclaim:

12 MORE FACE
INDICTMENT!

The story, quoting unidentified federal sources, predicts that various legislators who had been involved in the Washington Park Trotting Association stock bonanza, will be prosecuted by the U. S. Attorney's office. A list of the potential defendants includes Arthur J. Bidwill, Clyde Choate, George W. Dunne, William J. Lynch, Clyde Lee, John W. Lewis, W. J. Murphy, and George Schaller.

But it is a mistake — Project CRIMP is over.

On March 2, Judge Taylor formally dismisses the indictment which the government has held over the head of Miller and his secretary, Miss McInturf. The action is evidence enough no additional prosecution is planned. Miller has completed his contract; the government has no further use for him.

But the multimillion dollar civil case remains, growing in size with every passing day as penalties and interest pile up. Try as he might, Miller cannot bring it to trial. Only by doing so can he hope for personal vindication. For despite Royko's words, Miller has been badly hurt. Young men can shake off disgrace for there is time to build new careers, new images, but Miller is seventy-two and time is running out.

Meanwhile, time runs out for Joe Knight. Still under indictment, the director of financial institutions under Governor Kerner dies on May 2, 1973. A bachelor, he leaves an estate valued at $1 million. Two years later a federal judge rules that part of that estate could go to some City Savings Association depositors who were defrauded of $23 million during the period Knight allegedly supervised the institution.

On April 19, 1973, Kerner returns to the courtroom. Attorneys argue pro and con, and Kerner tells Judge Taylor:

"My real punishment, deserved or not, has already been inflicted. Twelve men and women of Illinois have found that I betrayed the public trust. Twelve jurors among the millions of citizens I have served chose to believe that I dishonored the high office of governor. No matter what the ultimate outcome of this case may be, that verdict has deeply and irreparably tainted the good reputation which I cherished. Years of imprisonment can never compare in severity to that punishment."

Judge Taylor calls the case "the most difficult and tense" he has encountered in twenty-three years. (In 1977 he presided over a somewhat similar trial which ended with a guilty verdict against Governor Mandell of Maryland.) Taylor throws out one bribery count and four mail-fraud counts, but many remain and he sentences Kerner and Isaacs to three years in prison and $50,000 fines.

Both men give notice of appeal.

On April 26, Kerner at last vacates his chambers, a six-room suite of offices, but he remains a federal judge on leave of absence, still drawing his salary of $42,500 a year. There is talk he may be impeached since he won't resign. Perhaps to quiet that talk, Kerner starts depositing his salary checks in an escrow account in the First National Bank of Chicago. They would stay there, he says, until his appeals are decided. Presumably, if he is forced to go to prison the money will return to the government. (It didn't. In April, 1976, Kerner withdrew it and closed the account.)

Meanwhile, a new chairman of the Illinois Racing Board, Anthony Scariano, demands that Balmoral's twenty-seven days of racing be canceled because the controlling stockholder and star witness in the Kerner-Isaacs case admitted during the trial that he told untruths about stock ownership to the Racing Board. There is irony in this situation. Miller's "untruths" were told to protect Kerner. The information about the stock deal was known, of course, to several people who instead of being punished for their role were rewarded: Lynch, who was made a federal judge; Schaller, who became a circuit judge; former racing commissioner McKellar, who heard about the deal in London and was not even rapped on the knuckles; and, of course, Marje Everett, who received kind words from Thompson *and* Kerner's attorney.

An appeal to the Illinois Supreme Court is made, and Scariano succeeds in getting Miller out of racing. Having previously lost his Chicago Harness Racing dates and sold his horses, the former chairman sells the refurbished track at Crete to the Edward J. DeBartolo Corporation of Youngstown, Ohio, and it gets the Balmoral dates back.

In Baltimore, meanwhile, Vice President Agnew faces indictment for kickbacks and other fiscal monkey business. He insists that before he can be indicted he must be impeached. Kerner agrees with this theory and states, "If there is no successful impeachment, there can be no indictment, and that applies to federal judges as well as to the vice president." But Agnew makes a deal, cops a plea, and resigns.

On October 1, 1973, Mrs. Kerner, daughter of Boss Cermak, topples from her chair in the kitchen of the Kerner summer home in Lake Geneva, Wisconsin, and dies almost instantly. The previous August she underwent brain surgery for cancer. Sixty-seven, she was three years older than her second husband.

The first anniversary of the conviction of Kerner and Isaacs arrives, and, ironically, a special three-judge panel of Court of Appeals judges marks the occasion by handing down its decision on the defendants' appeal. Three counts are thrown out. Conviction on all remaining counts is affirmed.

The special panel disposes of the "impeachment before prosecution" theory: "Protection of tenure is not a license to commit crime or a forgiveness of crimes committed before taking office," and it rules specifically "that a federal judge is subject to indictment and trial before impeachment and that the district court had jurisdiction to try defendant Kerner." As to the stock offer to Kerner, the panel states: "Significant evidence places the stamp of bribery on the transaction."

The counts dismissed involve evidence that three checks drawn by Knight as part of the distribution of proceeds of the stock sales had been cleared through the Federal Reserve Bank in St. Louis, after deposit by the recipients in Illinois banks. The government claimed this violates the Travel Act, which prohibits the use of interstate commerce facilities to distribute the proceeds of unlawful activity, but the panel concludes that "the use of interstate facilities here was so minimal, incidental and fortuitous, and so peripheral to the activities of Isaacs, Kerner and the other participants in this bribery scheme, that it was error to submit Counts II, III, and IV to the jury."

Thompson calls the decision "an unmitigated joy." Kerner says he will make a new appeal.

In March, 1974, Marje Everett gives an interview beside the swimming pool in Scottsdale. She has tried to buy the San Diego Padres, a baseball team, but National League owners turned her down. Now she is trying to buy the Oakland A's from Charley Finley. Baseball Commissioner Bowie Kuhn has been quoted as promising, "If she gets by the National League, she won't get by me." Marje doesn't want to talk about Kuhn, but she is willing to discuss William S. Miller. The "horrible tragedy" of the Kerner case, she says, was caused by Miller and only by Miller.

The vendetta continues.

Now it is June and on the 17th day, the Supreme Court by a vote of 8 to 0, with Justice Thurgood Marshall abstaining, refuses to review the Kerner-Isaacs case. July 9 arrives and the last door is shut as Judge Taylor refuses to change the sentence he has imposed, and gives the defendants until July 29 to tidy up their affairs. Observers thought Taylor was wavering until Thompson reminded him, "There is no warmth or humanity in the law. It isn't meant to be that way."

With five days of freedom remaining, Kerner resigns as a federal judge, proof that he has at last abandoned hope.

July 29 is a gray, misty day. Kerner arrives in style at the federal correctional institute at Lexington, Kentucky, the heart of the blue-grass racing-country. He drives up in his Mercedes-Benz, impeccably dressed in a suit of blue silk, and marches with face expressionless past waiting reporters into the prison where he is fingerprinted and listed as prisoner number 0037-223. In contrast, Ted Isaacs arrives in handcuffs at the federal penitentiary at Terre Haute, Indiana, a grim, gray fortress. Officials say, however, that he will be assigned to a minimum security prison farm nearby. Ultimately he will be transferred to the rolling hills of Lexington.

September comes. President Ford pardons ex-President Nixon, and a drive to win a pardon for Otto Kerner gathers steam. Even Mayor Daley suggests that the cause of equality would be served if Kerner is pardoned. No one mentions all those legislators, Democrats and Republicans, who were going to be prosecuted by Thompson for taking WPTA stock, but haven't been.

November brings an astonishing report: Special Agent Stufflebeam plans to quit the IRS to collaborate with his old enemy, William S. Miller, on a book about the Kerner case. With two *Chicago Tribune* reporters, Thomas Powers and Ron Koziol, Stufflebeam forms Reading, Riting and Research, Inc., but Miller isn't involved.

It is March 6, 1975, and word comes from Lexington that Otto Kerner is suffering from cancer. Within hours, the U. S. Parole Board orders him released. He has served seven months. Next day he enters a hospital in Chicago where, after tests, he undergoes surgery of the lung. It is July 28 before Isaacs is paroled and returns to Chicago. He remains largely invisible, while "the old man" — his term for Kerner — is feted like a triumphant hero. There is a difference, however; Isaacs is in good health but Kerner isn't.

Kerner dies May 9, 1976.

The controversy continues after death. Kerner's adopted children struggle loyally to clear the family name, and the sentimentalists weep openly and often. Details of the case begin to fade and the image of Mr. Clean is refurbished. The truth about Richard Nixon helps convince many that Kerner was but an innocent victim of a vindictive president. Lost, somehow, is the role of Marje Everett, but William Miller is not forgotten — he was smeared too thoroughly for that. He receives appeals from the Kerner children to "confess," either now or posthumously, that he lied about that famous meeting with Kerner on November 9, 1962, for that, everyone agrees, was the key to the conviction. Miller's counteroffer to open his files for inspection is ignored — the friends of Otto Kerner don't want to be confused with facts.

Isaacs, a man who lives in shadows, slips about Chicago being all things to all people. To Stufflebeam, Powers and Koziol, he presents himself as a collaborator of their book: he will write the true, inside story and tell how he was forced to sit silent as Kerner lied on the witness stand. He doesn't mention his role in making his attorney "go easy" on Marje, but he promises to expose Kerner and vindicate himself. To Anton Kerner, he tells another story: Miller is trying to get the two *Tribune* reporters to do a "hatchet job" on Marje and Otto. In the background also is Marje. Through her attorney, Papiano, she keeps in touch with developments that threaten unwelcome publicity, and she comes to Chicago on such occasions as the funeral of Judge Lynch, with whom the bottle has finally caught up.

In contrast to the publicity which surrounded the last days of Otto Kerner and the continuing argument over his guilt or innocence, is the silence that shrouds Miller's efforts to bring his civil tax case to trial.

On April 14, 1972, as the screws were being tightened on Miller, the Internal Revenue Service served him with a notice of a tax deficiency totaling $1,845,763, plus 50 per cent fraud charges for a grand total of $2,768,844. The bulk of the additional taxes demanded concerned racing stock and was explained by the IRS in this manner:

"It is determined that you purchased 227,500 shares of Chicago Harness Racing stock for $555,000, when the fair market value of that stock was $2,484,300. As a result you acquired stock with a fair market value which exceeded your cost by the total amount of $1,929,300.

"It is further determined that you caused to be purchased by Chicago Harness Racing, a corporation, which you controlled, 48,080 shares of Balmoral Jockey Club stock at a price of $30 per share when the fair market value of that stock was $45 per share. As a result, you acquired stock with a fair market value which exceeded your cost by the total amount of $721,200. Accordingly, it is determined that you received $2,650,500 from transactions for services performed or to be performed, and your taxable income is accordingly increased in the amount of $2,650,000."

In other words, the IRS based its formal claim on the same allegations that caused Marje Everett to testify at the Kerner trial that she was extorted by Miller. Here then the issues were plainly drawn — the government had to prove its claim that Miller indeed was the master-mind pictured by Marje and by Kerner's attorney, Paul Connolly.

Meanwhile, of course, the amount due grew as interest piled up with the passing of time. In addition, still another notice of deficiency for the tax years ending December 31, 1964, 1965, and 1966 was served on January 18, 1974. Involved were dividend income, business expenses, and certain capital gains of which the most interesting was explained as follows:

"It is determined that you realized a longterm capital gain for the year 1966 of $44,800, from the sale of your 28,000 shares of Chicago Harness Racing, Inc. stock. The gain is taxable income subject to the 50 per cent deduction provided by section 1202 of the Internal Revenue Code. Accordingly, income is increased $22,400," and a five per cent penalty is imposed.

This referred to the stock Miller arranged for Knight to buy — stock that was held in a street name by the broker, Sincere & Company, until Knight could pay for it. Some of it was sold to Kerner and Isaacs as part of the complicated dealing that enabled them to pay for the fifty shares of CTE stock.

Once again, another test of the mastermind theory is in the offing. It is 1976 before Miller's attorney, Matthias A. Lydon, a former assistant U. S. Attorney from Chicago, brings the case to trial in Miami. The key witness is the Everetts' former attorney, Henry D. Williams, who is in poor health and doesn't want to travel to Illinois. Judge Charles Simpson said he was going to Miami anyway, and so starts the trial there.

Williams testifies, and in a few minutes the complex theory of the Machiavellian Miller is in shambles. The witness tells why Webb Everett decided to sell stock shares held by newly organized Illinois Racing Enterprises to Miller and to dissolve IRE. It was done for tax reasons, Williams explains, and there was no pressure, no threats, no extortion. Nor was the stock sold for less than it was worth.

The trial moves to Chicago. The government is completely unprepared, offering no witnesses, no exhibits. Attempts to serve subpoenas on Marje and Webb Everett are reported to be unsuccessful. Miller, on the other hand, has 150 exhibits to present and a room full of witnesses.

Were it not tragic in its implications, it would be funny. The total tax bill now stands at $4,200,000 — and this is something that the seventy-five-year-old Miller has been living with for four years. One of the exhibits is an IRS memo dated August 9, 1973, which indicated that a review of the Kerner trial transcript "failed to find the support we seek." The same memo noted that "apparently Hemphill, Noyes, Hornblower & Weeks had valued the stock at $30. Also, several other individuals purchased shares of stock at the same $30." Yet the effort to prove it was worth $45 continued. If ever there were a case of the government making charges without facts to support them, this was it. Equally important, it was these false assumptions that had brought the investigation and subsequent indictment of Kerner, Isaacs, Knight, Miller, and McInturf.

It has cost Miller hundreds of thousands of dollars in legal fees, the loss of racing dates, and great damage to his health and reputation. A settlement is proposed. Some quick calculations convince Miller that to press for complete victory by continuing the trial will cost him more in legal fees than the proposed settlement. Agreement is reached.

Fraud charges are dropped, and with them the penalty. Miller pays $5,908.25, for 1964; $4,578.66, for 1965; $11,268.01, for 1966, and $58,552, for 1967. Instead of $4.2 million, the total is $80,306.92, and it is for such things as disallowed business expenses and hurricane damage to his Golden Beach home which were not accepted.

The real verdict at last is possible.

There wás no grand conspiracy by Miller or Marje Everett or Kerner-Isaacs.

There were men and women attempting to make a fast buck by doing *business as usual* with the politicians of Illinois.

And *there were* reformers such as Miller who in obedience to that "Chicago instinct" reported by Lincoln Steffens, sought improvement in racing by wheeling and dealing in a society not yet ready for good government.

There were unscrupulous men in the Nixon administration who were willing to use an angry woman's allegations to achieve their own political goals.

There were, in addition to these persons, the professional big-game hunters who enjoyed the sport of "getting Otto's ass."

There was also the press which played the game of easy headlines and let itself be used.

And, finally, *there was* the public which really didn't give a damn.

13
The Reckoning

The 1976 election brought the final triumph of the political operation known to very few as Project CRIMP with the victory of candidate Thompson in his campaign against the Daley Machine for governor of Illinois. Yet along the way it had also paid handsome dividends.

Although the case did not come to trial by the 1972 election, the project helped Nixon win big and contributed to his illusion that he had received a mandate. For a year prior to that election, the indictment was a knife poised to strike. Indictments of many legislators had also been promised. The publicity was continuous. That in the end the promised indictments were not returned is not *proof* a deal was made, but Mayor Daley's bungling of his hand-picked candidate's campaign in 1976 suggests the possibility.

Perhaps there's no connection, but Boss Daley died in December following his humiliating defeat in November. The final "crimp" in his activities had come, but of course the machine created by Kerner's father-in-law, Boss Cermak, lived on, as powerful as ever in Chicago. Of Daley the *Los Angeles Times* said: "He kept his power by keeping his promises."

The big winner it now appears is Thompson. Thanks to the Kerner case — and other moves such as the taking of a wife and the shedding of forty pounds — he emerged from the obscurity of 1970 to become governor of Illinois in 1977, and a potential Republican superstar. As the old generation passes, Thompson is right on schedule in his personal quest for the presidency.

Another winner appears to be Marje Everett. Her image became a trifle tarnished during the 1976 campaign when Thompson — who had called Marje "a public-spirited citizen" before the trial — found it

224

politically expedient to put the Kerner case in better perspective. On October 24, 1976, he appeared on WLS-TV, Chicago, and lied outright about his help to Marje in getting settled at Hollywood Park. Keeping a straight face, he insisted that California authorities "asked me one key question: 'Is Marje Everett guilty of bribery?' and I said, 'That's what my indictment says and she is.' She wasn't very pleased with that testimony."

Two California officials promptly denied Thompson's version, insisting he helped Marje instead of hurting her, but by then it was too late to matter in the campaign. Yet the facts are clear. Thompson's letter to the attorney general of California and his public statements before the trial prove he helped the woman who, at the time, was his key witness. His need for Miller was acknowledged indirectly in that WLS-TV interview when he admitted "her testimony wasn't all that great."

Marje got control of Hollywood Park, and soon the same sort of things that had happened in Chicago were being repeated in California. In the fiscal years ending March 31, 1976, and 1977, Hollywood Park spent $325,000 for political purposes. The bulk of this sum, $224,600, went to defeat Proposition 13 on the ballot which would have legalized parimutuel wagering on dog racing in the state. Interestingly enough, the political contributions were paid into a trustee account maintained by Marje's faithful attorney, Neil Papiano.

Papiano also ended up in control of the food concessions. His law firm was paid $369,000 in the fiscal year 1976 and $164,000 in the fiscal year 1977. Looking back, one can understand why the attorney became so agitated at the Chicago trial when defense attorney Wolfson was ripping his client apart on the stand.

There was also the inevitable bickering. Disgruntled stockholders complained and rumors of a feud among stockholders kept things in turmoil. As of this writing, Marje is still in business, but, obviously, she could use a friend to soothe ruffled feathers as Miller once did in Chicago. Her success remains the fact that in less than a decade she put together an improbable racing empire, disposed of it for a huge sum, and made a new beginning in the Golden West. Movie stars and politicians still pay her court and enjoy her hospitality in Hollywood and at her Arizona home.

Perhaps the largest winners were the late Mayor Daley's former law partners. Despite IRS recommendations they be indicted, they were not prosecuted. Lynch, as noted, moved to the federal bench before drinking himself to death in 1976. He left an estate valued at $1.5 million (before debts and taxes) and, of that, he left $25,000 to Mrs. Daley and another $25,000 to Daley's son. Schaller, who also became a judge, was left money and property valued at $237,364, by Lynch. How much he made on his own for his work for Marje may not be known until his death, but that it was in the hundreds of thousands of dollars is already a matter of record.

No need to list again the legislators who took stock in what to them had to seem the normal way of conducting state business. As usual, they got away with it despite additional recommendations for prosecution. This failure to prosecute may come back some day to haunt Jim Thompson, but the man who scores in politics by prosecution must pick his targets carefully. You don't use a shotgun when officials of both parties are feeding from the same trough.

Much the same can be said of the "respectables," those blue-ribbon businessmen who lent their names — willingly in some cases, stupidly in others — to protect the politicians. Well rewarded were they for their services, and they took the money as avidly as anyone else, proving yet again that the basic difference between legitimate business and organized crime is often one of degree; the gangsters are more free with their enterprise yet the objective is the same — fast bucks. Certainly there will always be corrupt officials to permit gangsters to operate just so long as there are businessmen who want to keep their options open — all their options including the right to bribe. The adage that a community gets the kind of newspaper, police department, and local government it deserves, still applies and Chicago is no exception.

When you have winners you also have losers, and in Project CRIMP the losers were those people it was necessary to hurt, or destroy, in order to play prosecution politics. Foremost among the losers was, of course, the late Otto Kerner, Jr. One can sympathize with his adopted children who have tried valiantly, if not always intelligently, to clear his name for he did sit high on Mount Olympus and terrible was his fall. Yet that sympathy has to be tempered by the knowledge that Kerner brought his troubles upon himself. He was stupid. No other word applies. He was also vain, and it was his stupidity that made him vain. For the scandal-ridden Chicago Machine, his value was in his image of Mr. Clean, yet it was that image that made him such a tempting target when Project CRIMP was activated. Had he told the truth, he might easily have walked away free, yet his ego was such he couldn't confess to human weakness. He compounded his folly by retaining an attorney who appeared convinced of *his* unique importance. Between defense attorney Connolly and Appellate Court Judge Kerner, the human being born Otto had no chance. It is perhaps ironic that Kerner's lasting claim to fame may be the boost his conviction gave to the career of a man aiming at the White House. Will he be remembered as is Alger Hiss?

Theodore Isaacs was also a loser, but he didn't have so much to lose. His importance depended upon his special relationship with the "old man" — Kerner — and with Kerner's retirement to the bench that importance had begun to fade. Isaacs lost a few months of his life to prison, but, like Kerner, he put himself there. Had he not interfered with his attorney, Warren Wolfson, and insisted Wolfson take it easy on Marje, the outcome of the trial could have been different for Isaacs. Wolfson, ironically, was a winner although he lost his case. He proved his ability, and was soon appointed to the circuit court bench. Yet one can't feel too sorry for his client. Isaacs returned from prison and began making himself useful to people who had, or might attain, power. It isn't inconceivable that he will find another man as stupid as his late friend, and make himself invaluable.

Joe Knight was hurt, of course, by his indictment, but he was a dying man. Perhaps his last months might have been more placid had he been spared public humiliation, but with both feet inside the grave it wasn't prison he worried about. Miss McInturf, although not called to testify at the trial, was hurt by the notoriety that accompanied her indictment. The gossips could make much of the fact that she was unmarried, a working woman, yet wealthy enough to lend Knight $40,000. Her defense cost heavily for F. Lee Bailey doesn't sell his services cheaply. The pre-indictment period was a time of harassment for Miss McInturf just as it was for her boss, and such episodes as the presence of federal agents in the bushes outside her apartment window added nothing to her peace of mind. The process of being indicted is no picnic, as this author knows from personal experience, and for a businesswoman with no political experience it can be most traumatic.

Finally, there was the big loser, William S. Miller. He, as Marje's original target, was the catalyst. Her failure to send him to prison remains a bitter disappointment according to George Mahin, the Republican who first heard her bitter litany. Like Kerner, Miller had much to lose. He was a successful businessman, for almost two decades an internationally known expert on racing, and he believed sincerely he had served his state and his fellowman. Honors had flowed in, including the degree of Doctor of Laws, *honoris causa*, from Saint Mary's College of Notre Dame. He was proud that he had won a reputation for integrity and for compassion; he was also proud of his ability to use the tools at hand to achieve as much improvement as an imperfect world allowed. That those Municipal League reformers of Lincoln Steffens' day were right in their approach, he believed sincerely. Good government was still impossible in Chicago so one played the game in the public interest.

That he was perhaps correct is shown in the fact that since he resigned as chairman of the Racing Board, since he sold his stable and retired his racing silks, since he was denied the right to operate racing meets, the Sport of Kings in Illinois, as elsewhere, has gone into a sharp decline. One reason is that greed brought overexposure — there are simply too many horse races and too few good horses. Moreover, the combination of televised sports events and the new freedom of the bookie provides more entertaining ways for the sucker to lose his money. When horse racing was the only game in town on which one could easily bet, it prospered. It no longer has that distinction, and as men who were truly interested in bloodlines and breeding quit, forced out by gangsters and greedy politicians, racing becomes less and less a sport and more and more a racket. The old mystique is largely lost, and the great Illinois scandal was a contributing factor.

Miller, who became fond of racing even as civilian police commissioners become infatuated with the private brotherhood of cops, was deeply hurt to see his dreams for racing sacrificed in the rush to get "Otto's ass." Yet he had other reasons to grieve. An elderly man, he was for four years threatened with personal bankruptcy as that multimillion dollar civil tax suit hung above him like a dark cloud. He lived with it, unable to believe as once he had that honesty was enough and would triumph in the end. Had he lacked the funds to pay a fortune in legal fees, he could have been ruined despite the overwhelming fact that the government had no evidence whatsoever to sustain the charges it had filed on the basis of Marje's allegations. When those charges were filed they made banner headlines on the front pages of Chicago newspapers, but when they were dropped there was only a small story buried deep inside. Obviously, publicity might have reflected on Thompson in the middle of his campaign so Miller's victory got little attention — a fact that could not help but irk a man who had valued the opinions of those once proud to call him friend.

The smearing of Miller, before and during the trial, was cold, deliberate policy. It began as Justice Department strategy, as part of the conspiracy theory, and it was continued in an illogical twist of reasoning by the defense. Marje Everett could have the best of both worlds and appear as both a government and a defense witness, but Miller was presented as the Machiavellian schemer who betrayed public trust and private confidence in an elaborate and mysterious plot for personal gain. The press so painted him and never bothered to undo the injustice. Indeed, the friends of Otto Kerner found it convenient to blame Miller for their idol's downfall, and their effort to win parole and then a pardon for the fallen hero consisted largely of innuendo against Miller who, they implied, bought immunity for himself by giving false testimony. Strangely, they harbored no resentment against Marje, apparently recognizing that although she started the whole thing her target had been Miller not Kerner. Too proud to answer, Miller retired to his home by the ocean at Golden Beach, Florida, and turned down an opportunity to take control of one of racing's legends, Hialeah — home of pink flamingos and red ink.

It wasn't until the 1976 campaign that Thompson — who had called Miller "a lovable rogue" — found opportunity to put Miller in better perspective. On that same television show in which he called Marje a "briber," he said that "Bill Miller is one of the toughest old birds I ever met in my life. Nobody could brainwash him, you know. [Is this an admission that he tried?] He held his own with me; he held his own with the federal agents and he told the truth at the trial and he was subjected to three days of the most rigorous cross-examination I have seen in sixteen years as a prosecutor, and his story stood up. And the reason that his story stood up was because it was corroborated by objective physical evidence including Governor Kerner's own diary."

There was no reason for Thompson to lie about Miller in 1976; he certainly had not helped him before or after the trial. Just nine days after vindicating the former Racing Board chairman, Thompson beat Michael J. Howlett by 1,376,905 votes, a record total. Obviously, and ironically, he carried his presidential candidate to victory on his coattails. Gerald Ford defeated Jimmy Carter in Illinois by only 103,656 votes out of more than 4,563,000 cast.

A crimp indeed.

Although the GOP lost nationally to a peanut farmer from Georgia, the party most unexpectedly found itself with a super nova burning brightly in a darkling sky where previously only black holes and fading comets had been observed. The politics of prosecution had paid off for Thompson just as it had in an earlier era when it rewarded Nixon in the Hiss case. With luck, and an impressive re-election as governor in 1978, Thompson could easily follow Nixon into the White House as the next *elected* Republican.

And that, perhaps, would be a most appropriate footnote to the strange saga of Project CRIMP.

APPENDIX

B. F. LINDHEIMER

NOTES AND ACCOUNTS RECEIVABLE AS AT DECEMBER 31, 1959

Total Forwarded		$180,075.25
CURRENCY BOX ACCOUNT		
By B.F.L. General		
Balance 1/1/59	$721,549.75	
Charges during 1959	128,700.00	
	$850,249.75	
Less: Credits during 1959	102,500.00	747,749.75
Total Notes & Accounts Receivable per Books 12/31/59		$927,824.98
(Exhibit A)		
RESERVES FOR ESTIMATED BAD & DOUBTFUL ACCOUNTS		
For Loans & Advances listed above	$ 55,000.00	
For A-D Accounts Receivable listed above	7,443.75	
For Currency Box Accounts listed above	700,000.00	762,443.75
ESTIMATED FAIR CASH VALUE OF NOTES & ACCOUNTS		
RECEIVABLE AS AT DECEMBER 31, 1959 (Exhibit A)		$165,081.23

CONTRACT RECEIVABLE			
PACESETTER HOMES, INC.			
On Sale of Hupe & Soehnholz Properties as follows:			
Hupe - 89.947 acres @ 4600.00 per acre		$413,756.00	
Soehnholz - 114.05 acres @ 4600.00 per acre		524,630.00	
		$938,386.00	
Less: Down Payments			
On November 4, 1959	$25,000.00		
On December 14, 1959	25,000.00	50,000.00	888,386.00
Less: Deferred Income			
Selling Price of Combined Properties		933,386.00	
Cost of Properties Sold			
Hupe	$142,005.28		
Soehnholz	115,925.49	257,930.77	
		680,455.23	
Gross Profit for 1959 (Schedule B-1)		36,256.68	644,198.55
Net Invest. in Contract Receivable 12/31/59 (Exhibit A)			$244,187.45

Page from Ben Lindheimer's secret journal with reference to his "Currency Box Account".

MARJORIE L. EVERETT

Dear W S:

The following memo is to confirm our telephone conversation of today.

At your earlier suggestion we have been holding:

For O.K.

25 shares of C.T.E. common — $25,000
10,000 shares of W.P.T.A. common — $10,000

For D.G.

5 shares of JCTE common — $5,000
2,000 shares of WPTA common — $2,000

We did not raise the above as you had suggested that I hold this stock until we received further instructions from you.

For your further information

MARJORIE L. EVERETT

You will recall that the common of Certain JCTE at the time Marje had a value of $1,000 a share.

I shall be pleased to either issue Certain stock or resit — or handle it in any manner you suggest

Kindest personal regards

Marge

November 8, 1962

P.O. BOX 7 • ARLINGTON HEIGHTS, ILLINOIS • • • Clearbrook 5-4300

Very important memo from Marje to Miller about Kerner-Isaacs stock. It was misread at trial and thus put into the record incorrectly.

November 12, 1962

Mr. Theodore J. Isaacs
804 Greenleaf Avenue
Glencoe, Illinois

Dear Ted:

This will confirm that I have purchased for you and paid for
on behalf of yourself and/or your nominees fifty (50) shares
of Chicago Thoroughbred Enterprises, Inc. at the issuing
price of $1,000.00 per share.

According to our understanding, I will hold these shares in
my possession as collateral for your note to me of this
date for $50,000.00 bearing interest at the rate of 5% per
year (simple interest), with the further understanding that
your note will be paid on or before November 15, 1966.

Kindest personal regards.

Very truly yours,

Mrs. Webb A. Everett

MLE:mc

A backdated letter actually written in 1966 as part of the coverup for tax purposes.

Marjorie L. Everett
Executive Vice President

Divisions of
Chicago Thoroughbred Enterprises, Inc.

February 8, 1966

The Honorable William J. Lynch
Lynch, Schaller, Reilly & Cassidy
33 North LaSalle Street
Chicago, Illinois 60602

Dear Senator Lynch:

of CTE:

Enclosed are the following stock certificates

No. CS 160 dated February 8, 1966 for 25 shares
issued in the name of Marjorie L. Everett

No. CS 159 dated February 8, 1966 for 25 shares
issued in the name of Marjorie L. Everett

Inasmuch as Mary Carroll is on vacation, would
you kindly ask Mr. Schaller to sign these two certificates.

Sincerely yours,

La Verne Naslund

Secretary to Mrs. Everett

Enclosures

*These certificates have been endorsed by me
and I believe you said you would guarantee
my signature. Thanks*
Marje

Copy of letter forwarding the stock certificates of Kerner and Isaacs. Note handwritten note by
Marje.

CHICAGO HARNESS RACING, INC.

N⁰ 3544   2-1 / 710

P. O. Box 72 • HOMEWOOD, ILLINOIS   Feb. 2 19 66

PAY

Amount $2,606.38

TO THE
ORDER
OF

Account S

CHICAGO HARNESS RACING, INC.

THE FIRST NATIONAL BANK OF CHICAGO, ILL.

CHICAGO HARNESS RACING, INC.   N⁰ 3544

ENDORSEMENT ON ATTACHED CHECK BY PAYEE IS ACKNOWLEDGMENT OF THE PAYMENT IN FULL OF ITEMS SHOWN HEREON.	STATEMENT OF ACCOUNT	ACCOUNT	
		1006	$ 600.00
		712	1,375.00
		1020	631.38
		Total	$2,606.38

Attachment #1

December 31, 1965

MEMORANDUM TO ACCOUNTING DEPARTMENT:

Would you please have each of the following
companies issue its check payable to Account S as follows:

CTE $2,913.88 (one-half each to AP and WP)

Balmoral   2,913.88

WPTA   2,913.88

CHRI   2,913.88

This is to reimburse Account S for certain expenses.

Please return the checks to me today. Thanks.

Mary
MC

Two records referring to Marje's slush fund, "Account S".

235

M E M O S H E E T

CHICAGO THOROUGHBRED ENTERPRISES   Arlington Heights, Ill.

10/7/68 Palluck mb	Marge Everett called me at home Sunday night to advise that she had agreed to a deal whereby her shares of CTE would be acquired by a conglomerate company for $10,000 per share. She was not at that time able to indicate the name of the buyer and said this would be done after public announcement on the following Tuesday. She will obtain a convertible subordinate debenture which will give her annual income in excess of $1,000,000 annually, a ten year management contract, and full authority in running the business. The purchaser will tender for the remaining shares at the same price. Marge said this will put her in an excellent personal position whereby she can retire her debt, which is slightly less than $1,500,000, with us, and will enable her to do certain philanthropic things which she has in mind.

     The purchaser is apparently particularly interested in the development of the land at both Arlington Park and Washington Park and indicated to her that they would make available $8,000,000 for such purpose in the next year. This would include major improvements at both tracks--completion of the grandstand expansion at Arlington and enclosing all of the grandstand at Washington Park. Also, CTE will continue its banking relationship with us, and in fact will probably be enhanced. Marge said the acquiring company was impressed with the job we had done for CTE and wanted no changes whatsoever.

     Ed Weisl was apparently the key factor in arranging the deal, although Ned Janotta had been working with him on it. The entire group met with the purchaser last Wednesday, Thursday, and Friday, and the deal was concluded late Friday. She said that Henry Williams was already working on her estate planning, and I suggested our Trust Department could be helpful to her and would welcome an opportunity to have our people work with Mr. Williams. She said she would keep me posted in that respect.

Copy of first page of an internal bank memo dealing with Marje's plans to sell out to Gulf & Western.

36-04-303-1-1 (CHI-SP-14)
36-13-145-1-1 (CHI-SP-28)
36-04-255-1-1 (CHI-SP-42)
36-14-221-1-1 (CHI-SP-44)
FINAL

OTTO KERNER is employed as a Federal Appellate Court Judge, Seventh Judicial Circuit, at Chicago, Illinois, and formerly served as Governor of Illinois, 1961-1968. THEODORE ISAACS is an attorney currently engaged in his own practice and formerly served as Director of Department of Revenue, State of Illinois. WILLIAM S. MILLER is an officer and executive of various horse racing companies operating a race track at Crete, Illinois, and was formerly Chairman of the ILLINOIS RACING BOARD. JOSEPH E. KNIGHT is currently retired and was the former Director of Financial Institutions, State of Illinois. ISAACS, MILLER and KNIGHT were all appointed to their respective State positions by KERNER during his tenure as Governor of the State of Illinois.

These cases were originated as a result of information developed during inquiries made with respect to Project CRIMP. These cases were assigned to both Special Agents WILLIAM WITKOWSKI and OLIVER P. STUFFLEBEAM and were initiated as follows:

	Date Preliminary	Date Full-Scale
OTTO KERNER	June 12, 1970	December 7, 1970
THEODORE ISAACS	January 5, 1971	January 5, 1971
WILLIAM S. MILLER	May 8, 1970	June 18, 1971
JOSEPH KNIGHT	June 18, 1971	June 18, 1971

Internal Revenue Agents JOHN MARSHALL (resigned June 12, 1971) and JOHN LUBKE, Group 515, were assigned to assist in the investigation of these cases. OTTO KERNER was first notified of the investigation on July 15, 1970, and warned of his constitutional rights when he was interviewed regarding his income tax liabilities (Exhibit 1, Memorandum of Interview). THEODORE ISAACS was first notified of the investigation on January 13, 1971, and warned of his constitutional rights when he was interviewed regarding his income tax liabilities (Exhibit 2, Memorandum of Interview). On May 20, 1970, WILLIAM S. MILLER was spoken with on the telephone (Exhibit 3, Memorandum of Telephone Conversation) and he said that he already had learned of our investigation. JOSEPH E. KNIGHT has not been interviewed subsequent to the opening of the investigation of him and he has not been informed that he is currently under investigation.

On March 25, 1971, during an interview, KERNER said that PAYTON FORD, Washington, D. C., was representing him as his attorney (Exhibit 4, Memorandum of Interview).

- 3 -

Page 3 of the IRS report recommending prosecution of Kerner. Note the reference to Project CRIMP.

memorandum

to:

from:

subject: Prosecution Memorandum
ARTHUR J. BIDWILL
NEAL BIDWILL
CLYDE L. CHOATE
ALOYSIUS L. CRONIN
GEORGE W. DUNNE
JOHN W. LEWIS
WILLIAM J. LYNCH
ROBERT T. McLOSKEY
JOHN P. MEYER (MERTYCE MEYER)
GEORGE J. SCHALLER
PAUL A. ZIEGLER

This memorandum covers the proposed prosecution of the above listed

individuals for violations of Title 18, Sections 371, 1952 and 1341

of the United States Code. In addition, it is proposed that the

following individuals be named as unindicted co-conspirators:

> MARJORIE L. EVERETT
> CLYDE LEE
> WILLIAM S. MILLER
> WILLARD J. MURPHY
> DONALD J. O'BRIEN (?)
> EVERETT R. PETERS (deceased)
> WILLIAM POLLACK (deceased)
> PAUL POWELL (deceased)

> STATEMENT OF FACT:

Corporate Background

During November, 1960 CTE Inc. (hereinafter referred to as CTE) was

incorporated as a Delaware Corporation authorized to conduct business

within the State of Illinois.

Internal Revenue Service

First page of IRS memo proposing prosecution of various legislators, two of Marje's attorneys, both ex-partners of Mayor Daley. Nothing happened.

238

memorandum

to: Mr. Edward T. Joyce
Attorney, Criminal Division

from: Paul J. Schaeffer
Attorney, Project CRIMP

subject: NEWSPAPER PUBLICITY   September 15, 1971

The enclosed article appeared in the Chicago Today, September 15, 1971,
five-star final edition.

(b) (3)

I have brought the article to the attention of the IRS inspection agents
who, at the request of Commissioner Walters, are investigating possible
leaks in connection with "Project CRIMP," and I discussed with Inspection
the implications of this article's appearance in the newspaper.

While there is no definite information relating to the source of this and
similar disclosures to the press, all of the information contained in these
articles is in the possession of William S. Miller and his confederates.

(b) (3)

It has also come to the attention of the project attorneys that Miller held
a two-hour press conference in which he discussed with reporters his involvement with Kerner and Isaacs in the acquisition of Race Track stock.

(b)(3)
(b)(5)
(b)(7)(C)

Of course, the possibility that the leaks to the press are coming from
persons participating in the investigation cannot be and is not being
overlooked by the Inspection service.

Internal Revenue Service

This memo, obtained in censored form, confirms the manner in which the press was manipulated,
and raises a question: How did the Government know what information was possessed by WSM at
this pre-indictment stage of the investigation.

239

United States Department of Justice

UNITED STATES ATTORNEY
NORTHERN DISTRICT OF ILLINOIS
UNITED STATES COURTHOUSE
CHICAGO, ILLINOIS 60604

JRT:SKS:lcm
71 CR 1085

January 10, 1972

Honorable Evelle J. Younger
The Attorney General
State of California
600 State Building
Los Angeles, California 90012

Re: United States v. Isaacs, et al.,
71 CR 1086

Dear General Younger:

As you are aware from our conversation in Los Angeles on Friday, January 7, 1972, Attorney General John N. Mitchell has referred your letter of December 10, 1971, to me for appropriate response.

This office has provided a copy of Indictment 71 CR 1086 to members of your staff and an additional copy is enclosed with this letter. This indictment was returned on December 15, 1971, in the United States District Court for the Northern District of Illinois, Eastern Division, before Acting Chief Judge Richard B. Austin.

The return of this indictment is the culmination of an 18-month investigation by the Intelligence Division of the Internal Revenue Service, United States Treasury Department.

Unfortunately, while this office would like to respond to your request for the facts of this case, the rules of the United States District Court for the Northern District of Illinois, Rule 6 of the Federal Rules of Criminal Procedure, the guidelines of the Department of Justice, and the canons of ethics prohibit us from disclosing or commenting on the factual basis of this indictment.

In addition, because of the unusually widespread public interest in this case by the news media and the public, any comments or statements by any persons involved in this lawsuit, including Mrs. Marie L. Everett, could raise questions of prejudice to the right of the defendants to a fair and impartial trial.

- 2 -

Honorable Evelle J. Younger
The Attorney General
State of California
Re: U.S. v. Isaacs, et al.,
71 CR 1086

January 10, 1972

The trial of the captioned case is expected to be held within the next twelve months, and we will make complete transcripts of the trial available to members of your staff as they become available.

We can, however, respond to your questions regarding Mrs. Everett's status. This investigation was initiated after Mrs. Everett voluntarily informed agents of the Internal Revenue Service of certain facts. She has not asked for, nor has she been granted immunity. There are, of course, no criminal charges pending against her.

If we can be of further assistance, please do not hesitate to contact us.

Very truly yours,

JAMES R. THOMPSON
United States Attorney
Northern District of Illinois

JRT:SKS:lcm

Enclosure —
Copy of Indictment

Letter U. S. Attorney Thompson wrote to California Attorney General on behalf of Marje Everett. He denied in his 1976 gubernatorial campaign that he tried to help her and called her a "briber."

240

17 North Dearborn St., Chicago, ...

Department of the Treasury

District Director
Internal Revenue Service

Date: APR 14 1972 | In reply refer to: A:R:SN

TELEPHONE 353-1084

Mr. William S. Miller and
Mrs. Catherine G. Miller
222 West Prospect
Ottawa, Illinois 61350

Sir and Madam:

This is your legal notice that a determination of your Federal income tax liability for the taxable year 1967 discloses the following:

Tax	Addition to Tax Under Section 6653(b)	Liability of Mrs. Catherine G. Miller limited to Deficiency in Tax
$1,845,763.00	$922,881.00	$1,845,763.00

The attached statement shows the computation of the deficiency and addition to tax.

Neither this notice, nor any action taken by the Internal Revenue Service in connection with it, affects other sanctions the law provides.

The amount you owe will be assessed for collection, as required by law, at the end of 90 days from the date of this letter, unless you contest this determination by filing a petition with the United States Tax Court within that time.

You can obtain a copy of the rules for filing a petition with the Tax Court by addressing a request to the Clerk, United States Tax Court, Box 70, Washington, D. C. 20224.

Sincerely yours,

Johnnie M. Walters
Commissioner

By: Roger C. Beck
District Director

Enclosure:
Statement

WILLIAM S. MILLER
666 North Michigan Avenue
CHICAGO, ILLINOIS 60611

September 13, 1976

Commissioner of Internal Revenue
of the United States of America
230 South Dearborn Street
Chicago, Illinois

Sir:

I respectfully refer to a decision in the United States Tax Court covered by Docket No. 5779-72 that my income tax deficiency for the taxable year 1967 was $58,552.00. My check in that amount is attached hereto.

As of this date, I have not been informed of the amount of interest due, if any, in connection with subject assessment.

Yours very truly,

WSM/fm
Enc.

Two items that tell a long story: one the notice of tax deficiency served on William Miller in 1972, and, two, the final settlement.

WASHINGTON PARK TROTTING ASSOCIATION

CERTIFICATE NUMBER	NUMBER OF SHARES	ISSUE DATE	NAME ON CERTIFICATE	ACTUAL OWNER	$1.00 PER SHARE PURCHASE PRICE	SALE DATE	$5.00 PER SHARE SALE PRICE	TO WHOM SOLD
1	15,000	4/62	Charles Wacker III	Same	$15,000	9/66	$120,000	To C.T.E.
2	5,000	4/62	Ralph Atlass	Same	5,000	9/66	25,000	To Treasury
3	10,000	4/62	Ralph Atlass	5,000 Wm. Lynch / 5,000 George Schaller	5,000 / 5,000	9/66	25,000 / 25,000	To Treasury / To C.T.E.
4	5,000	4/62	Ralph Atlass	William Lynch	5,000	9/66	25,000	To C.T.E.
5	5,000	4/62	Harold Anderson	Same	5,000	4/17/67	25,000	To Treasury
6	10,000	4/62	Harold Anderson	5,000 Edna Hayes / 5,000 Webb Everett	5,000 / 5,000	9/66	25,000	To C.T.E.
7	5,000	4/62	Harold Anderson	Webb Everett				
8	1,000	4/62	Webb Everett	Webb Everett				
9	1,000	4/62	Webb Everett	Webb Everett				
10	1,000	4/62	Webb Everett	Webb Everett				
11	1,000	4/62	Webb Everett	Webb Everett				
12	1,000	4/62	Webb Everett	Webb Everett				
13	1,000	4/62	Webb Everett	Webb Everett	20,000	9/66	100,000	To C.T.E.
14	1,000	4/62	Webb Everett	Webb Everett				
15	1,000	4/62	Webb Everett	Webb Everett				
16	1,000	4/62	Webb Everett	Webb Everett				
17	1,000	4/62	Webb Everett	Webb Everett				
18	5,000	4/62	Webb Everett	Webb Everett				
19	5,000	4/62	Webb Everett	Webb Everett				
20	1,000	4/62	William Lynch	William Lynch				
21	1,000	4/62	William Lynch	William Lynch				
22	1,000	4/62	William Lynch	William Lynch				
23	1,000	4/62	William Lynch	William Lynch				
24	1,000	4/62	William Lynch	William Lynch				
25	1,000	4/62	William Lynch	William Lynch	20,000	9/66	100,000	To C.T.E.
26	1,000	4/62	William Lynch	William Lynch				
27	1,000	4/62	William Lynch	William Lynch				
28	1,000	4/62	William Lynch	William Lynch				
29	1,000	4/62	William Lynch	William Lynch				
30	5,000	4/62	William Lynch	William Lynch				
31	5,000	4/62	William Lynch	William Lynch				

No.	Shares	Date	Seller	Buyer	Amount	Date	Amount	Note
32	1,000	4/62	Lawrence Marsh	Same	$ 1,000	9/66	$ 5,000	To C.T.E.
33	1,000	4/62	George Schaller	Same	1,000	9/66	5,000	To C.T.E.
34	1,000	4/62	Henry D. Williams	Same	1,000	9/66	5,000	To C.T.E.
35	97,000	4/62	Wacker, Everett, Lynch, Trustees	Same (Trust Cert. Issued)	97,000	N/A	N/A	
36	1,000	4/62	Wacker, Everett, Lynch, Trustees	Same (Trust Cert. Issued)	1,000	N/A	N/A	
37	7,000	7/64	William J. Lynch	Paul Powell	7,000	5/67	42,000	To Treasury
38	7,000	7/64	William J. Lynch	Clyde Choate	7,000	5/67	42,000	To Treasury
39	5,000	7/64	William J. Lynch	George Dunne	5,000	10/66	25,000	To Treasury
40	7,000	7/64	William J. Lynch	Willard Murphy	7,000	5/67	42,000	To Treasury
41	3,000	7/64	William J. Lynch	John Lewis	3,000	5/67	18,000	To Treasury
42	3,000	7/64	William J. Lynch	Robert McLoskey	3,000	9/65	15,000	To Treasury
43	2,000	7/64	William J. Lynch	Robert McLoskey	2,000	9/65		
44	7,000	7/64	Ralph Atlass	William Pollack	7,000	5/67	42,000	To Treasury
45	24,000	7/64	Charles Wacker III	Arthur Bidwell	24,000	4/66	96,000	To C.T.E.
46	1,000	7/64	Charles Wacker III	M. Fagot (John Meyer)	1,000	12/67	6,000	To Treasury
47	2,000	7/64	C. Wacker (Peter F. Biggam)	Paul A. Ziegler	2,000	10/70	20,000	To C.T.E.
48	10,000	7/64	C. Wacker (Peter F. Biggam)	5,000 Neal Bidwell	5,000	6/66	25,000	To Treasury
				5,000 Everett Peters	5,000	6/66	15,000	To Treasury
49	12,000	7/64	C. Wacker (Peter F. Biggam)	7,000 Peter F. Biggam	7,000	10/70	70,000*	To C.T.E.
				2,500 J. J. Kennedy	2,500	10/70	25,000*	To C.T.E.
				2,500 A. L. Cronin	2,500	10/70	25,000*	To C.T.E.
50	7,000	7/64	George Schaller	Clyde Lee	7,000	9/66	35,000	To Treasury
51	5,000	7/64	George Schaller	Same	5,000	9/66	25,000	To Treasury

*Less Sales Commissions Paid

From IRS accountants, stock transactions of Washington Park Trotting Association.

243

CERTIFICATE NUMBER	NUMBER OF SHARES	DATE PURCHASED	NAME ON CERTIFICATE	ACTUAL OWNER	PURCHASE PRICE
13	50,000	2/64	Wm. J. Lynch	25,000 Wm. Lynch	$10,000
				25,000 George Schaller	10,000
14	5,000	2/64	George Schaller	George Schaller	2,000
15	5,000	2/64	Wm. J. Lynch	Wm. J. Lynch	2,000
16	5,000	6/64	Albert R. Bell	Albert R. Bell	2,000
17	10,000	2/64	Harold H. Anderson	Milburn P. Akers	4,000
18	350,000	2/64	Modie Spiegel, Harold Anderson & Albert R. Bell as trustees	see Appendix C	
19	VOID				
20	10,000	10/63	Lawrence E. Marsh	Lawrence E. Marsh	4,000
21	25,000	8/62	Harold H. Anderson	Harold Anderson	10,000
22	10,000	2/64	Harold H. Anderson	7,500 Harold Anderson	3,000
				2,500 Margaret Luft	1,000
23	VOID				
24	50,000	4/64	Ralph Atlass	William S. Miller	20,000
25	15,000	2/64	Ralph Atlass	Ralph Atlass	6,000
26	50,000	11/62	Modie J. Spiegel	Modie J. Spiegel	20,000
27	25,000	11/62	Crowdus Baker	Crowdus Baker	10,000
28	5,000	11/62	Elmer F. Layden	Elmer F. Layden	2,000
29	2,000	2/64	Erva T. Butler	Erva T. Butler	N/A
30	25,000	11/63	Bacon, Whipple & Co.	Charles Wacker, III	10,000
31	7,500	11/63	Albert R. Bell	Paul Powell	3,000
32	7,500	11/63	Albert R. Bell	Clyde Lee	3,000
33	25,000	12/62	William T. Brady	William T. Brady	10,000
34	10,000	12/62	William T. Brady	James Hayes	4,000
35	10,000	unknown	William T. Brady	James Hayes	4,000
36	15,000	11/62	William L. McKnight	James Hayes	6,000
			(McKnight sold 15,000 shares to Hayes on 8/66 for $1.20 per share and continued acting as nominee)		
37	1,000	7/64	George W. Howard	George W. Howard	400
38	2,000	10/63	Janice L. Marsh	Janice L. Marsh	800
39	5,000	2/64	Alice Weisl	Alice Weisl	2,000
40	50,000	2/64	Peter F. Biggam*	Neal Bidwill	20,000
			*original nominee was Ralph Atlass		
41-43	see certificate #29		Still Outstanding		
44-45	2,000	5/65	Sincere and Company*	Francis Lorenz	800
			(*transferred prior to sale to #93 nominee Joseph Knight)		
46-55	10,000	5/65	Sincere and Company*	Faith McInturf	4,000
			(*transferred through certificates #74, 77, 82, 88 as nominees)		
56, 57, 68	28,000	7/66	Sincere and Company*	14,000 Otto Kerner	5,600
				14,000 Theodore Isaacs	5,600
			(*transferred prior to sale through certificates #75, 76, 78, 79, 83, and 84 as nominees)		
58-67	10,000	5/65	Sincere and Company*	Joseph Knight	4,000
			(*transferred prior to sale through certificate #92)		
69	10,000	5/65	Ralph L. Atlass	Ralph L. Atlass	12,000
70-71	see certificate #27		Still Outstanding		
72-73	see certificate #13				
74, 77, 82	see certificates #46-55				
75, 76, 78, 79, 83, 84	see certificates #56, 57, & 68				
80	227,500	9/66	Balmoral Jockey Club	Balmoral Jockey Club	555,000
81	227,500	10/66	Illinois Racing Enterprises	Illinois Racing Enterprises	555,000
85	see certificate #31		Still Outstanding		
86	5,000	5/67	Faith McInturf	Faith McInturf	10,000
87	25,000	4/67	Faith McInturf	Faith McInturf	50,000
88	see certificates #46-55		Still Outstanding		
89	14,000	5/67	Joseph Becker	Joseph Becker	28,000
90	see certificate #56, 57, 68		Still Outstanding		
91	see certificate #81		Still Outstanding		
92	see certificates #58-67				
93	see certificates #44-45				
94	14,000	7/67	Faith McInturf	Faith McInturf	28,000
95-96	see certificate #94		Both still outstanding		
97	see certificates #58-67		Still Outstanding		
98	see certificates #44-45		Still Outstanding		

CERTIFICATE #99 AND UPWARD UNISSUED AS OF JUNE 3, 1970

(For Certificates #1-12 see certificate #18 and Appendix C)

SALE DATE	SALES PRICE	NUMBER OF SHARES SOLD	SALES PRICE PER SHARE	TO WHOM SOLD	NEW CERTIFICATE NUMBER	FROM TRUST CERTIFICATE NO. (APPENDIX C)
9/66	$ 50,000	25,000	$2.00	Balmoral Jockey Club	80	New Issue
9/66	50,000	25,000	2.00	Balmoral Jockey Club	80	
9/66	10,000	5,000	2.00	Balmoral Jockey Club	80	New Issue
9/66	10,000	5,000	2.00	Balmoral Jockey Club	80	New Issue
9/66	16,250	5,000	3.25	Balmoral Jockey Club	80	New Issue
10/66	20,000	10,000	2.00	Retired to Treasury	-	New Issue Appendix C
5/65	12,000	10,000	1.20	Ralph Atlass	69	TC #30
10/66	50,000	25,000	2.00	Retired to Treasury	-	TC #3
10/66	15,000	7,500	2.00	Retired to Treasury	-	TC #18
10/66	5,000	2,500	2.00	Retired to Treasury	-	
5/65	4,000	10,000	.40	Joseph E. Knight	58-67	TC #22
5/65	800	2,000	.40	Francis Lorenz	44-45	
	4,000	10,000	.40	Faith McInturf	46-55	
7/66	5,600	14,000	.40	Otto Kerner	56-57	
7/66	5,600	14,000	.40	Theodore J. Isaacs	& 68	
9/66	30,000	15,000	2.00	Balmoral Jockey Club	80	TC #26
9/66	162,500	50,000	3.25	Balmoral Jockey Club	80	TC #1
10/65	100,000	25,000	4.00	Holders Investment Co.	70	TC #5
5/67	10,000	5,000	2.00	Faith McInturf	86	TC #7
N/A	N/A	N/A	N/A	Still Outstanding*	N/A	TC #20
9/66	81,250	25,000	3.25	Balmoral Jockey Club	80	TC #25
N/A	N/A	N/A	N/A	Still Outstanding*	N/A	TC #28
9/66	15,000	7,500	2.00	Balmoral Jockey Club	80	TC #29
4/67	50,000	25,000	2.00	Faith McInturf	87	TC #9
2/67	30,000	10,000	3.00	Retired to Treasury	-	TC #14
2/67	30,000	10,000	3.00	Retired to Treasury	-	TC #27
2/67	45,000	15,000	3.00	Retired to Treasury	-	TC #11
10/66	2,000	1,000	2.00	Retired to Treasury	-	TC #19
N/A	N/A	N/A	N/A	Still Outstanding	N/A	TC #21
9/66	10,000	5,000	2.00	Balmoral Jockey Club	80	TC #23
9/66	100,000	50,000	2.00	Balmoral Jockey Club	80	TC #17 N/A
3/70	unknown	2,000	unknown	Lawrence White	98	Transfer
N/A	N/A	N/A	N/A	Still Outstanding	N/A	Transfer
5/67	28,000	14,000	2.00	Joseph Becker	89	Transfer
5/67	28,000	14,000	2.00	Norman Becker	90	
3/70	unknown	10,000	unknown	Lawrence White	97	Transfer
9/66	20,000	10,000	2.00	Balmoral Jockey Club	80	Transfer N/A N/A N/A
						N/A
10/66	555,000	227,500	(average) 2.44	Illinois Racing Enterprises	81	Transfer
5/67	555,000	227,500	(average) 2.44	William S. Miller	N/A	Transfer N/A
N/A	N/A	N/A	N/A	Still Outstanding	N/A	Transfer
N/A	N/A	N/A	N/A	Still Outstanding	N/A	Transfer N/A
7/67	28,000	14,000	2.00	Faith McInturf	94	Transfer N/A N/A N/A N/A
12/67	2,000	1,000	2.00	George Schaller	95	Transfer N/A N/A N/A

From IRS accountants, stock transactions of Chicago Harness Racing, Inc.

245

VOTING TRUST CERTIFICATE NUMBER	OWNER OF RECORD	BENEFICIAL OWNER	DATE ISSUED	NUMBER OF SHARES	PURCHASE DATE
1	Modie Spiegel	Modie Spiegel	2-8-64	50,000	11-27-62
2	Modie Spiegel	Modie Spiegel	2-8-64	37,500	11-27-62
3	Harold Anderson	Harold Anderson	2-8-64	25,000	11-27-62
4	Harold Anderson	Harold Anderson	2-8-64	37,500	11-27-62
5	Crowdus Baker	Crowdus Baker	2-8-64	25,000	11-27-62
6	Crowdus Baker	Crowdus Baker	2-8-64	37,500	11-27-62
7	Elmer Leyden	Elmer Leyden	2-8-64	5,000	11-27-62
8	Elmer Leyden	Elmer Leyden	2-8-64	7,500	11-27-62
9	William Brady	William Brady	2-8-64	25,000	12-3-62
10	William Brady	William Brady	2-8-64	62,500	12-3-62
11	William McKnight	William McKnight	2-8-64	15,000	11-27-62
12	William McKnight	William McKnight	2-8-64	22,500	11-27-62
13					
14	William Brady	James Hayes	2-8-64	10,000	12-3-62
15					
16					
17	Ralph Atlass	Neal Bidwill	7-1-64	50,000	2-19-64
18	Harold Anderson	Margaret Luft 2,500 Harold Anderson 7,500	—	10,000	4-27-64
19	George Howard	George Howard	7-1-64	1,000	7-1-64
20	Erva Butler	Erva Butler	7-1-64	2,000	2-4-64
21	Janice Marsh	Janice Marsh	7-1-64	2,000	10-21-63
22	Ralph Atlass	William Miller	7-1-64	50,000	4-22-64
23	Alice Weisl	Alice Weisl	7-1-64	5,000	2-19-64
24					
25	Bacon Whipple & Co.	Charles Wacker	7-1-64	25,000	11-5-63
26	Ralph Atlass	Ralph Atlass	7-1-64	15,000	2-19-64
27	William Brady	James Hayes	—	10,000	—
28	Albert Bell	Clyde Lee	7-1-64	7,500	7-1-64
29	Albert Bell	Paul Powell	7-1-64	7,500	7-1-64
30	Lawrence Marsh	Lawrence Marsh	7-1-64	10,000	10-15-63

From IRS accountants, stock transactions of Chicago Harness Racing, Inc. Voting Trust, 350,00

COST (40¢ PER SHARE)	FROM CHR STOCK CERT. OR TRUST CERT.	DATE TRANSFERRED OR DATE SOLD	NUMBER OF SHARES	TRANSFERRED TO STOCK CERT. OR TRUST CERT.	SALES PRICE
$20,000 –	SC 11	4-15-65	50,000	SC 26	N.A.
15,000 –	SC 12	7-1-64	7,500	TC 22	$ 3,000 –
		7-1-64	5,000	TC 23	2,000 –
		7-1-64	15,000	TC 26	6,000 –
		7-1-64	10,000	TC 30	4,000 –
					$15,000 –
10,000 –	SC 3	4-15-65	25,000	SC 21	N.A.
15,000 –	SC 4	7-1-64	10,000	TC 18	$ 4,000 –
		7-1-64	500	TC 19	200 –
		7-1-64	2,000	TC 20	800 –
		7-1-64	25,000	TC 25	10,000 –
					$15,000 –
10,000 –	SC 7	4-15-65	25,000	SC 27	N.A.
15,000 –	SC 8	7-1-64	37,500	TC 17	$15,000 –
2,000 –	SC 9	4-15-65	5,000	SC 28	N.A.
3,000 –	SC 10	7-1-64	500	TC 19	$ 200 –
		7-1-64	2,000	TC 21	800 –
		7-1-64	5,000	TC 29	2,000 –
					$ 3,000 –
10,000 –	SC 1	7-27-65	25,000	SC 33	N.A.
25,000 –	SC 2	2-8-64	10,000	TC 14	N.A.
		7-1-64	42,500	TC 22	$17,000 –
		—	10,000	TC 27	4,000 –
					$21,000 –
6,000 –	SC 6	4-15-65	15,000	SC 36	N.A.
9,000 –	SC 5	7-1-64	12,500	TC 17	$ 5,000 –
		7-1-64	7,500	TC 28	3,000 –
		7-1-64	2,500	TC 29	1,000 –
					$ 9,000 –
N.A.	TC 10	7-27-65	10,000	SC 34	N.A.
$20,000 –	TC 6				
	TC 12	4-15-65	50,000	SC 40	N.A.
4,000 –	TC 4	4-15-65	10,000	SC 22	N.A.
400 –	TC 8				
	TC 4	4-15-65	1,000	SC 37	N.A.
800 –	TC 4	5-3-65	1,000	SC 41	N.A.
		5-3-65	500	SC 42	N.A.
		5-3-65	500	SC 43	N.A.
800 –	TC 8	4-15-65	2,000	SC 38	N.A.
20,000 –	TC 2				
	TC 10	4-15-65	50,000	SC 24	N.A.
2,000 –	TC 2	4-15-65	5,000	SC 39	N.A.
10,000 –	TC 4	6-2-65	25,000	SC 30	N.A.
6,000 –	TC 2	4-15-65	15,000	SC 25	N.A.
4,000 –	TC 10	4-15-65	10,000	SC 35	N.A.
3,000 –	TC 12	4-15-65	7,500	SC 31	N.A.
3,000 –	TC 8				
	TC 12	4-15-65	7,500	SC 32	N.A.
4,000 –	TC 2	4-15-65	10,000	SC 20	N.A.

shares Chicago Harness Racing Stock, Analysis of Certificate #18 Chicago Harness Racing, Inc.

Index